Scared to Life

JILLIAN WEBSTER

Elifant Publishing, LLC

Copyright © 2015 by Jillian Webster

Cover illustration copyright © 2015 by Jessica Hurley

Cover design by Jessica Hurley

Interior book design by Bookfly Design

Editing by Bookfly Design

Author photograph by Heather Applegate

I have tried to recreate events, locales, and conversations from my memories of them. In order to maintain their anonymity, I have changed the names of some individuals and places. I may have also changed identifying characteristics and details such as physical properties, occupations, and places of residence.

Printed in the United States of America

ISBN 978-0-9861888-0-0

First Edition

Table of Contents

For Dad
And Grandpa and Granny.
My anchor
And my wings.

"*Though we travel the world over to find the beautiful, we must carry it with us or we find it not.*"

—*Ralph Waldo Emerson*

Mui Ne, Vietnam

I can still hear you
as if you were still standing here,
still standing next to me.

I can still hear the life in your heartbeat,
the music in your laughter.

But you are not here.
No,
you are a million miles away.

I stand now,
alone in the world.

I stand quiet,
stable,
despite losing the secure grasp of your hand,
the strength of your stature.

I knew you once,
many lifetimes ago,
during a time when I thought I knew myself.

But in a glimmering instant,
my worlds collided,

my earth shattered,
leaving a silent sliver of myself to be reborn.

Now here I am,
having passed through expanses of oceans and cultures,
lands and lifelines of humanity
humbly dwelling day to day throughout this world.

I have witnessed the poetic,
heart-wrenching beauty of this world's people,
and its tattered cloak of
everything you'd hope it to be.

But it's a lie,
a beautiful, jumbled masterpiece of postcards and photos,
all desperately trying to prove
that we've made it after all.

Looking back, the life I've lived seems like a millennium of
*   moments,*
all woven together in a sacred mess of a story.

Did this all really happen?

Did I really live through this?

Did my eyes really witness such exquisite chaos?
Such exotic beauty?
Such raging
biased
hostility?

What an extravagant, explosive, and fascinating story to tell!

What a wonderfully liberating life to have lived!

I followed my heart
and in the end,
my heart has led me home.

Everything has changed,
yet everything remains the same.

I will always love you.

Disfellowship: to "remove the wicked man" or woman from the congregation.

—*The Watchtower,* July 15, 2011, p. 22

I

I'M NOT SURE what I was thinking about the night I
called my mother. I'm not even sure why I was calling;
I think it had been a while since we last spoke. She hadn't
been happy with me for quite some time, and I couldn't
blame her. She didn't understand why I was leaving, and
I didn't know what to tell her. But I remember that evening, I remember as if it were just yesterday. How could I
forget? It was the last conversation I was allowed to have
with my mother.

Listening to the repeated rings on the telephone line,
I'm preparing to leave a message when my mom picks up.

"Why are you home?" I ask.

I figured she'd be mid-prayer at the Kingdom Hall
of Jehovah's Witnesses this time of night. I casually lean
against the customer service kiosk and smile at a passing
shopper. It is an uneventful Thursday evening, with only an
occasional body meandering through Circuit City's open
glass doors to wander the aisles of assorted electronics
and televisions. The sun is setting outside, giving the sky
an iridescent blue haze that tells you darkness will soon
be coming. The chirping birds are narrating the day's
events among the few scattered trees in the parking lot.
There seem to be a lot of them compared to the small
amount of trees. Their songs echo off the wall behind me,

giving the illusion that they are as much inside the store as they are out.

"I didn't feel well," my mom responds quickly, almost absently.

"Are you okay?"

There is silence. The store's other line rings through. Another coworker answers and transfers the call to the warehouse before walking to the back office to start our closing duties. A customer exits the building, lugging plastic bags stuffed with CDs and office supplies. The outside light continues to fade.

"Mom?"

"They're disfellowshipping you tonight."

All of a sudden the chirping birds seem so loud, almost suffocating in their intensity. I grip the phone, alarmed and unsteady as her words hang midair before crashing into me like shrapnel.

Meanwhile, an elder walks warily toward the podium in front of a congregation of Jehovah's Witnesses I once called family. Book bags are casually shuffled through, another elder standing along the back wall clears his throat, and Bibles rest in laps while unsuspecting Witnesses await what shall happen next. He walks the two carpeted steps up to the stage and places himself behind the simple podium.

"So what does this mean? Mom? Can I at least come over and say goodbye?"

"No."

The elder unfolds a piece of paper and makes eye contact with the man standing along the back wall. They both look away.

"This is to inform you that Jillian Webster has been disfellowshipped from the congregation."

The silence is broken as a dear friend breaks down into sobs and is led out of the room. The elder leaves the podium and finds his seat next to his family. The meeting resumes with the next Bible lesson.

II

THERE IS NOTHING LEFT between my mother and me but silence. There are no words, no deep truths to lay out on the table and dissect for the betterment of our souls. Our wounds are deep and gutted, our memories corroded and few. Our story is not a common one, not one you typically hear when meeting a new friend or coworker. It's not a common story, but it's my story.

When I was a toddler, my mother had hit rock bottom. It was 1987. Her marriage to my father was ending, her mother was dying after a long and hard battle with cancer, and her alcohol addiction was slowly suffocating her. She had lost herself, but to be realistic, I don't believe she had ever really had herself. Battles with a distant and abusive father had left wounds cratered so deep within her that she caved in on herself to the point of becoming unrecognizable.

Then came a knock on the door. They had smiles on their faces and all the right answers. They were a port in the storm. No matter what had happened or what will happen, they provided the shelter my mother had always craved. They called themselves Jehovah's Witnesses, and my mother threw herself into their arms and into a whole new life-consuming addiction.

As a Christian sect, the Jehovah's Witnesses follow the same basic guidelines of belief when it comes to worshiping one God, the Father—or Jehovah, and finding salvation through the Son, Jesus Christ. They believe the Bible is the inspired word of God and follow the rules and guidelines God has set out through His word, although they have their own translation of the Bible, which has been a large source of debate with other sects of Christianity. Some key differences include the Jehovah's Witnesses' rejection of the Trinity doctrine, celebrating holidays, and eternal damnation through hellfire. They also believe eternal life in Heaven will only be granted to 144,000 believers, while all other Witnesses will live forever in an earthly paradise.

The guidelines for how one should live are also all claimed to be derived from Scripture, although those put forth by the Jehovah's Witnesses include many more than mainstream Christianity, and if one should break any of these rules, especially if that one is unrepentant, it is grounds for shunning from the religion. These rules prohibit sex before marriage, drunkenness, divorce, cheating, lying, smoking cigarettes, using drugs, homosexuality, disagreeing with the religion, association with a disfellowshipped person, getting a blood transfusion, attending any other Christian church, artificial insemination/surrogate motherhood, gambling, joining the military, performing yoga, celebrating any holiday including birthdays, leaving the religion, saluting the country's flag, or involving oneself with politics—to name a few.

I spent the majority of my life up until I was nineteen years old as a Jehovah's Witness; it was how my mother, who has always truly believed in the religion with all her being, had raised us. I, too, believed in their teachings of God and the way life should be lived, although I never had much of an option. The teachings of the Jehovah's Witnesses are serious and strict and to be followed without question.

Throughout my teenage years, I went back and forth and in and out of the Kingdom Hall's doors—plagued with guilt and fear of doing wrong, but reminded ever so constantly by my heart: *This life was not meant for me.* It didn't matter though, I had been taught my entire life that this was "The Truth," and my young and malleable mind had always believed it.

By the age of sixteen, I had finally been approved for baptism. It was the next step in becoming a true Jehovah's Witness, and I had a congregation of brothers and sisters who loved and supported me. I had made the most significant decision you can make as a Christian: I dedicated myself to God and his organization of Witnesses.

My deep satisfaction lasted a total of four months.

For the next two years I continued to go back and forth. There were months I felt strong in my resolve to make my strict Christian life work. I'd sit in the hallway at school during lunch and read my Bible, cut off from my "worldly" friends (the Jehovah's Witness's term for those not affiliated with the faith), and I spent every Saturday going door to door, preaching the "good news of God's Kingdom." I tried so hard to be a part of the clean and Christlike life that the Witnesses had laid out for me, but I was lying—to myself, to the brothers and sisters of the congregation, and to my mother. This was not on purpose of course. I was in the throes of a confusion so vast that all I could do was stumble my way through, doing everything I thought I was supposed to, yet everything I knew I wasn't, by listening to everything but my own heart. I was trying to grow up and compose my identity, and doing so in ways only a fumbling teenager could by disappointing everyone almost as much as I disappointed myself in the vain hope that one day...I'd figure it out.

Inevitably, there were times during that period when my young and persistent heart would win me over and I'd disappear from the Witnesses completely. I would live the life I had desperately yearned for with social events and days out with my worldly, non-Witness friends, who had missed me so dearly during my times of withdrawal. I was free to be whoever I wanted to be, which typically involved being a giddy, daydreaming, flirtatious teenager. But each night I'd fall asleep carrying the guilt of a fugitive, turning my back on God and ignoring phone calls from worried sisters and elders, all begging me to come back to them. At this point I was living with my non-Witness father who, despite never understanding or agreeing with my choice to be a Jehovah's Witness, didn't challenge my position either. My mother was the complete opposite. Worried, she would often remind me that it was Satan putting doubts in my head.

Eventually my confusion would wrap around me so tightly that, out of sheer misery, I felt the best option was to go back. It was The Truth, and I had disobeyed. I'd crawl back to the elders and confess all my wrongdoings, and they'd immediately inform the congregation I was being monitored so parents would know not to let their children spend time with me alone. Everyone would know I had done wrong, and I was being punished.

At eighteen, my whole world started to dissolve. Looking back now, I can see that in reality I was starting to grow up and was learning to think for myself. The Witnesses had disfellowshipped me earlier that year for smoking cigarettes. A brother of the congregation had driven past me and seen the cigarette in my hand with smoke streaming out of my cracked car window. I wasn't attending the meetings at this time, but I had no intention whatsoever of leaving the one and only Truth and losing my family and congregation of friends. The congregation's elders spent months trying to contact me, but I wasn't ready to come back, so they announced that I was shunned and not to be spoken to.

I was completely devastated. I immediately abandoned my "evil ways" and returned once again to the flock. But now I was no longer one of them. The once warm and welcoming faces were cold and distant. At the order of the organization, the congregation—including my mother, stepfather, and three younger siblings—refrained from making eye contact or speaking with me.

I was to attend religious services and sit by myself until the elders thought I had repented long enough to be reinstated into the organization, "at least three months," they told me. A month earlier, I had gotten into a serious car accident that totaled my car. Since I did not have transportation, the elders allowed my mother to drive me back and forth to the meetings. I was to sit in the back seat of her van, and no one was to look at or speak to me. Like obedient sheep, that is exactly what we did.

"Few things can hurt us more deeply than the pain we suffer when a relative or a close friend is expelled from the congregation for unrepentant sin. How we respond to the Bible's direction on this matter can reveal the depth of our love for God and of our loyalty to his arrangement. ... How should we treat a disfellowshipped person? The Bible says: ... 'Do not receive him into your homes or say a greeting to him. For the one who says a greeting to him is a sharer in his wicked works.' (2 John 9-11) We do not have spiritual or social fellowship with disfellowshipped ones. *The Watchtower* of September 15, 1981, page 25, stated: 'A simple "Hello" to someone can be the first step that develops into a conversation and maybe even a friendship. Would we want to take that first step with a disfellowshipped person?' Is strict avoidance really necessary? Yes ... it is a matter of loyalty to God and his Word." (*Keep Yourselves in God's Love*, p. 207)

I spent three months going to two meetings a week and sitting alone in the back of my mother's van. We would usually arrive at the meetings early to socialize with the other members of the congregation, so I'd sit in the dark van by myself and sneak in when the opening prayer began.

I spent each and every day alone, repenting and begging God for mercy. I wasn't allowed to spend time with anyone who was not a Witness, for they were worldly and God would disapprove. But I wasn't allowed to spend time with any Witnesses either because I was considered wicked. So I spent three months *alone*, every day and every night, reading the Bible and crying for forgiveness. I had no one. I had never felt so low in my entire life.

After months of solitude and reflection, I was reinstated into the congregation. The elders called me into a meeting to assess whether I was truly sorry for smoking cigarettes. I held my head in my hands and cried the entire time, telling them how deeply repentant I was. They agreed I could be allowed back into the organization.

The night they announced that I was reinstated, the members of the congregation did not react. The religion discourages Witnesses from celebrating anything that has to do with rebellion. But as soon as the last amen was uttered after closing prayer, I was surrounded by people hugging me and welcoming me back. I had everything. This was the moment I had been waiting for.

Little did I realize, those three months of being completely alone had given me an immense opportunity to grow. I had thought being back in the congregation would make me feel whole again—I would know I was finally where I belonged, and I would be happy living the life outlined in their teachings. But this was not at all the case. For the first time in my life, I could see the judgment; I could see all the conditions required for love and acceptance. The Witnesses believe that everyone who turns them away was given their chance, and when God ends the world, most of those people will die, especially anyone calling themselves a Christian who is not one of Jehovah's Witnesses. This felt so wrong.

Once again, I was inhabiting a life where I did not belong, but this time it was different. I was *exhausted*. I was sick and tired of trying to be someone I wasn't, struggling to fit into a mold I had outgrown. I had spent my entire existence dreaming of a life I could never have, bottling a soul that could never be freed, the entire time afraid of the loss and the deadly wrath of a prohibitively conditional God. And I just couldn't take it anymore.

I felt empty inside. My mother told me to fight it, that it was the Devil putting doubts in my mind, but it wasn't right—that sort of conditional love. After all that hard work, after *all those months* of studying the Bible and repenting, I found my heart just wasn't in it. For the first time in my life, I felt like I could see clearly. I felt brave enough to stand up and say, "I don't believe in this anymore, and I don't need you." I had gotten what I wanted, only to realize it was no longer what I needed.

I was nineteen years old when I left the Jehovah's Witnesses, and I have never looked back. Of course my initial absence did not go by unnoticed. From the very first missed meeting, I started a tactic of avoidance I had known very well throughout my teenage years—ignoring phone calls and, for that matter, anyone who had any association with the Witnesses. I couldn't talk to them; I didn't have any of the answers. All I knew was that something wasn't right or, more accurately, *it was all wrong*. It wasn't anything I could explain or defend. I was following my heart, listening to my gut that had been persistently telling me for years to *get out*.

At the time, the teachings were so strong in my young mind that despite *knowing* I was leaving God's organization of "safety" and "love" for Satan's unlawful and wicked world, I left anyway. I was scared and guilt-ridden, following an inner voice I barely knew. It was only a matter of time before they disfellowshipped me—again.

This was where it all ended for my mother and me. My separation from the Jehovah's Witnesses had also inadvertently wrapped my mother in her own version of confusion by creating a label for myself that did not allow her to see me.

"What if we have a relative or a close friend who is disfellowshipped? Now our loyalty is on the line, not to that person, but to God. Jehovah is watching us to see whether we will abide by his command not to have contact with *anyone* who is disfellowshipped." (*The Watchtower*, April 15, 2012 p. 8)

For years my mother went back and forth between her own maternal yearnings and the strict admonishment of the Jehovah's Witnesses to not see me. She'd send me letters to meet "sometime soon" and more letters days later breaking all our newly made plans. "My loyalty is to Jehovah," she'd write. "I am willing to die for you, but I will not die *with* you." I would ask her if she wanted me to be in her life, and she would reply with a simple, "I don't know." I could only react with gasps and sobs.

The last time my mother invited me into her home was six years ago. Sitting across from me on the couch in her living room, she held her head in her hands and cried for her sorrows and regrets over my childhood. Of course she never meant for any of this to happen. For the first time in her life, she had found a place to belong and a reason to live after existing so long without one. Unfortunately, that "reason" was a life I could never live.

I love my mother and I'll always miss her. I'll always feel the sting at times when a young woman should be able to have her mother. We don't talk now. I'm not allowed in her home to see her, my stepfather, or my little brother who lives with her. My two other siblings have grown up and moved out. Like my older brother who is uninvolved with the Jehovah's Witnesses, they do not participate in the religion, and throughout the years, we have found our way back to each other.

I am also the only one of my siblings who has been baptized as a Jehovah's Witness, and because of this I am the only one who is disfellowshipped. One cannot be officially "shunned" if she is not officially bonded to the religion by baptism. This makes me the only sibling in the family whom my mother does not speak to. There have been family dinners where I am not allowed to attend, along with other events throughout the years this "arrangement," as the Jehovah's Witnesses call it, has affected our entire family. But in most cases, I am the one at the event while my mother, stepfather, and younger brother are not around. I have an incredible extended family who, because they are not involved with the Jehovah's Witnesses, support and love me—despite my apparent shortcomings.

Many have asked if I regret getting baptized as a Jehovah's Witness, because had I not, this whole mess could have been avoided. I do not. Each decision we make throughout our days paints a wide array of colors into the tapestry of our lives—some darker than others. The decision I made to become baptized was sincere, coming from a place as good and righteous as any when you decide to devote your life to God. And I was young—too young by most standards to make a decision that would be upheld for the rest of my life. Just like many things, there is a time and a season. I grew up, I learned to think for myself, and I moved on. Because of the choices I have made and risks I've taken, I do not take this life for granted. Because I've lost so much to live this life, I love it that much more.

I have also somehow found my way back into a relationship with God—an unconditional God, one who loves
us all, despite how our labels on earth have categorized us.
Like Elizabeth Gilbert once said when asked what sort of
God she believes in, I too believe in "a loving God." Beyond
that, I have no other answers.

I could say so much more about my mother, make judgments while fingers point in every direction besides my own,
but that isn't the point. I've spent my entire life judging
and being judged, and I don't want to do it anymore. This
is not a story about what happened to me; it's a story about
what I did *in spite of it*. That's the thing about the human
spirit. We endure. We all have pains and scars and battles
we'd rather not fight. But every moment we have the choice
to allow the badness to pull us down or to let go and fly.

There are countless disfellowshipped Jehovah's Witnesses throughout the world, all trying to live their lives
in the shadow of a religion that has rejected them. We
feel the pain, some more than others, of a decision that
will haunt us until the day we die. Some will crawl back,
unable to bear the weight of the consequences from a
God who would forever condemn them. Others, however,
will move on with their lives, find the strength in their
storms and the rainbows in their teardrops. I choose to
walk with the latter.

I lost a lot the day I walked out of the Kingdom Hall
doors, but through all the heartache and tears, I learned
that to live a life based on fear, and to continue on as the
shell of a person I had become by ignoring my heart, *was
not a life worth living*. Turning my back on everything I'd
ever known, covered in a film of fear and doubt, I made

a vow, a vow that still determines my decisions down to this very moment, this very written word:

I will never, *ever* live a life based on fear.

It took years to sort through the religious teachings of man and find myself, and even longer to learn to live with the rejection of my mother. Months after the disfellowshipping, she wrote to me that she didn't believe for a minute I was going to have the life I was looking for. She told me it wasn't that she didn't want me to have it, but she felt the possibility just didn't exist. Reading this at twenty years old left me devastated. I had spent my entire childhood dreaming of *that life*—it was everything I had ever wanted but never had. I wanted to go to college—an aspiration commonly discouraged by the Witnesses—and travel the world, passionate and free. I wanted to live in a big city, unencumbered from the stress of worrying about money and the dullness of existing in a life unlived. I was going to find where I belonged—live the life I had previously given up for the acceptance and love from my family and religion.

I had a choice in that moment whether to allow this judgment to affect my decision to continue on the path I had started. I refused. Her lack of faith in the stand I had made only strengthened my determination to succeed. Once I started college, it was like nothing else mattered. I knew I was on my way.

After graduating, I moved straight to Chicago. In the years that followed, I traveled the country, solidified friendships and relationships with the rest of my family, and lived in a high-rise overlooking the city. I had finally found the life I had longed for, with one huge exception: my childhood dream of traveling the world.

Even though I had almost everything I wanted, my life still didn't feel right. No matter what happened, no matter how much I wanted to, I couldn't shake it. There was an undeniable longing, a calling to a certain destiny demanding to be lived. The same inner voice that had guided me from the beginning whispered constantly to me to follow this dream, tapping on my shoulder daily to the point of madness, finding me in my dreams at night.

I had to go. I had to see what would happen. I didn't know why exactly, and I didn't know how, but I knew with all my heart that it was meant to be. Somewhere, out there, was a place where I belonged—the life I had been looking for. And whatever life was calling out to me could only be found by living it.

I was scared to death. It took three years of unending doubt and agony to finally give up my life in Chicago to live the next. Year after year, journal after journal, I grappled with self-doubt and the incredibly limiting fear of being different from everyone around me. It was a long road, but in the end I surrendered, put everything I owned in storage, and left knowing deep down that I would never come back. In a way, I was right—just not in the way I could have ever imagined.

The Journey

Chicago, Illinois

How can I explain what I am feeling now? I'm desperate to put my world into words, and I hopelessly fail every time.

The misty rain coats the outside of my windows tonight. The Sears Tower is whittled down into a nub as the surrounding clouds take over the city and all its glory. The sights and sounds are muffled in the deep trenching rain and wind. Everything is quieted in the overwhelming noise of raindrops blanketing the steel and cement of the city. Everything is quiet, like my whole life, moving in slow motion.

*Almost immediately after arriving in Chicago three and a half years ago, I started seriously considering traveling the world on my own, but the logical, responsible part of my brain came up empty-handed. I needed a reason. **Why** on earth would I give everything up to face this big, scary world alone? I couldn't find a reason other than passion and a certain persistent pull that could only be described as fate.*

In the beginning, to my younger self, this answer wasn't good enough. So I wrote. I wrote letters to myself while pleading with God to give me the strength to live my destiny despite my intense fear of facing the world on my own.

Of course being afraid was not an unknown or unfamiliar territory to me, but this was by far the biggest and scariest dream I'd ever had. It was also the most fascinatingly exciting and life-changing. This degree of passion is sometimes followed by the same extreme degree of fear. It took me a while to realize this.

So here I am, three long years later. I have surrendered. I still don't know why I'm leaving, but I'm not going to interrogate myself anymore. I trust the pull, the gut feeling, the passion in my heart. It's definitely been a process, but I can say now that the confusion disappeared as soon as the questions fell away. I have accepted the grace of my angels and the teardrops of the demons that used to haunt me at night.

My whole world is about to change. Everything I've spent my entire life working for is disappearing as a new and foreign life is appearing. One chapter ends as another begins. All the comforts I relish are fading into nothing: my job, my new car, my hefty savings, my beautiful home in downtown Chicago—it's all about to disappear, and all I'll have is myself. It'll be the world and me, with no buffer and no apparent luxuries except time. All I'll have is time.

I'm definitely freaked out. I have no idea what lies ahead of me. And there is no way to prepare, no way to know what to expect, no shoulder to cry on or hand to hold.

I have no idea what to expect of **myself**. Will I charge through each day and meet it with confidence? Will I cry myself to sleep in the beginning? Will I stay until each country physically kicks me out? Or will I be ready to go home after six months?

How will my body react? Will I get sick? Will my stomach recognize or process the extreme change in food and bacteria?

I keep searching for security in another's eyes, something that will bring me comfort in knowing I am not alone and that I will be safe. But this isn't that sort of path I'm following. This isn't about safe and secure. I've had that. I have that now…yet I find all I crave is the adventure. There are no other options but to follow my love, let go, and fall.

So fall I will; I will dive fully into the depths of everything I am and morph into completely new dimensions. I will never be the same. Nothing will ever be the same. I've prayed and now it is time, time to let myself live this life I have fought so hard for. It is time to fly.

Europe

Dublin, Ireland

I NEVER THOUGHT FOR A SECOND that I'd be calm sitting here. I imagined my hands sweating and shaking, my heart pounding, my mind racing. Instead, I sit at O'Hare International Airport, calm—almost bored. I look innocently around at my fellow passengers and let out a sigh. This is it.

Faint hints of perfume and body odor waft through the stagnant air. The woman and her screaming baby have just left their seats one row over from me, and I pray that doesn't change. If I had a companion, we'd probably be talking about all this. Instead, the lashes of my eyes are still soaked from my final goodbyes, and my face remains streaked with the stains of my teardrops. So here I sit, alone. Calm. *Huh. I didn't see that coming.*

~

I arrive in Dublin at 6:50 a.m., but my body clock says it's 1:00 a.m. I didn't sleep on the plane. I'm exhausted and my stomach has a knot the size of my head. It feels weird—odd—to be in this Irish city so tired and lost. I strap my "average sized" backpack to myself after getting off the bus, and I instantly regret packing so much. It's heavy. It's so heavy and I'm so tired I actually panic for a second that I can't breathe.

It's a cool sixty degrees here despite being summer, but the temperature and the drizzle of rain fail to keep me cool as I break a sweat wearing this gigantic monkey-like pack wrapped tightly around me. *Dear God, what am I going to do?*

I'm lost. The hostel directions are vague at best, so I find myself repeatedly asking for directions. I must look miserable because the city workers keep flashing me "poor little hippie" looks as they clean the streets from last night's party.

After wandering aimlessly through the city for about forty-five minutes, I finally find my hostel. It is now 7:45 a.m., and I'm so tired I wouldn't think twice about sleeping on a park bench. Check-in, I'm told, is at 2:30 p.m.

"Please," I beg. "I just came in from overseas and am exhausted. Aren't there any beds open?"

The young man behind the counter stares at me blankly as he slowly shakes his head. I stand there for a moment, staring back at him, lost for words as I consider the predicament I'm in. I have to stay awake. What am I going to do?

And still, we stare.

After wandering the small and sleepy hostel, I find its common room filled to the brim with old soiled couches and banged-up coffee tables. I drop my bags into a corner and curl up on a ripped cushion of what used to be a love seat. Despite the few random strangers loitering about the room, I desperately pull my jacket over my weary eyes and try to get some sleep.

To my horror, it only takes about thirty seconds before the room fills with a noise I can't escape. *Clank!* My blood-shot eyes scrunch and peel open. *Clank, clank, CLANK!* Workers just outside our hostel's open windows are throwing what sounds like empty beer bottles into an even larger pile of empty beer bottles. Every five seconds, my body jolts awake from its semi-coma of slumber as loud clashes of glass echo off Dublin's old brick buildings lining the street.

I am so tired. *What am I doing here?* This is so surreal. I pull myself into a nauseatingly upright position and look at the meaningless faces around me. I make small talk with a couple of young guys from Toronto, one of whom wakes me up an hour later after I apparently passed out mid-sentence and offers me their room to sleep in while they head out to explore the city. I happily accept.

As I crawl into bed, I am horrified to hear outside their open window a worker just below cutting wood with a chain saw. I want to stick my head out the window and shout, "*Screw you!*" But instead I smile. What can I do? *Just sleep, Jill,* I whisper to myself. *Maybe, just maybe, when you wake up, the aching fear and overwhelming nausea will be gone.* I keep hearing Diane Lane's voice from *Under the Tuscan Sun* after she purchases a villa in the Tuscan countryside: "Just because you have a nauseous pit in your stomach and the sudden urge to weep doesn't necessarily mean you've made the wrong decision."

Even though I kind of expected feeling this way, experiencing it doesn't come any easier. Hours later, after I eventually settle into my room and awake from my second nap of the day, I feel slightly better—a little stronger to take on this magnificent city. I grab a map and familiarize myself with my surroundings, giving me just enough confidence to not feel so hopelessly lost. I wander into the streets of Dublin, through an area of town called Temple Bar, a neighborhood people often compare to the French Quarter in New Orleans.

The streets are narrow and lined with pubs, overflowing flower boxes, and live music on every corner. As I listen to the plethora of street performers, I have to remind myself every so often to breathe. I feel like every step I take on the uneven cobblestone is like the first step of a newborn, like every effort to walk farther on is like pushing through streets of ankle-deep, rapidly hardening cement. At the same time though, my insides are screaming in pure delight. There are weights on my ankles yet wings on my back. I'm terrified and exhilarated, wanting to laugh and cry, if only breathing didn't feel so foreign.

When I arrive back at the hostel, I meet my roommates: four men from Australia, two girls from Louisiana, and another lone female traveler from Brazil. Everyone is so nice and down-to-earth. We instantly form friendships and decide to go out together that night.

It doesn't take long to make friends in this nomadic life I've started. We all know—despite our different backgrounds, religions, and opinions—we need each other. We are each other's families now. And so we hold on to each other and take care of each other and don't let go until we have to. This is my first experience with this unexpected bond and, I am told, it certainly won't be the last.

We join in the common room (the former loathe of my life) as a young Australian guy with messy blond curls picks up a guitar. We look around and smile as we start singing George Michael's "Faith." One young woman takes my cup and pours a mixture of Jameson and Coke for my first, very much needed drink of my trip.

We head out into the rain-speckled cobblestone streets and hop from pub to pub, ending the night at a club filled with drunken eighteen-year-olds vibrating in a sea of bodies beneath bright green strobe lighting and techno music. I'm not used to feeling old at the alarming age of twenty-six, so I drink in the moment, and the tequila, and stumble home giggling with my new horde of friends at 2:00 a.m.

The next morning, while most people at the hostel are off on tours of the countryside, city, and pubs, I head out into the city alone. I spend the next three days alone, coexisting with what can only be described as a dense fog. I feel awkward. I'm starving, but even food fails to provide any comfort, as my anxiety and depression-laden state has chased away any hope of an appetite. The cold and rainy weather feels more like November than August, with a constant wind and rain that chills me to the bone.

Back at the hostel, the large wooden windows of our room are always open. Each evening, wafts of cool night air drift in with the sounds of people on the street talking and laughing while the bands below persistently play music. They have an assortment of instruments, and the main artist in front works a flute like I've never seen. His fingers open and close, moving up and down the sleek silver as he sways to the music. People passing by can't help but stop and clap their hands. The music starts early in the afternoon, and it doesn't stop until early in the morning. I wake up from my afternoon nap and hear Irish music. I get ready and take a shower and write postcards and hear Irish music. It is in this blanket of notes when I start to realize this really is a charmed life.

By the third morning, with the jet lag wearing off and my appetite slowly seeping back into my system, I start to feel like myself again. I've just awoken from a dream where

I was back at home and this life had never existed. I sit up and look around, relieved to see I'm not home. I've never been so far from home in my life. I roll over in my squeaky bunk bed and genuinely smile for the first time since arriving in Dublin. Looking out the large open window, I see the sun finally shining and Ireland smiling back at me. This is all starting to feel right. I can't believe this is my life, and it's only just begun.

I pull my earplugs out and look around my crammed room with bunk beds lining every square inch. *Empty.* The beds have been stripped bare with pillows thrown about. The only evidence of life is one lonely hair band left in the middle of the floor. Gone, all gone. I forgot in our frenzy of Guinness and music last night that everyone was leaving this morning, off in different directions to continue their journeys. It's sad in a way, forming friendships and seeing smiles on faces that actually started to mean something. The life of a nomad—within hours the room will fill up again with new faces, and just like that, the hope of new friends will begin again.

I feel bad that Ireland had to be my first stop. I was too busy being scared out of my mind to really see its splendor. I could have started my trip anywhere; even Disney World wouldn't have shaken me from my state of grief and panic. But in Dublin, at least in my anxiety and uncertainty, I had the company of a country whose people know what it's like to hold on tight when your world gets tipped on its side.

Looking back, knowing I could have been anywhere my first few days, I'm glad I chose Ireland.

Chicago, Illinois

So I let go of my travel dream, for months I let it go…but it never let go of me. Whenever I talk to people who are doing or have done something like it, this tight feeling of sadness grips my chest, accompanied by what can only be described as a pure ache.

Regret.

If I don't do this, I will forever regret it.

*Last night I had a dream that I was leaving to do my world trip. I was exhilarated, nervous, excited—not scared…not like I am now. I was off to Belgium. Then, out of nowhere, I was home, telling people that I just came back from Europe. I had this **treasure**, this experience, this fully lived-in dream. And then I woke up, and I was sad all over again. This dream forever haunts me. Every time I let it go, it stays with me, reminds me, finds me in my dreams.*

The problem is I have all these thoughts of how it could be, and I don't want that life! I start whining to myself that I'd live in a dirty hostel, broke and lonely, with eighteen-year-olds and loud, all-night parties.

But who says it has to be that way?

It could be magical…and on my terms.

Then one of my dental hygiene patients, my last patient of the day, tells me about this horrific freak accident that caused the death of her sister.

"*That's why,*" *she says as she looks up at me through tear-filled eyes,* "*you can't put things off, or make excuses as to why you can't do anything. Don't say, 'Maybe when I'm fifty I'll do that.' Because you never know when your time is. So you've got to **live** your life—no excuses! This is not a dress rehearsal.*"

As she is saying this, a resounding "*Yes!*" *screams from within me.*

And I smile inside.

This always happens. The dream awakens and there's always someone around the corner saying, "*Yes, you can.*" *I then shake my head with nothing but fear empowering my whimpers.* "*No! I can't.*"

And always, this wisdom of the world whispering quietly back to me, "*Yes, yes you can.*"

So I'm going. I have to. I have to! God, help me actually stick with this. God, help me live this lifelong dream. I have to do this. God, help me do this. Have mercy on me and let me fly, and may this life be all that it is cracked up to be.

Dublin Airport, Ireland

STANDING IN LINE at the Dublin Airport, I can hear everything around me like the sounds themselves are on megaphones. There is no buffer of a conversation of my own, no companionship, no distractions—just life, blaring around me like music to my ears.

There isn't much room between us—the people in line and myself. I can't help but eavesdrop on the two men behind me. They have beautiful British accents and are joking with each other about their favorite brand of toothpaste. In my boredom, I turn around to see the faces that belong to these stories, and in an instant everything changes.

He is tall and handsome with light-brown eyes. We stare at each other and smile for what seems like an eternity, but realistically is only seconds. I am beaming. I bashfully turn away, desperate to talk to him.

Our line inches forward a couple feet. We stop again. They start talking about how great their trip was and how friendly everyone in Ireland is. The line slowly shifts again. We are even closer now, and I purposely reposition myself so I am only half turned toward them. I look at him again. He is staring right at me.

"So where are you guys headed?" I ask nonchalantly.

"Back to London. You?" he responds, smiling.

"Off to Amsterdam to visit a friend."

"What were you in Ireland for?" God, his accent is beautiful.

"Well, I'm on a pretty big trip, so this was my first stop."

The small talk continues as our line slowly moves toward security. By the time we hit the conveyor belts, I think I'm in love. He smiles and I giggle. It's downright embarrassing.

As I remove my shoes and jewelry, I panic for a moment when I realize our time is up; this is when we will part ways. I act cool as I go through the motions: wait for the hand wave of the security officer, walk through the metal detector, and grab my things on the other side. As I repack my bags and put my shoes back on, I stall as long as possible, wanting to give him a sufficient chance to do…something. I don't know, what can he do? *Something!* I don't want this to be the end.

I casually look around as I put my second sandal on. *Where did they go?* I spot them standing in the airport hall, looking at me. He points down the corridor and raises his eyebrows. "Coffee?"

I smile.

At the airport coffee shop, England asks me what I want. My mind instantly responds, *You. All of you.*

Coffee, he's talking about *coffee.* I don't know what to order and, wanting to avoid sounding like I am high maintenance, I ask for a black coffee and end up pouring in a mountain of sugar to make it somewhat palatable. We find a tall table with no chairs and use it as a base to lean on.

As I awkwardly crunch my coffee, we talk about where we're from and what's next in line for our week.

"You should come to London," he mentions slyly. "I could show you around."

I look up at him and smile. "I'd love to."

We exchange numbers, and I secretly pat myself on the back for getting an international phone for the trip. He gives me a somewhat awkward hug, as we have only known each other for fifteen minutes, and promises to call me. Walking toward my terminal, I fight the urge to squeal. *He. Is. Adorable! I'm going to London? I'm going to London! How romantic! We're going to fall in love and get married and have very tall babies.*

I fight with my water bottle to open the cap, and as I pull off the top, my hand squeezes the cheap plastic and water sprays all over my face. All I can do is laugh. "Crazy woman," the locals must think. I am crazy, crazy in love with Connor. Connor...oh, I never got his last name... or his age. Oh well, his name is Connor, and I'm going to London to go on a date.

Amsterdam, The Netherlands

AFTER LANDING at Amsterdam Airport Schiphol, I take the train into the city. Leaving my bag in storage, I stroll out of the station and know I have stepped into another world. The streets are lined in narrow, uneven brick buildings with large, white, molded windows. Sexual paraphernalia crowds the shop windows while throngs of bikers pass in every direction. The smell of weed is in the air.

It's warmer here, seventy degrees and sunny. After being in Ireland, this alone makes me incredibly happy. I walk the streets just elated. *What is this place?* It's like I stepped into an alternate universe, like the air is different or the humans are a unique subspecies.

As I walk along a tree-lined street and its aligning canal, I see a large gathering of people looking down at the passing boats and screaming while triumphantly throwing their hands in the air. I find myself spending the next two hours joining them. I meet John, a local who approaches me and strikes up a conversation in Dutch.

"Oh, I don't speak Dutch," I apologize.

He responds in English, informing me that it was actually a compliment because I am skinny, blond, and sans backpack. Every tourist here seems to wear a backpack.

I smile and thank him, not mentioning my large pack sitting in storage.

I squeeze into the crowd overlooking the canal and stand shoulder to shoulder on the cobblestone to witness a hilarious show of unorganized chaos. We are at a particular spot where the canal becomes extremely narrow, just wide enough for two small boats or one large boat to get through. It is also a gateway from the larger sea into the city canals, so many, many boats are trying to get through simultaneously. I shall call this game "Bumper Boats" or better yet, "I'm-Too-Laid-Back-to-Give-a-Rat's-Ass-What's-Going-on-Around-Me Boats."

The point of the game is this: how many unconcerned, happy Hollanders can you get through the canal at one time? But there is a catch: on the city side of the narrow opening two perpendicular canals merge together to go through the narrow passageway into the ocean. This is fine until the very large and longer tourist boats try to get through from the other side. The captain lays on the menacing horn in a fair warning that he is coming through. Some boats stay back, which is boring, but most try to squeeze through. This is where the fun begins for us spectators. We scream and shout, "Ooooohhh nooooo!" as some barely make it through and then cheer them on as they successfully squeeze by.

But what about the boats that decide against it and back up? They have an eye on the situation in front of them but not in back. That's where we come in again. We watch to the right as a boat or two creeps through and then look back to the left as a boat backs up into a gaggle of waiting boats. "Ooohh oh!" We point and scream, then scream and laugh, and on and on we go. The boaters scramble to throw their rubber buoys in between their boats so they don't hurt the precious wood. *Boink!* They bounce playfully off one another, propelling the initial boat in the opposite direction, once more into another oncoming boat. "Oh, oh! OH!" we all scream and watch as the older man jumps up and buoys his boat again. Everyone claps at his success at avoiding any damage. He smiles and bows. It is so hilariously unstructured. And instead of stressing out as most people would, followed by a ruined evening and a strongly worded letter to Congress, everyone just shrugs their shoulders and laughs. They slowly chug their incredibly unique boats up and down the canals, listening to music, grilling, and probably getting high as all hell.

Now I understand why everyone loves this place. It's amazing.

Riccardo calls. He is off work and ready to meet up. Riccardo and I met last year in Rome when a couple friends and I had decided to spend our evening sitting at a fountain, watching people and smoking cigarettes. *When in Rome.* I had bought a sad excuse for a lighter that only worked about thirty percent of the time. As I flicked away for some sort of spark, Riccardo walked up, like the Italian gentleman he is, to give me a light.

Two hours later our group had tripled. We had a guitar and were singing "Sweet Home Alabama" while drinking beer and passing around a joint. It was 2:00 a.m. and I swear we had made friends with half of Rome. Riccardo and his friends met up with us multiple times while we were in Rome, and we have kept in touch ever since. He is now living in Amsterdam with his girlfriend, Aurelie, and has invited me to stay with them.

I walk away from the commotion of "Bumper Boats" so I can hear better. Riccardo has a thick Italian accent, and sometimes I need all the concentration I can muster to understand him.

"Where are you?" he asks.

"Uhhh…I'm kind of by the train station, next to a coffee shop called The Bulldog."

"Jill, there are hundreds of coffee shops and almost an equal amount named The Bulldog."

"Oh, right. I'm by a canal…"

"*Jill.*"

"Oh God, I know, I'm sorry! Okay, the street I'm on is…" I speed walk until I find a street sign. "Bloom…en…kejk?"

"What?"

Forty-five minutes and three phone calls later, we find each other. I run up and hug him as we each extend compliments of how wonderful it is to have an opportunity to meet again. We stop on the way home for a beer, and he tells me about Aurelie, who is from Paris. It's a little difficult to find something to talk about when our only conversations have been premeditated messages on Facebook, but as the time passes—and our blood alcohol level rises—the conversation starts to flow better as well.

I notice as we walk home that each building has a large wooden plank with a hook attached to the molding framing the roof. Riccardo explains to me that because of the very narrow stairwells in the Netherlands, it is impossible to move furniture into the homes. So they attach a rope to the hook and pulley the furniture above the streets and through the windows. And he isn't kidding. As soon as we walk into his building, I find myself awkwardly climbing the tiny little steps up to his apartment, eventually giving up and taking them two at a time.

I'm introduced to sweet Aurelie, and the large marijuana plant they named after her that is sitting in a sun-drenched corner of the living room. I then excuse myself to take a much-needed shower. Oh, I am so grateful to be able to shower without wearing flip-flops or dry heaving when my naked rear accidentally touches the side of the slimy community shower stall. I'm also relieved to have my very own private bedroom, and so soon into my trip.

∼

Later, as we get ready to leave for dinner, Riccardo and Aurelie tell me they fixed up a bike for me to ride while I'm here. It's a standard bike, with taller handlebars and a ladybug bell that sits on the front. I have a thing for ladybugs, so this small detail makes me very happy indeed. The bike seats are much higher here, so as I take off from a standstill position, I have to stand on the pedal to get onto the seat and instantly start pedaling to avoid losing my balance. I can't remember the last time I've ridden a bike, so I'm quite the wobbly mess when I start.

As we head off to the restaurant, Riccardo patiently leads us at a slow pace until I get the hang of it. The sidewalks here are like biker expressways, which intimidates the hell out of me. This is especially the case when we have to stop at the biker traffic lights and then pick up again in the midst of a sea of professional bikers. I can't just *go*, because the effort of *going* involves getting up on my seat from a standstill and starting to pedal. I then wobble and weave as I gain some momentum and balance, often pushing other bikers off the path and sometimes going a little off the path myself. I wouldn't be surprised if, by the time I leave, there is a "WARNING!" poster with a sketch of my face plastering the city.

Eventually, as we head out of traffic to the edge of town, the sidewalk clears once again and we are left with minutes of pure unaccompanied bliss.

Bikers heading in the opposite direction approach us.

"Jill, stay to the right!" Riccardo tips his head and yells from ahead. I panic and go to the left.

"I'm sorry, I'm sorry!" I shout as the bikers pass between us. My wheel bobs to the left and almost slips into the tram tracks in the road. A car whizzes by and practically nudges me into a nearby canal.

"Try not to get hit by car, no?" Riccardo yells. I giggle nervously. *Tomorrow, I think I'll walk.*

The three of us pedal to Riccardo and Aurelie's favorite coffee shop and bar. Sitting on the deck overlooking a canal, I watch nervously as he puts a weed and tobacco mixture into a thin piece of paper and licks the edges so they stick together. I haven't done this in a while.

"Just smoke it like a cigarette," they tell me.

I can do that.

It's nice, not like college where people sit around and get stoned all night. It's just a light *haze*.

We sit outside and talk about our opinions and beliefs and passions. It's hilarious to see a French woman and an Italian man in love. Aurelie is so matter-of-fact, while Riccardo doesn't understand why we can't all just get along and "how come money has to rule the world?" I love this so much about travel, learning about others' cultures and thoughts and ways of life. It's intriguing and eye-opening and makes me feel truly alive.

As we bike home, the cool night air almost flows through me. I look up and see a shooting star burn across the midnight sky.

Amsterdam, The Netherlands

I once read a quote somewhere stating that real travel—not going on vacation—is rarely glamorous. I think of that quote often, as I am often uncomfortable. I am a foreigner, so therefore everything is foreign to me. I don't know what that sign says. How do I eat this? And how in the hell do I flush this toilet?

Riding my bike in Amsterdam, I have a general idea of which direction to head in, but I have no idea where I'm going. This sometimes leads me to cut a corner last minute and realize one second before it happens that I am about to run smack into a curb. The only thing I can do is brace myself. This is kind of like traveling and I suppose life in general: sometimes you have to just show up and brace yourself.

The worst part so far has been my travel days—leaving a city I was just starting to figure out, only to throw myself into a completely new environment. I often get a little lost, walk at least one time in the wrong direction, get frustrated, and turn around. The whole time I am carrying around a backpack the size and weight of a chubby eight-year-old. No matter how cold and rainy it is (which is northern Europe almost every day), I start sweating, my hips and lower back start to ache, and I can't breathe in a full breath of air. This... this is not glamour.

But then I look around and realize I am somewhere completely new. With eyes wide open, I wander the streets of an entirely unique city. That's the beautiful thing about traveling the world, especially alone: every day is something new. Every day brings new experiences, different food, intriguing people. You never know upon waking up what new adventures the day will hold. I get to do whatever I want; I get to live my authentic life, wholly, and just be. As I write this, I am sitting at a street-side café, drinking a couple beers on a Tuesday afternoon and watching a completely new world pass before me.

The great explorers never had easy lives, but they sure were grand and monumental and life-changing. Now, I understand that I am not a grand explorer, and many have passed this way before me. But every time you embark on any new exploration—whether it be starting a family, going to school, getting a dog, or moving to a new city—it is all a learning process and can always be scary. No one can do it for you, and no one can take that experience away from you.

I am still learning to love my uneasy feeling, and I have to be patient with myself, as it has only been a week. I have traveled many times before, but to do it alone and for so long is a completely exotic and alien expedition. It's such a tremendous undertaking that it is inevitable there is going to be somewhat of a learning curve.

Tomorrow, I head for Paris, one of the most romantic cities in the world. Connor is meeting me there for the weekend. An additional ticket to London was too expensive, so instead of forgetting the whole thing, we are now meeting for our date in Paris. Sounds reasonable to me. This is either incredibly romantic or incredibly stupid. But what an experience it will be! We are both putting ourselves out there and hoping it will be worth it.

*This is my life now. This is my once-in-a-lifetime opportunity. So I'm going to continue to follow my heart, take risks, and have faith that it will **always** be worth it. Because when the lights go out, you only answer to yourself.*

And in the end, what will ever be a good enough answer?

Paris, France

COMING UP FROM THE MÉTRO, I instantly lay eyes on him. The escalator stairs lead up to a broad open square surrounded by expensive hotels and cafés with large ornamental doorways and windows.

Oh *God*, is that him? I squint my eyes to see better. He is skinnier than I remember and his pants are falling down… is he punk? Oh shit, what have I gotten myself into?

I slowly inch toward him, trying to avoid direct eye contact. *If that is him*, I think cowardly, *I'll run.* His face comes into focus—nope, not him.

Relief showers over me.

My phone starts to vibrate. It's him. I answer immediately. "Hey, Jillian, I'm here. I see you, look to your left. More, more—there! See me?"

He is standing by a table at a hotel café overlooking the square, waving his arms. Tall, attractive, and slightly pale, my English gentleman reenters my world.

I smile and casually walk over to him, nervous and excited.

"You look stunning," he says as he kisses my cheek.

This, of course, is not by accident. I have spent the last two hours prepping, straightening my hair by sections and doing my nails. I am wearing a floor-length black dress with a heart-shaped neckline and an eye-catching silver shell necklace. He is in a blue-and-white-striped button-up

Ralph Lauren shirt and dark jeans. We sit and enjoy an overpriced drink—I have a white wine and he has a beer—and talk over blushing cheeks about how crazy it is that we are both in Paris. His accent is thick, sometimes leaving me having to guess what he is saying. He is charming and down-to-earth, and it doesn't take long to remember why we both jumped so quickly at this opportunity.

We are in his "neighborhood" for the weekend. Since I have been in Paris five days already and am now familiar with the Métro lines, I offered to meet him somewhere close to his hotel. He is staying just blocks away from the Louvre, in a charming neighborhood that is considerably nicer than my current choice of residence.

We head out after our initial drinks to a restaurant with a sultry vocalist who sings French melodies resembling the likes of Norah Jones. I proceed to learn more about my date for the next three days: he is young, one and a half years my junior at twenty-four years old, and owns a family business with his father in the suburbs of London.

As we sit in candlelight and "Norah" belts out romantic melodies, I'm practically floating on a sea of romance. I've already practiced signing my new name in my head, and I see visions of Connor and Jillian Juniors frolicking in the British countryside, when I turn to see my future husband texting away under the table. Taken aback, I shrug it off for now and turn my attention back to "Norah."

Hours later, we end the evening at Buddha Bar, a chic and trendy restaurant close to the Eiffel Tower that charges us a very steep thirty-four euros for two mojitos. At about twenty-two U.S. dollars per drink, this mojito is by far the most expensive beverage I have ever had. We then split a rainbow roll, my favorite sushi roll, resembling a rainbow because of the different fish and avocado placed on top. It's twenty euros for six pieces, but it's heavenly. I'm addicted to sushi and haven't had it in almost a month, making it the perfect dessert.

It is here, under the watchful eyes of a two-and-a-half-story Buddha, that we share our first kiss. Connor is an amazing kisser, and I think the Buddha approves. We sit together for hours, listening to music and getting to know each other.

Later on in the early morning hours, we wander outside and share a goodnight kiss in the evening glow of the Eiffel Tower. The tip of the tower has two very prominent searchlights that remind me it's time to go home.

"Please, don't..." he whispers as he begs me with his eyes. I hesitate.

"Please." He brushes his lips along the skin of my neck. "Don't go."

God, his accent is beautiful. He pulls away and holds my face in his hands. I smile. And he kisses me for hours.

~

The next day we greet Paris at an outdoor café with two espressos, some sunshine, and jazz. It has been very cloudy and cold here, which seems unusual for August and is quickly becoming an unbearable thorn in my side. I am irritated as I wake up to see an overtone of gray skies and clouds on a fairly regular basis.

Today though, the gods smile upon us and bless us with uninterrupted blue skies for the entire day. I couldn't be happier, feeling the warm rays of sunlight on my face, and as Connor and I share a kiss and a smile, I privately thank God for the much-needed change of scenery. Paris has quite literally shown me a cold shoulder this past week. From my lack of company to my lack of directions, this hasn't exactly proven to be the city of love.

~

Six days prior.

I'm lost—again. Damn it! Why do the hostel directions have to be so vague? I look again at my notes: *When you come out of the Métro, across from the Habitat, across from the McDonalds.*

I look around as my useless directions scrunch between my fingers. I see the Habitat, but no McDonalds. I walk up to a tall and slightly aged gentleman leaning against a lamppost and ask if he speaks English.

"*Excusez-moi? S'il vous plaît, parlez-vous anglais?*" I stutter, desperate for some sort of eye contact.

He shakes his head no, looking in my direction for a brief moment and then promptly looking away. This is my first experience in Paris being treated like a homeless person (which I am), and it certainly won't be the last.

I continue my investigation with a couple of women smoking outside a bank entrance. They are tall and elegant with expensive shoes, pressed slacks, and beautiful brown flowing hair. I slowly walk up as they chat away, hoping my day-old hair in a messy ponytail and overflowing backpack don't tempt them to pick up stones and throw them at me.

They each pull out their iPhones to try to find my mystery hostel, and then proceed to send me in the completely wrong direction.

And I was in such a good mood.

I pass an elderly woman, dreadfully hunched over her cane as she shuffles down the uneven Parisian cobblestone. That'll be me in another six months, guaranteed.

After twenty minutes and three breakdowns, I find it! It's old and beautiful, with dimly lit, red-carpeted, winding staircases and opera music playing quietly over the conspicuously placed speakers. There is no common area, I am told, which is unfortunate since it's how I made half my friends in Dublin.

I meet my new roommates—two young men from South Korea who speak very little English. The only contact we have over a period of three days is an exchange of smiles and their offering of friendship by leaving little candies on my pillow that I find upon waking up every morning.

I unpack a little and shove what I can under my hollow metal bunk bed. Both men shove their noses into their laptops to avoid conversation. I suppose I'll be greeting Paris alone.

As I start my first exploration, I pull out my cell phone and call my older brother, Andrew. I haven't spoken to him since I left home, so just the sound of his voice brings tears to my eyes.

"Jill! How are you?" he excitedly asks.

"Uh, I'm okay," I wobble in return.

I attempt to muster some sort of composure and we talk for a couple minutes, catching up with a select few newsworthy events and promising to keep in touch.

After we hang up, I let myself feel sad for a glorious five whole minutes, then put on my iPod and head for the Eiffel Tower. I decide to get off the Métro a little early so I can walk through some of the beautiful neighborhoods surrounding the tower.

The buildings are everything I've grown up watching in movies: light in color, black roofs, and tall open windows with flower boxes lining every floor. There are cafés and *cragh-saunts* and beautiful women in scarves of every color. My red scarf and I fit right in. I'm not really sure where I'm going, so I keep my eye on the tip of the tower peeking over the buildings as a sort of beacon to keep me heading in the right direction.

The clouds start to dissipate, and the sun embraces this old European city in all its splendor. The park trees clear away and I see it, the Eiffel Tower. Harry Connick Jr. is singing "A Wink and a Smile," giggling children are running around, and body odor is in the air. If the cities I've been in so far on this trip had to have one smell associated with them, Dublin would be rain; Amsterdam, weed; and Paris, definitely BO. Beautiful city—awful smell. I'd rather smell Amsterdam any day.

I wander around the tower grounds and take photos. How many photos can one tourist possibly take of the Eiffel Tower? Many. Too many. It's just so incredible; pictures don't give it the reverence it deserves.

I find a park bench, determined to wait until dark to see the tower light up and watch the world go by while I listen to my iPod. I wish I could tell you that some beautiful man approached me and we ran into the French sunset holding hands, but instead I pass the time by joining the people perched along the benches next to me. We all follow the same routine: look left, watch the crowds walk by, scan them from top to bottom, then stare at their shoes until they are down the road. Repeat, repeat, repeat.

It is now 8:55 p.m. and the Eiffel Tower has just lit up. It's *glorious*. The whole structure is sparkling with little white lights covering the tower from top to bottom, emitting a purely magical glow.

A couple days later, I decide to stroll along the famous Rue Cler, a street in Paris that is considerably old and lined with flower shops and cafés. I have to say, I find it a little disappointing. It looks like every other street in Paris but with no cars. That's it, not really worth the trip over here.

So I look for a restaurant within my means to sit outside and watch the increasingly anticlimactic world roll by. Out of sheer laziness, I settle on a Chinese buffet and make friends with some very curious pigeons. One in particular sits by my feet and keeps me company while I eat what appears to be some sort of mystery meat coated in MSG. I keep thinking of that scene in one of the last episodes of *Sex and the City*, where Carrie is in a bakery in Paris eating a croissant and is kept company by a large and patient dog begging for her scraps. I have a feeling my bird friend has the same intentions.

After I fill my monthly quota of brown food coloring and gelatin meat, I decide to head once again to the Eiffel Tower. I know it must be close, but I can't see the tip over the tall buildings surrounding me. After a few left turns, and a few more wrong ones, I find my way to the tower of love, admiration, and trinket sellers in gorilla suits. I spend the rest of the afternoon lazing about on the busy lawn of what used to grow grass in front of the tower, writing and listening to music.

I decide to write myself a little pep talk. I need this today, as I am feeling a little overwhelmed with the life I have created for myself. It is cold here, both the temperature and the people, and I have never felt so lonely in my entire life. Four days have passed since I first watched the Eiffel Tower light up, and I have continued to watch it every night since. I've wandered the streets of Paris and the halls of its world-famous museums. I've had breakfast alone, lunch alone, and all but one dinner alone when I met up with a friend who lives in Paris.

I feel so guilty at this point, having to write myself a pep talk when there are beggars to the left and right of me who would dream of just *one day* of my life. I also hate admitting that this dream life of mine, as exceptionally free and uniquely adventurous as it is, is hard—really hard—and lonely, and uncomfortable. It's no-one-to-talk-to-even-though-you-are-surrounded-by-people uncomfortable. It's never-quite-sure-of-where-you're-going-or-what-you're-doing uncomfortable. This puts an edge on my existence. I'm uncomfortable yet more alive than ever, which is why I'm living such a dichotomous life of extremes. I'm in love yet drowning in insecurity. I just haven't exactly figured it out—this life of mine—or learned to accept my discomfort yet. And that's okay. I know I'll figure it out eventually. I always do.

Then, in the middle of my heart-wrenching confusion, in the middle of the lawn under the shadows of a grand monument, a ladybug lands on my arm. *A ladybug!* Ladybugs are a sign of good fortune! I'm so happy that, as it sits there, I grab my camera to take a picture. But as I aim the lens, it lifts its wings, *shits* on me, and flies away. *Not nice.* A ladybug is supposed to be the friendliest bug! It's the only bug that I'm not afraid of. I feel like a unicorn just flipped me off. In my horror, I attempt to wipe "the cutest little piece of fecal matter" off my arm, only to smudge it deeper into my skin. I'm starting to get the feeling that this whole traveling the world bit is going to require thicker skin… and some hand sanitizer.

~

Connor and I spend our first full day together exploring the highlights of Paris. Since it is his first time in Paris as well, we decide to start off by heading to the Arc de Triomphe. The tickets to the top are nine euros each, but only 4.5 euros for people under the age of twenty-five. He laughs at me about the trials of being old as I tell him the museums here are free if you are under twenty-six.

"Wow! That is *so* great since that is the only reason I've come to Paris!" He winks at me.

I smile, but I'm irritated. I've never been one to waste time feeling old, especially considering the fact that *I'm not.* But it's summer holiday at this time, so the hostels and night scene are shoulder to shoulder with giggling, smart-ass, pimply teenagers. I feel ancient.

Paris is not exactly equipped with its fair share of elevators, so it comes as no surprise that to get to the top of the Arc de Triomphe, you have to climb a winding, narrow staircase of three hundred steps. I pant and wheeze my way through every step while Connor waits for me at several of the landings.

"You're not out of breath, are you?" He pokes at me.

"It's the weed," I gasp, remembering Amsterdam, and humbly shamble on.

The scene at the top is sublime, giving us uninterrupted panoramic views of Paris. We sit and take photos, all the while trying to figure out the rules of the road below. We stand essentially at the bull's-eye of a circle with about eight different roads merging into one circling the Arc. We watch, horrified, as the cars zoom around each other as if each owned an invisible force field protecting them and leaving each driver with no consequence whatsoever for driving like a maniac.

Next stop: the former "ode to loneliness," the Eiffel Tower. Thirty minutes into the line, we learn the only way to the second level tonight is by stairs…all seven hundred of them. As I take a deep breath and begin my journey, I realize I may have never been so out of breath in my entire life, but the view at the top—what an amazing view. The sun is disappearing below the Parisian buildings, canvasing the city in a blanket of luminescent orange hues.

As we make our way down, the tower lights power on and we heighten our speed. The glimmering white lights are turning on soon, and Connor has never seen the tower shimmer. At step 380, only about halfway down, the twinkling lights start up.

"Go, go, go!" I yell to Connor.

The lights only flash for a couple minutes each hour, and we want to see the show close-up. I feel like we are in the center of a disco ball as we clank down the metal stairs that form the vertebra of the tower. By the time we reach the bottom, hearts pounding and out of breath, the show is over. "It's okay," we say. "We'll catch it next hour."

We walk along the Seine in search of a restaurant, preferably one with classic French food, low lighting, and a good view. We cross to the opposite side of the river and stumble upon the tunnel where Princess Diana died, almost thirteen years ago to the day. It's chilling standing above the very place where she took her frightful last breaths. There are love letters and roses all over the tunnel, as well as written memories and prayers for a princess who captured our hearts and left us all too soon.

We find a perfect table at a restaurant with outdoor seating, right across the street from Diana's tunnel, where we have uninhibited views of the Eiffel Tower across the river. The tables are small and intimate, adorned with crisp white cloths and petite tabletop lamps to set the mood. I couldn't think of any place better to sit and enjoy each other's company for the last night that we have it.

Connor is easy to get along with, and our conversations are effortless. It has the potential to be a great romance, or at least a great story of a romance that I'll be able to tell when I'm gray-haired and senile. I'll rock away in my creaky old chair and remember the days when love and poetry ruled the world.

I can't, however, get past the sneaking suspicion that my Prince Charming sitting across from me, texting away under the table, may not exactly be on the market. We didn't sleep together last night, although I very much wanted to. He didn't bring protection and didn't push the issue of sleeping together either. What sort of man spends hundreds of pounds to meet a woman in Paris for the weekend and doesn't bring protection? He didn't seem to care and I wasn't about to interrogate him. So we ripped each other's clothes off, made out…and then went to sleep.

I watch him as he clicks away at his phone.

"That's rude," I pronounce in my best motherly voice.

"I know, I'm sorry," he says and continues typing.

What a stupid accent. No, I take that back. It's still gorgeous.

"Can you excuse me for a sec? I'll be two minutes. I need to call my mum. She has no idea where I am." He smiles as he stands and pushes his chair in.

As I watch him at the curb, kicking dirt and mumbling into his phone, I can't decide which is worse: if he really did have to call his mom so desperately that it had to be during dinner, or if he's actually calling his girlfriend. He's probably telling her some story about running into an old friend or having a business meeting with a new contractor for the family business. Either way, he's a shiesty bugger, and I disconnect myself immediately, chalking it up to a fantastic story and romantic fling, deciding right then and there not to take any of it too seriously. Besides, what's the point of traveling the world alone if you have to carry the baggage of a new boyfriend?

Connor returns. "Sorry, love, my mum's such a worrier."

"Of course," I say slyly. "I would worry too if someone left the country like that and didn't tell me."

We both smile. *Bastard.* Oh well, he sure is pretty to look at.

The server finally comes around, and Connor orders pan-seared veal and I order a fish I have never heard of.

They bring my dish out, grilled with scales intact and eyes wide open, staring at me.

"Oh, nice. *Merci?*" I doubtfully remark.

The server, reading my obvious expression, asks if I would like him to prepare it for me by removing the scales and head. Smiling, I respond with a nod.

I take a bite and start to realize that my food, just like my company, may be lacking somewhat in the quality versus quantity category. There is a whole dish of bland in front of me. Connor's dinner, however, is astonishing. I pick at what tastes like moist dish sponge while Connor is next to me having an out-of-body experience.

Later, as we enjoy our crème brûlée under the moonlit sky, we watch the Eiffel Tower light up again like a fireworks show on Fourth of July.

As hard as I try to "not take it all so seriously," I still can't seem to get over his secretiveness. If there is one thing I've learned over the years, it's if it walks like a duck, and quacks like a duck…well, you know the rest.

"I think I'm going to head home after this," I announce as I push myself away from the table.

"Really? Why?"

"I don't feel well. I have a headache." Classic excuse.

"Please stay with me. Please? It's our last night."

I hesitate. Arguments are shooting back and forth inside my head. *Screw him! Let him hump his pillow tonight while he dreams of his girlfriend.* The other side rebuts: *Oh come on, it never would have worked anyway. Besides, it is a fling, right? So fling! Fling around the bedroom with your clothes off. It's Paris! Que sera or whatever. No regrets, remember?*

And with that, Little Jack Horny and I walk hand in hand

under the pseudo moonlight of the neon lights of his hotel. No condoms, no sex, no deep romance. But we *flinged*, and it's still a great story, no matter what Danielle Steel may say.

～

Sunday is gray again and unfortunately arrives all too soon. Despite my doubts or judgment of his character, Connor has still been good company in a lonely city. And the kisses haven't hurt either.

After a last wander through the city and a couple of farewell beers, I accompany him to Gare du Nord, the northern train station in Paris where we say our "see you laters." We have every intention of trying to meet once again (*what the hell*), but for now, our weekend fling in Paris may remain just that…a fling.

I'll never know what was the real issue with Connor— whether he secretly had a girlfriend or maybe he just really loved his mom. Either way, it wasn't meant to be the romance I had hoped for. We texted each other a few times after we parted ways, but as I suspected, those fizzled too.

Looking back at our chance encounter and our weekend together, I can't help but think, gratefully, what an amazing experience to have lived, and a new friend, if anything, to have made.

I spend my last day in Paris perched along the Rue du Rivoli, next to the Louvre, sipping wine and writing in my leather-bound notebook. I help myself to another delightful bite of my Nutella crepe and smile. Love or no love, my life is still a fairy tale.

Michigan

I have tried to let it go,
I have tried to move on,
release the grip,
forgive.

Many affirmations later,
I am still breathless with the pain.

And so we talked.
I spoke softer words,
so the harsher ones wouldn't have room.

I soared beyond my maturity
and apologized for words unspoken.

I felt her deep anger,
and she listened to my tears.

There was a letting go,
a certain sorrow beyond our ability to understand.

I've lost the capacity to control these sad circumstances,
and a frustration that must be released.

The loneliness has multiplied.
I feel even more now earth's gravity clinging to me.
My feet unable to lift
and move away from this place.

"I don't know," she said quietly,
"if these words sound hollow...
but I do love you, Jill."

At that moment, I released my breath
and exhaled my rejection.

I cried for all the things she's said,
and all the things she never will.

I keep saying to myself,
"I must somehow release the grip.
I must somehow grieve my loss.
I must somehow move away from this place."

So here, have my tears.
And save yourself from the doom I will obviously inflict by your
     association with me.

They say time heals all wounds.
Dear God, I hope so.

Until then,
I will "cope"
and say affirmations
and "forgive."

Until I can breathe again...

Nice, France

A S MY FOOT STEPS OFF the train platform, choirs of
angels raise their voice in joyous song, giggling cherubs lift my pack, and I start floating in midair. The sky
and ocean share equal shades of a deep blue, so deep you
don't know where one ends and the other begins. I am in
the south of France. I have stepped through the gates of
heaven, and heaven's name is Nice.

Just five and a half hours from cold and dreary Paris, I am
in the presence of glorious warm weather, deep blue ocean,
and tall and slender palm trees lining the coast. The stone
buildings here are painted in white, yellow, and rose hues,
with red and orange tiled roofs and white wooden shutters
on the windows. The cypress and palm trees all seem to
point and sway as if dancing to music in a Dr. Seuss movie.

I am deliriously happy.

I don't want to see another tourist attraction, forty-five-
minute-long line, or my stupid fleece ever again. I am going
to walk the narrow cobblestone streets, eat ice cream, smell
the overflowing flower boxes of roses, and lie in the ocean
until I melt away completely. I'm trading in my scarf for
my bikini, my leggings for my sundress—praise the sweet
baby Jesus, it's warm at last!

The train ride here was amazing. Sitting first class in a
high-speed train skirting the coast of the French Riviera,

I passed the time glued to my window, repeating quiet whispers of gratitude for the astonishing beauty and uninterrupted blue skies and sea.

After two weeks of almost nonstop cold and rain, Nice is like Southern comfort food to the starving. I'm not saying it's been awful spending the past two weeks in those incredible and culturally exquisite European cities—it was unbelievable. I'm just so damn happy to finally be able to relax in the warmth of the sun again, to soak the blisters of my weary feet in the salty ocean waters and feel the sand beneath my toes. To top it all off, I have found a hostel right in the center of town with a five-minute walk to the beach. It doesn't get any better than this.

I rise early at 8:30 a.m. with the enthusiasm of a child. As I slip on my bikini with price tags still attached, I can barely contain myself. I am going to the beach today, and I'm not going to leave—*ever*.

By midday, I have reunited with some new hostel friends I met the night before, and we line up along the shore. We have one Canadian, one American, one Englishman, and two Australians.

Unfortunately, there is no feeling of sand beneath our toes today. The beach is filled entirely with pebbles or, more accurately, large stones. We each bring along a bamboo mat from the hostel to cushion us from the somewhat harsh surface, but this does not faze anyone. We are sitting on the coast of the French Riviera. It is seventy-eight degrees and sunny. What do I have to do today? Nothing. What am I doing tomorrow? Nothing. I'm on a vacation from my vacation.

Later on that evening, a group of us are enjoying beers in the common room when we meet Kate, a young Canadian woman who has just arrived in Nice. I invite her to join us for dinner in a part of Nice known as Old Town, only blocks away.

We make our way through block after block of the evening street markets, filled with tables of eclectic jewelry, knickknacks, and souvenirs, and keep an eye out for a restaurant that suits. As I browse through the plethora of glitz and glitter, the girls in my group whisper and point. "If you like this, you will love Thailand!"

Dinner that night is at an establishment serving typical French fare and seafood with heaps of tables overflowing onto the street. This area of town does not allow cars, so the restaurants have their outdoor seating under intimate, low-lit white tents filling the road.

I hit the jackpot tonight; not only am I sitting outside and enjoying dinner in Nice, but I am enjoying my meal with a great group of new friends. There are Tom and Jess, an Australian couple traveling around Europe during their summer holiday at "Uni"; Rochelle from London who is doing the same; and now Kate, who is traveling for three weeks alone "just because." We sit around our table and drink a couple carafes of red wine and order our feasts for the evening. Jess and Rochelle each order their own pizza, Kate has an enormous helping of spaghetti, and Tom and I? Well, we really hit the jackpot—unlimited servings of French fries and mussels.

As we inform the servers how we want our mussels seasoned, another worker places a giant metal bucket in front of us for scraps. My first bucket of mussels is seasoned with garlic and white wine, the second is lemon and parsley, and my third bucket is doused in white wine and onion.

Yes, that's three buckets of mussels. I think for a moment I may have died and gone to heaven, and maybe Tom and I are racing because all you can hear at dinner is the *clink, clink, clink* of empty mussel shells being thrown into the communal bucket.

In the process of the evening, I find out that Kate just happens to be leaving Nice the same day as I am and also just happens to be going to the same area of Italy: Cinque Terre, or "The Five Villages." We form an instant bond, talking as if we were old friends who grew up together, so it doesn't take us long to agree that exploring Italy together would be a fine idea indeed. We all talk about this phenomenon over the buckets of mussels: how when you are traveling and putting faith in the unknown, things just seem to...work out.

The next morning, Kate accompanies me to the train station so I can book my Italy tickets, and then she helps me book a room in the hotel where she will be staying in La Spezia, a small town just seven minutes by train from the first village.

Tomorrow, I will hop a train to the place BBC Travel and Lonely Planet nominated this year as the number one travel destination in Europe. I now have my *own room* at a hotel and a wonderful new travel mate to explore Italy's magical Five Villages with. I can't get over the way this has all fallen into place.

After my next destination is officially set up, we meet up with Rochelle at the hostel and the three of us head to Cannes for the day.

Cannes is gorgeous with its white-sand beaches, palm trees, and "lifestyles of the rich and famous." I don't think

I have ever seen so many deeply bronzed bodies sprinkled with white curly hair. There are no beautiful young Fabios surrounding us lucky ladies today, possibly Fabio's grandparents. With protruding bellies and brightly colored Speedos, they would surely all qualify for the senior citizen's discount at Big Boy. Once again, this is no matter. The three of us lie on the beach, giggling and whispering to each other, "We're in *Cannes!*"

Unlike the shoreline in Nice, the beaches here are filled with sand. But similar to Nice, they are topless. Since I have already fully participated in topless beaches in Spain and Mexico, I don't hesitate for a second to find a spot, plop down, and remove my bikini top. With our toes in the sand, heads tilted back, and bikini tops in a heap next to us, there is nothing left to do but relax in the sun and discuss at length the lives we have temporarily abandoned back home—Rochelle's brothers and sisters, my home in Chicago, and Kate's mom.

Kate confides in us about the emotional—yet not physical—loss of her mother, who has caused Kate to grieve over her mother's rejection through bits and pieces of denial and intermittent bursts of therapy for most of her life. This is my first time in a long time meeting another woman who shares the emotional loss of a mother and, surprisingly, on my trip it won't be the last. We all seem to be driven in the same way, attracted to the same unconventional paths in life.

"How do you do it?" Kate looks at me.

"Do what?"

"You seem to be okay with it all."

I look at her, hesitating. "I'm not okay with it. I'm not okay with it at all. I'll *never* be okay with it."

She sighs and looks out at the ocean. "So how are we supposed to move on? How are we supposed to…be okay with it all?"

"I used to have dreams"—I inhale deeply—"every night, where I was back with the Jehovah's Witnesses. I'd see their smiling faces, and my mother and I would wrap our arms around each other and hold each other. They'd tell me it was okay that I left, and they were *happy* for me, and that the whole disfellowshipping 'arrangement' was no longer valid. I was so happy. I remember feeling like I was smiling through my entire body. And I was so *relieved* that I no longer had to carry such a burden. I could finally have my family back.

"And then I'd wake up. I'd lie in bed all morning and cry. I'd pray to God to take away the pain, to make the Jehovah's Witnesses stop, to help me find someone to make them stop, make them talk to me again, make them give me my family back…make them do things that they are never going to do. Every morning I'd mourn my loss over and over again.

"When I turned twenty-one, two years after my disfellowshipping, I found out my mother was getting baptized, and I knew. I knew that was the official end. Up until then, we'd still have occasional contact because *technically* she couldn't get into trouble for speaking to me. Our communication would be irregular and full of dysfunction, as her guilt governed her every move, but at least I still had hope. Once one is baptized, however, the rules become hard and permanent.

"I was in college and living with my grandparents at the time. I walked into the living room, my face swollen from tears, and crawled into my grandfather's arms. He didn't say anything; he already knew. I shoved my face in his shoulder and said, 'I think I need to talk to someone.' That's when I started therapy."

Kate gives me a long and commiserative look. "I'm in therapy as well."

"I think it's good to talk it out. I think it's good to do whatever you have to do to move on. That's what you have to do to 'be okay with it all.' You have got to find a way to let the broken pieces go." At this point, I'm not sure if I'm speaking to Kate anymore...or to myself.

"Easier said than done," Kate mumbles.

"I know. I used to be so bitter that I had somehow 'failed' and was robbed of the one love that was supposed to be unconditional. The only thing that helped me was having compassion. I stopped blaming myself, I stopped blaming *her*, and then year after year, book after book, journal after journal, I've slowly found myself...moving forward."

We sit in silence and watch as a couple seagulls hover and swoop around us.

"It's going to keep happening," Kate says after a while.

"What?"

"The rejection," she says. "It's not like our mothers have passed away. They're still here, and because of that, the rejection will find a way to repeat itself, over and over again. So then what?"

"I'm not sure. I'm still figuring that out. I guess I've been hoping the worst is behind me."

I glance at her with an uncertain smile.

"We'll figure it out," she says. "We don't have any other choice..."

"Unfortunately, life doesn't give you the option of whether or not you want to deal with some things. Some things just *happen*." I grab a handful of hot sand and watch it slowly drain from my clenched fist. "And then you have a choice: you either let it swallow you whole, or you move on. So I guess when the rejection repeats itself, let it hurt for a while. And then when you're ready, peel yourself off the ground, stand on your own two feet, and keep moving. That's all I know."

"Do you ever wonder..." Kate hesitates. "Do you ever wonder how losing our mothers has affected us as adults?" She scrunches her nose at another half-nude elderly woman passing by our towels. "I mean—what consequences does a woman without a mother figure in her life have? Am I displaying 'classic' symptoms or neurosis?"

"Well, you are a little nuts," I joke.

"I'm serious. They say that women without a father figure tend to have a harder time with relationships with men... but what about mothers? I don't feel I have a hard time with relationships with my female friends."

"I'm not sure. I've searched out of curiosity for the same thing, but there's not a whole lot out there. It's just not that common, I suppose."

Kate says nothing. Rochelle excuses herself to grab some food.

I add, "The *tiny* amount of research I did find says that motherless women can be quite critical of themselves and others. It also mentions that we tend to be pretty nontraditional and driven."

"Sounds about right. There are a lot of famous women who are motherless. Did you know that?"

"Like who?"

"Okay." Kate sits up. "Like Oprah…and Ariel."

"Ariel? Ariel who?"

"From *The Little Mermaid.*"

"She's fictitious."

"Still. Most of Disney's main female characters have been motherless."

I ponder the list of heroines and smile. *She's right.* Sleeping Beauty, the Little Mermaid, Cinderella, Princess Jasmine, Belle…there have been many. I suppose they all fit that typical motherless persona, one who is adventurous and free-spirited, or one who has had to make her own rules because she didn't have that female role model to guide her. Motherless women tend to have a little more freedom to create a new way of life for themselves.

And free we are today. In the heat of the midafternoon sun, I excuse myself to cool off in the ocean. I wander out into the water, far away from the noise of human voices, and lie back to float and become one with the waves. The salty ocean water laps over my ears, so all I can hear is the sound of my own breathing.

Breathe in, breathe out.

The sun washes over me and I close my eyes.

Breathe in, breathe out.

I think back to my last days in Chicago, how incredibly afraid and alone I felt. I think about all the late-night phone calls about how strongly I felt about living this dream but couldn't find the courage to do it. I remember sitting at the bus stop in Chicago, feeling my heart *pound* with anxiety and having to remind myself every so often to breathe to calm my fears about the life I am living *right now*…the life

I've always dreamed of. The past two weeks have been such a whirlwind. I've been too busy to fully realize until now... *I'm doing it.*

My eyes well up with tears as I bask in the sun in this beautiful place called Cannes, a place I would have never experienced had I closed my eyes and shut my heart to the possibilities. This would be just a dream, and I would still be living a life shackled in fear.

But I never gave up; in fear and insecurity I never let go. And now here I am. I lift my head above the water and look around as the sea twinkles back at me.

I made it.

I made it.

Thank you, God. I have finally made it.

Somewhere in France...possibly

O KAY, SO THIS ISN'T EXACTLY IDEAL. I guess I couldn't have picked a prettier train station to get off at the wrong stop. This place is surrounded by mountains, spacious blue skies...and completely deserted. My first train was late, so if I had been *paying attention*, I would have realized that getting off the train at the time on my ticket wouldn't be right.

Instead, I'm studying all the neatly printed details of my handful of new train tickets for the next week when I suddenly realize it's exactly the time quoted on my ticket. Panicked, I jump up and watch as papers and iPod accessories spill off my lap and tumble chaotically to the floor. I crumple the mass of contents into my arms while simultaneously hauling my substantially bloated backpack and barrel through the helpless victims who happen to stand in my way.

"*Excusez moi! Excusez moi!*" The passengers standing between me and the open doors to the platform stare at me and laugh. I do not find this funny. The train jolts forward just as my foot reaches solid ground. Relief showers over me.

And then I look around. This is...not my train station. This is not my train station? Nope, not my train station.

So now here I am in some random French town. I am on my way to meet Kate in Cinque Terre, which, because of construction, I have to take four different trains to get to… *all* of which I am now going to miss.

I look around and exhale. Not having a companion along to either buffer or accelerate my fears, I decide—well, actually, I don't decide anything. My mind flips a switch into all-out panic, opens Pandora's box of negative scenarios, and proceeds to hurl them at me like a troubled teenager with Tourette's.

Oh, this is just fantastic. What in the hell do I do now? I am so screwed. I'm scared. I'm anxious. I don't feel safe…

Okay, Jill, take a deep breath. Am I dying? No. Am I in any immediate danger? No. Then it's fine. I'll figure it out. I'll just get on the next train out, and then the next train from there, and do what I have to do to get to Italy. There are no other options here but "Good going, blondie, now figure it out."

But what if I get in trouble? What if the conductor asks for my ticket and when he sees that I'm not supposed to be on that train, he yells at me in French? Everyone will turn to look at me and shake their heads because of course I won't understand because "of course" I don't speak French.

Okay, Jill, deep breath. I guess I'll say, "Oops, I messed up," and I'll figure it out from there. Unless, of course, a female attendant approaches me. Then she'll behave like every other French woman I've come across and will look me up and down with sheer disgust and stare at my shoes. Seriously, women. Stop with the staring!

As I approached the bus stop in Nice this morning, every single woman waiting turned around and inventoried my outfit from the top of my head down to my shoes. It was the sort of response you'd expect if you wore a stripper dress to a bar mitzvah. I was scrutinized as if I had a butt cheek hanging out from under my shorts or had a little nipple action with a see-through shirt. But I had none of those things. Today, I am wearing a black sundress with short sleeves and—might I add—*matching* black flip-flops. I am aware that, as a single young woman in this country, I am expected to represent myself better and wear nicer shoes, but this is not an option for me. So they stare. And I stare back. And then I move on.

Eventually, another train arrives that takes me to my next station in Ventimiglia. I have no idea if I am in Italy or still in France anymore, but this is the least of my concerns. I am standing under a giant electric board displaying all the departures and times. The next train to Genova isn't for hours.

I wait in line for twenty-five minutes and am greeted by the grumpiest old Italian man I have ever met. I explain to him that I got off at the wrong stop and have subsequently missed all my trains. He mumbles a couple sentences as he shakes his head and prints off a new itinerary. But the final city on this paper does not say "La Spezia," which is the town I need to be in.

"Sir, I have to go to *La Spezia*."

He mumbles more incomprehensible words in complete annoyance.

"*Scusi?* I don't understand."

He rolls his eyes, grabs my papers, and writes, "La Spezia 18:45" and underlines it aggressively. I look at it. "So the train is now going to La Spezia?" I am getting to my hotel *today*, damn it.

He throws his hands in the air and *shoos* me, yelling, "Walk! Walk! Walk!" I stare at him in shock. I have just been shooed by a complete stranger. I haven't been shooed since I was a toddler. What*ever*. At least I know I'll be on the next train to Genova, which is only one stop away from my hotel. As long as I keep inching toward Cinque Terre, I'll be fine.

With three hours to kill, I decide to take my pack and wander the new city I am in. I can see water at the end of the road, so I make the ten-minute hike and keep my eye on the prize. I find a bridge over a river leading into the sea. Behind me are mountains upon mountains speckled with homes and churches. I throw my backpack on the ground. *Ahhhhh.* I can breathe again. I think for a second about feeding the ducks, but my growling stomach reminds me they are probably better off than I am.

～

On the train to Genova, a middle-aged couple from the UK sits across from me. At first we don't speak much, only exchanging smiles and hellos. My pack is propped up next to me, and within minutes of laying my head against it, I am asleep. I wake up often in attempts to close the gap between my upper and lower jaw. I'm not the most attractive sleeper; as soon as I fall asleep, my head tips back, unfortunately leaving my lower jaw behind and causing my mouth to open as wide as physically possible. This is not ideal, especially when sleeping directly in front of strangers.

After I wake up, we start talking and end up bantering back and forth for hours. They are a lovely couple, and when waving goodbye through the train window at their stop, I realize another gift this trip continues to give me. This world is so full of unique and kind people (and a couple not-so-kind people). Every person I meet has a different story, a different outlook, a different opinion. Each encounter leaves a small imprint on my life. Because I am traveling alone, I talk to people on trains and planes and airports, in Laundromats and bars and hostels. As I ponder this, I think of Kate and my roommates in Ireland and smile. I probably would have never become friends with these people if I had my own agenda with others.

I feel so lucky to have the courage to travel solo. Because I am alone, I am gaining the entire world.

Chicago, Illinois

*Dreaming this dream, I have many thoughts. Some things I just know like, "There's no place like home," or I have a heart-breaking inability to remain content. I know a big part of me may not know how to just **be**.*

*I think of my travels-to-be and of my picky stomach and digestive tract, or of the friendships I'll make because we'll all be so starving for companionship. I'll look at the beautiful homes and relationships of the locals and realize that life really is very simple, no matter where you go. Maybe I'll realize that I had it perfect after all. I'll realize that I could have the best of both worlds: exhilarating travel with loved ones **and** my perfect piece of paradise that I call home.*

*But this travel dream has been an itch, a "knowing" for **years**. No matter how hard I try, I can't shake it. As soon I become settled and happy, something whispers...this unmet need makes itself known again and again. I am trying to ignore something that can't be ignored. I am letting fear and "what ifs" decide for me.*

I keep trying to talk myself out of going, telling myself that I don't need to live abroad to feel passion. This is true. But for some reason, I feel deep down that it is absolutely necessary for me to go. I don't know where I'll end up, who I'll meet, or what will happen, but I feel that I'll look back and thank the grace of God every minute of every day for giving me the courage to leave.

I also can't help but feel if this trip would be miserable and worthless, it wouldn't tug at my intuition for so many years. Something tells me to stop imagining this scary future because it wouldn't be that way. But I can't help but assume that I'll be dirty, afraid, sad, and lonely with fake companions and stuck in smelly old hostels. I see myself stressed.

So what do I listen to? What do I do? Every time I've traveled smaller trips with friends, I've asked myself, "What if I were here alone?" and the answer is always negative. I'd tell myself to leave it alone for now, but then I can't relax. Not having a plan makes me very unsettled.

I think that traveling the world would be this amazing gift—and a nightmare. It would encompass such grand dreams, yet the fear and the ever-constant struggle of trying to be "honest with myself" leave a deep confusion in me. A part of my brain asks, "Why keep fighting it?" while another says that it's just history repeating itself—me always being unsettled. Maybe I just need a hobby, something to be passionate about, something a little more…normal, something else—anything else.

*My whole life I've lived in my head. When I was a child in a painful and sad place, with nothing but silence surrounding me, I could find comfort in the fact that I was going to save myself. I **knew** I was going to save myself, that I was going to make a beautiful life with love, comfort, and peace. "One day… one day this will all be worth it," I'd tell myself as I drifted off to sleep. "One day I will be living my dreams." I romanticized those dreams, as young girls tend to do, and (thank you, God) they've almost all come true. I fought hard. I fought so very hard that it took all I had. I never gave up, and with faith I forged through some very dark times.*

And now here I am. I am in the most amazing city in the world. I live in a beautiful apartment. I have comforts, a wonderful career as a dental hygienist, and a substantial savings account. I am closer than ever with my family, I'm traveling with girlfriends throughout the country, and I even went on a ten-day trip to Italy and Spain a few months back. Yet I find myself craving more. What?

My older brother told me tonight, "When it's right...you just know." And he's so right. Every time something has been flat-out right or wrong for me, I just knew. Not a moment too early, not a moment too late. At the right moment, I just knew. I always do...when I allow myself to listen.

So despite not understanding, despite all the battling back and forth, something inside me just knows. I don't want to spend the rest of my life dreaming of what could have been. I'm so sick of hearing of people traveling and feeling instant guilt, remorse, or jealousy. I feel like chasing down college kids screaming, "Study abroad! Study abroad!" like a crazy madwoman. This is not a dress rehearsal. Somehow I need to find the strength to do this.

I saw Karen from Australia today. I love her. She comes into the office and I think, "That is me!" I tell her about my dreams of travel and living abroad, and I ask her, for motivation to stay, "But isn't life basically the same everywhere you go?"

She answers, "Oh sure! You get used to the cultural differences and settle in. You go to work, you go to the pub with your mates, you eat and drink."

So I tell her how maybe my dream of living abroad is just not worth it, maybe it's all romanticized in my head, and she says, "Oh, but it's so much fun and so incredibly worth it! I don't regret doing what I did for a second!"

So I say, "Sometimes I think I don't know how to be content...that maybe I need to stay here and learn to be happy."
She smiles. "That's exactly how I was. You're young. One
day you'll meet someone, in a place you could call home, and
you'll be older and more grown-up...and you'll be surprised
how quickly you settle."

"But I'd be leaving so much behind...I have a great job."

"That'll all be here when you get back! Your friends will be
here, your Mum and Dad, and there are great jobs all over!
You'll find another one, or another niche. I've left perfect jobs
before, but I always end up finding myself someplace that makes
it all worth it."

Then she adds, "I just have had faith my entire life that
everything works out."

It was then that I realized once again how much I fight
this—day after day, year after year. I look around and see how
wonderful my life is, and I'm afraid to leave it, afraid to give
it up for something "less than perfect." But I was the one who
created this life for myself, and I can do it again. And this
apartment and city will always be here, waiting for me when
I am ready to return.

The biggest issue shouldn't be the fear of leaving so much
as the fear of staying—the intense regret awaiting me, ready
to settle in with me, reminding me of what could have been.
I know this feeling already. Whenever I get settled, whenever
I meet someone and settle with him, I almost get resentful of
him—of our relationship—because I feel like it is holding me
back. This dream follows me everywhere I go.

The last thing Karen says to me before walking out the door
is, "You need to just do it, Jillian. Just **do it**. Stop thinking so
much and go."

Yes, the thinking part. I do think too much. This I know.

I head home after work, walk into my apartment, and open my blinds to allow the sunlight to pour over me.

And I doubt all over again.

Cinque Terre, Italy

MY TRAIN FINALLY PULLS INTO the La Spezia station. I made it, and all in one piece! I take my first taxi ride alone on this trip in a leather-interior BMW to my new home, a bed-and-breakfast in the heart of town.

"Uh, *un problema*," the older woman wavers from behind the hotel's front desk.

Well, actually, she says a lot more than that, but it's all in Italian. All I really understand is "problema." What I'm getting is that I can only stay one night, even though I have reserved and paid for four. I'm looking at her with a bewildered expression, I'm sure, as she goes on and on…in Italian.

"I'm sorry," I say. "I don't understand you."

She doesn't respond.

"No understand!" I yell. "No *capisce…o*?" I'm confused. Is it *capish? Capisco? Comprende?*

She then proceeds to speak to me louder and slower in Italian. The next five days end up being this same scenario: every day she rambles off, asking us questions and making conversation in Italian. Every day, I look at her and tell her I don't understand her. I didn't understand her yesterday, I don't understand her today, and I'm pretty sure I won't understand her tomorrow. But this makes no difference.

I hear words on this first evening like *domani* (tomorrow?), *problema, una notte,* and *piano.* I know she's not talking about a piano, but she keeps pointing down the hall saying, "*Blah blah blah, Italian Italian, piano.*"

"I just don't know," I say, completely exasperated. "I don't understand you, and I don't know what I am going to do."

She picks up the telephone and dials a number—I'm assuming to find someone who can speak English—but no one answers. Finally, after bantering back and forth in English and Italian, neither of us understanding the other, she asks for my passport, copies my information, gives me my keys, and mentions that damn piano again.

"Okay?" I ask. "*Oui?* I mean, *si?*"

"*Si.*"

"*No problema?* Four nights?" I question while holding up four fingers.

"*Si.*"

And that, my friends, is how you negotiate with an Italian.

My hotel room is adorable, with doilies and lace, floral wallpaper, and *more than one* pillow. I have a balcony and my own bathroom, and it smells so good! No stinky boys for five whole days! After a refreshing hot shower, I walk around the corner and order a pizza with cheese and capers and something else Italian. To complete my first evening in Italy, I ask where the closest gelato restaurant is, but no one understands me. Ah well, best to go to bed now. Tomorrow is a big day.

I curl up in my own bed, in my own room with the doors to my patio wide open. The fresh Italian air soothes me to sleep. I sleep for eleven hours. I love Italy.

The next morning, I meet Kate at 10:00 a.m. in the hotel lobby, and together we make our way to the train station to start exploring our first of the five villages,

Riomaggiore. The train between the villages clings to the rocky cliffs around them, weaving in and out of the mountains and carving its way through patches of vineyards and forest foliage.

Stepping off the train, I look at my surroundings in complete disbelief. *What is this place?* A place like this actually exists? I know I am still early in my trip, but I am going to say this now: if there is one place every person must see before they die, it's Cinque Terre.

As we make our way into Riomaggiore, we are met with a steady uphill climb. The streets are narrow and steep with the rare car placed conspicuously along the curb. Small alleys head off in every direction with clotheslines draped across the buildings, and children's voices float along the pathways like the soothing scent of fresh baked bread.

We did not bring our swimsuits, and we kick ourselves all day as we watch happy-go-lucky folks of all ages jumping off moss-covered rocks into the welcoming waters below. We walk up, up, up along narrow, winding streets and climb countless stairs, passing flourishing vineyards and lemon trees, old churches and family-run restaurants.

At the top of it all, we overlook the magnificent village below, blanketing the mountains and practically spilling into a deep blue sea. The beauty of it all is so exquisite I almost cry. I look at Kate and inform her of this. She responds matter-of-factly, "Oh, I've cried twice already."

It all feels so surreal, like walking through a movie set, or being in a parallel universe where life is simple again, where beauty is found in the little things and no actual effort is put into feeling…alive. These Italians, these Italians know how to live.

We make our way to a path that leads to the second village, Manarola. This twenty-minute walk along a paved trail hugs the cliffs overlooking the Mediterranean Sea. Soon into our walk, we begin to encounter small, various padlocks hanging along the railings and nets covering the mountainside. Welcome to Via dell'Amore, a path where lovers from all over the world whisper promises of love and adoration while closing a lock around a fixed point on the path and throwing the key over the cliff to forever seal their bond.

Throughout our short journey, we pass by hundreds of locks—some shiny and new like the lovers that clasped them, others rusty and tested by time, stubbornly holding on to something that may have passed decades ago. I ponder this as my fingers sweep along the abundance of clasped metal—how many are still holding on when their lovers have let go. But this is not the message of this passageway. It tells us love, at any time in our lives, is always a beautiful thing to be cherished. And how comforting to see in a world of constant change, these locks are still holding on. It sends chills down my body to see them. It is all *so romantic*.

Manarola, in my opinion, is even better than Riomaggiore. After looking around, I feel a surge of excitement as I realize it's one of the most photographed of the five villages. It's the village I'd gaze upon late at night in Chicago while dreaming of the possibilities. And now, with the sun kissing my face and a new friend by my side, here I am.

We wander aimlessly with our necks craned and mouths open, taking picture after picture everywhere we turn, *click, click, click*. The best part about being here is the sheer joy of exploring what's around every corner. The buildings are so colorful and old with peeling paint, exposed brick, and intricately carved iron balconies adorned with flower boxes. The shutters garnishing each building are a dark green—no doubt to coordinate with the towering green mountains that engulf each village. This place is what Disneyland is to a child…it's magical.

In a souvenir shop, I ask the owner what restaurant she as a local would recommend.

"Oh, definitely Billy's. It's just up the hill," she says with a smile.

After walking a steep road going up, up, up, we figure we must have passed it. We stop and ask another local. "Oh, *si*. Just continue up the road, go past the church in the square, and then it's to the right, up the steps…" and on and on he goes.

Just up the hill…puh.

After passing the square and the church, we spot a sign for Billy's on an old stone wall pointing up to another alley with…more steps. Up, up, up we go, through a narrow alley with small chirping birds as our accompanying music. It's quite the trek, but it's away from the tourists, which is perfect and exactly why I asked a local.

Billy's is an old, family-run restaurant with a large out-door patio and a million-dollar view overlooking the village, the surrounding mountains, and the sea. After walking through the restaurant gate, we walk down another twenty steps onto the patio and sit at a table nestled up against an iron railing overlooking the entire world. Jackpot.

We order a heaping plate of black seafood pasta stained from squid ink and a grilled, rare tuna steak. It's incredible. Our beverages, just like our conversation, are steady and dependable with a consecutive lineup of Birra Moretti beer. We also enjoy a little limoncello, and a "Sardinian Coca-Cola," aka Vicks VapoRub mixed with black licorice in a bottle. Not my favorite item on the menu but it was on the house from Billy himself, so we smile and drink it anyway, just to be polite.

Billy is an older Italian man in his mid-sixties who runs the establishment with the help of his family. Born and raised in Manarola, he lives "right up there," as he points above us to the homes on the mountain, with his eighty-seven-year-old mother and his ninety-four-year-old father, his wife, and his children. How in the hell a ninety-four-year-old man can walk these hills and steps is beyond me.

Billy is charming and kind, allowing us to sit out on the patio for four hours alone while he essentially closes the restaurant (we had no idea). Kate and I have so much in common and so much to talk about that we are shocked when we hear the old church bell down the road ringing five o'clock.

We spend the next couple days wandering the narrow, winding cobblestone streets of each of the five villages: Riomaggiore, Manarola, Corniglia, Vernazza, and Monterosso. Every day we eat savory, just-off-the-boat seafood at outdoor cafés, sip crisp Italian wine, and do a small version of cliff-diving in Manarola.

With our things tucked neatly between the rocks, we jump into the crystal-blue waters below. Kate straps on her goggles with attached snorkel and dips her head below the calm blanket of water. She instantly snaps back up screaming, "Oh my God! Look at all the fish swimming at our feet!"

"Oh God! No!" I shriek in a frenzy, furiously kicking my feet in an attempt to scare any fish approaching me. Our giggles echo off the rocky cliffs and reverberate in the waves. It's a nervous laughter for me, but eventually I take her goggles and look down at the world below. It's astonishing. Miniature bright blue-and-yellow-striped fish confidently swim around our feet, as if they know we are meant to be a part of their world. I'm nervous being in such deep waters with nothing to hold on to, but when I remember how high the salt content is, I finally relax and kick my feet up to float on top of the ocean.

After our dip, we explore an incredibly narrow and at times unstable trail between the fourth and fifth villages that winds along what feels like thousands of steps carved into the mountains of Cinque Terre. We have to push our bodies into the side of the mountain to allow the fellow hikers passing in the opposite direction to carefully slide past us. I grin to myself throughout the one-and-a-half-hour hike, as I look just beyond my footing to see a steep drop down the side of the cliff.

"In America, you'd have to sign a waiver to hike this!" I yell to Kate.

It's really too bad too, as we miss a majority of the hike's views because we are too busy watching our footing (and getting eaten alive by mosquitoes). But what a *feeling* to arrive in Vernazza from the mountains above!

～

I still stand by my initial comment on the first day here: Cinque Terre is the most stunningly beautiful, charming, and magical place I have ever seen. I hope to return here someday soon, say hello to Billy, and float once again in its pristine waters.

I head now to Berlin, where the city is thriving and the weather—cold and rainy. I carry with me a renewed love for *Italia*, a few new sun-kissed freckles, and a few more mosquito bites.

Cinque Terre has forever captured my heart.

Somewhere in Switzerland...

I WAS PRETTY SPOILED in Cinque Terre, sleeping peacefully in my own hotel room that smelled of freshly washed laundry and floral potpourri. I believe I said exactly, "No stinky boys for five whole days!"

Well, folks, the party's over. I am in a second-class sleeper car on a train to Berlin. What the hell! My Eurail pass is all first class! Because someone messed up, I now have to smell *feet* for the next twelve hours.

I walk into my room for the evening, which is the size of a small closet with six beds crammed inside, three on top of each other. One of my roommates greets me with an enthusiastic wave and a smile. I return his smile but inwardly curse like a sailor. I've had this type of roommate before, in Paris. His body odor hits me like a thousand punches to the face.

There is a postcard on my bed featuring a happy-go-lucky woman in her blue-and-white-pinstriped pajamas and a fluffy white puppy, who also just happens to be wearing matching blue-and-white-pinstriped pajamas, cuddled up next to her. It has "*Doppelte softness, doppelter komfort*" printed on the front with views of Venice just outside her large open window. And she has *four* pillows? I pick up the card in disgust and look at my new bunkmate.

"What in the hell is this?" I interrogate him as if he personally put that card there to torture me.

He waves enthusiastically and smiles. He doesn't understand. "Wonder if he understands how a shower works," I bitterly mumble to myself as I kick and shove my pack under the metal framework of my bunk.

I decide to go to the dining car after, of course, opening our window for "fresh air," aka emergency oxygen. To get to my dinner, I walk through seven cars, half of which are first-class and smell somewhat normal. I mutter, "This is bullshit" through all seven cars.

I pay seven euros for a bottle of water and a sandwich, the cheapest items on the menu, and take a seat next to the window. My sandwich consists of "*belegt mit hinterschinken, salami und gouda.*" I pick up one of the squares only to watch the "bread" crumble as I bring it to my mouth. I chew slowly. *What is this?* I think I may be eating a poo sandwich. They wouldn't feed this shit to cows.

Okay then, no dinner for me. What do I do now? I consider hanging myself with the plastic curtain on the window, but something tells me I'm being slightly dramatic. Then I remember I hid a Vicodin in the corner of my backpack for emergency purposes. This is definitely an emergency.

I breathe through my mouth as I force myself back into my tin can for the night. Dinner tonight is leftover potato chips, water, and a big white pill, dinner of champions... or crack addicts. Either way, I'm sleeping tonight.

As I stare outside the window above my mattress, I realize how peaceful it is to be on a train at night; golden lights flash by, along with thick outlines of trees and mountains. The life of a traveler isn't always easy. It's actually the hardest thing I've ever done, but it's also turning out to be incredibly eye-opening. I smile as I remember Italy. Besides, apparently whatever doesn't kill you will make you stronger, and this smell is definitely doing the trick.

The Vicodin has just kicked in and just in time, as my new roomie has made an executive decision to slide the window closed. Next stop after my self-imposed la-la land: Berlin, fresh air, and real food. I can only go up from here.

Here's hoping…

Berlin, Germany

ALL WINTER LONG this past year, all I did was research, hours and days and months of research on what to do, where to go, and how to say hello in the different cities and countries I might find myself in. I laugh to myself now as I walk down the street leading out of one of Berlin's train stations. I don't know anything about Berlin, nor do I have any idea about the next two cities I'll be visiting. None of this was part of the plan. I'm going completely off word of mouth from fellow travelers.

It's cold and rainy here, which is a bit of a shock after being in the French and Italian Rivieras. People still look at me as we pass each other, but for reasons different than the glares I received in France. I am completely underdressed. I have my stupid fleece on again with short, slate-colored capris and bright silver gladiator sandals…not exactly cold and rainy gear.

Berlin is so different from the other cities I've seen so far. When I first arrived, I looked around at the anticlimactic metropolis and my first thought was, *And? What was all the fuss about? What is so special about this city?*

The answer?

Everything.

You know that one incredible friend you have who you didn't like in the beginning? We all have one; you meet her, judge her, and label her. You think, *eh,* but as soon as you turn your back, she sneaks in and steals your heart forever.

This is Berlin.

I'm somewhat at a loss for words to explain this city, but here is my best shot. It's a classic northern European city with a mix of cement and cobblestone—a sort of clashing of old and new worlds. It has all the chains and shopping a girl could ever ask for, along with almost two hundred museums and a world-famous zoo. But mixed in with all the current new-world comforts, there is old-world charm and a stormy past that chronicles among some of the darkest days in history. Besides Hitler and the Nazi regime, World War II, and the genocide of a staggering eleven *million* people during the Holocaust, there is the Berlin Wall. For those of you who are rusty with history, here is a very quick overview.

World War II ends, Hitler cowardly commits suicide, and other German leaders fall off the face of the earth. Berlin is left to be divided between four major world powers: the Soviet Union, the United Kingdom, the United States, and France. At first all is well, but after a while the countries controlling Berlin start to not get along (*shocking*), setting into motion the dividing of Berlin (and Germany) into East (the Soviet Union) and West (the United Kingdom, the United States, and France). In the middle of the night the Soviet Union erects a wall out of defiance against the "fascists" and forbids anyone to cross it. Thirteen thousand marriages end, families are separated, and thousands of jobs are lost. Just imagine—your children head off to Granny and Grandpa's for the night, which just happens to be on the other side of town, and you wake up the next morning with barbed wire and military snipers down the road. You don't see your children again for years.

Separated from their loved ones and facing deteriorating living conditions in the East, people try to cross the wall, risking their lives every second. At certain points there are three walls to cross. If you get across the first wall, you are met with a bed of nails. If you make it past that and the snipers, you have to climb over another wall and are met with raked gravel. Not so scary? Every step you make leaves a trail for the snipers to find and shoot you dead.

In November 1989, because of a domino effect of events and huge misunderstandings (understatement), the Berlin Wall falls. Today, at the East Side Gallery, a portion of the remaining wall features paintings by artists from all over the world. The artwork is fantastic and opinionated, depicting the different artists' views of life, love, homosexuality, and the choking hold of religion. Hitler would freak.

Before the wall, there was the Nazi regime and mass genocide and communism and burning books and war and more war and more war. Nine out of ten buildings in Berlin were bombed to destruction during World War II...twice. This city was completely left in desolation and rubble.

Like I said, *very* dark history.

The general mindset of the inhabitants of Berlin would be a mix between San Francisco (Berlin has the third-highest gay population in the world) and New York City. There is a "free to be you and me" and "live your own life" freedom about it, yet possibly an even stronger "be yourself and if you aren't, we don't give a fuck." About twenty-five to thirty percent of the people I pass on a daily basis don a pleasant yet edgy mix of Mohawks, spiked dog collars, and pencil skirts. It's Marilyn Manson meets Marilyn Monroe. Actually, I have been properly warned before arriving that if you "overdress," aka wear heels and a dress out to some of the clubs here, you will not get in.

~

Upon arriving at my hostel, I meet two of my roommates, Steph and Chris from Australia, who are also traveling solo and invite me to join them on a pub crawl tonight. We walk a couple blocks to the meeting point, collect our free Becks beer, and, as we wait for the group to form, listen to a band on the street playing "Sweet Home Chicago." I am thrilled, experiencing a little taste of home in this foreign city.

Our leader, a thirty-something spunky woman with short, brown hair and thick, black-rimmed glasses, takes our group of about twenty to four different bars and one club. The nightlife here is quintessentially German, with loud, low-lit, smoke-filled bars and drip candles stuck to the old wooden tables. The city we wander and the bars we fill are a blend of rusty metal and wood, brick walls and graffiti, and Mohawks and cigarettes.

The third bar we visit is in an old, abandoned warehouse with a live band consisting of a cello, drums, guitar, and piano. The various open doors in the back of the building lead to an outdoor bar, with the busted-up brick and broken windows of the building lit by streams of blue and red lights. In other words, coming from Chicago where everything is shiny and new, this place is rad.

As we listen to the band, clouds of cigarette smoke swirl around us with strong hints of weed mixed in. I ask

Simone, our fearless leader, if pot is legal in Berlin.

"Well, technically it's not legal to smoke, buy, or sell marijuana, but it is legal to carry ten grams on you."

"How much weed is ten grams?" I ask, amused.

"Enough for about forty joints."

Hilarious.

∾

Thursday morning, Steph, Chris, and I head to the Holocaust Memorial and Jewish Museum. It is under a memorial site built specifically for the six million Jews who were viciously murdered during World War II. I've seen my fair share of Holocaust photos, movies, books, and documentaries, but to be in a museum in Berlin, where it all started, seems especially significant. We each grab a headset with a narrative provided by the museum and dissect its contents at our own pace.

I wander through each of the rooms filled with family photos and stories, timelines, personal accounts, and letters home. I listen in horror to an account of a Nazi soldier writing home to his wife, feeling my heart pound harder and faster as he brags to her about the privilege of being part of a mass shooting.

"At first" he says, "my hand would shake when I pulled the trigger. But then, after shooting around the tenth truckful of Jews, I was a pro at it. I knew exactly where to shoot without wasting too many bullets. And when we'd shoot the babies out of the mothers' hands, they'd fly through the air and we'd shoot them again to make sure they'd land in the pit below. I thought about our two babies at home when I did this, knowing if these monsters had the chance, they'd do things one hundred times worse to us."

A letter written by a Jewish woman paints a picture of the beaten-down souls her people possessed. After looking at photo after photo, I keep thinking, *How are these people appearing so calm? Why are they not screaming and crying?*

Because most of them were already dead.

The woman writes:

"What's the point? Why keep living? There's no more family to love, no friends left to hug, no home to return to. They are going to murder me today. I am going to die. I am so afraid, but this life is worse than death. To hold out any longer would be beyond human endurance."

Feeling depleted and heartbroken, I find myself in a completely dark room except for the subtle lights under about a half dozen white benches in the middle of the floor. Light coming from projectors displays a name on each of the four walls with a year of birth and a year of death underneath. A sound system reads the name, a very short history of that person's life, and then how they died. Once that name is done, it disappears, and a new name with a new timeline of a shortened life appears.

The five minutes I force myself to sit there, the vast majority of the names read have timelines of life spanning between eight and twelve years. The museum is two and a half years old. The Room of Names reads names nonstop, twenty-four hours a day, seven days a week. For this system to read the names of all the six million murdered Jews will take six years, seven months, and twenty-seven days. And that is just the Jews. Almost that same number, five million others, were murdered alongside them. It's a hard number to grasp, but I bet if this room read the eleven million names in entirety, it'd take at least twelve *years*.

Leaving the museum, exhausted and depressed, we are done for the day. We head back to the hostel to do absolutely nothing but allow the images of the atrocities to slowly soak into our memories—a small price to pay in remembrance of our dear brothers and sisters.

∿

The next morning, Steph and I decide to head to the zoo. The Berlin Zoo is world-known and one of the biggest zoos in Europe. It's refreshing. What is it about spending time with animals that makes people giggle like schoolchildren? I have been to a lot of zoos in my life, and this is one of my favorites. I have never seen so many animals interacting the way I do here. The whole zoo is an open-air concept, so, except for the panda and ape enclosures, there are no walls or cages, just a moat-like ditch surrounding each exhibit.

The sun is shining, there's a gentle breeze, and the animals are out and alive. The seals are barking, the monkeys swinging around, and the panda has set up camp right in front of the glass separating him from us. I don't know if it's because the weather is perfect or it's the time of day we're here or maybe the animals just like Germany, but the Berlin Zoo does not disappoint.

The only exception is the gorilla, an incredibly handsome yet grief-stricken silverback. As soon as we walk up, he looks us both directly in the eyes and then looks away. I look at Steph.

"He's gorgeous."

She nods.

"Isn't he the saddest gorilla you have ever seen?" I add.

"It's depressing," she says and walks away.

I sit there with him for another couple minutes, pondering what he could be thinking. He bites his nails, just like we do, and watches us as much as we do him.

He knows.

I'll never forget the sadness in his eyes. Eventually he wanders to the back of the room, curls in a ball as he covers his head with a blanket, and doesn't move.

After the Berlin Zoo and another mouth-watering kabob, we head to the train station. Steph has researched a day trip for us to get out of the city today. Well, maybe "research" is a little strong, or maybe the Internet was incorrect, but we never make it to our destination. Intuitively knowing we were in for a ride, we hesitate at the ticket kiosk. Should we just skip it? This whole thing sounds complicated—what if we get stuck out in the sticks?

"Let's just do it," I say. "It'll be an adventure! But just in case, let's get some roadies."

Thirty seconds later, we are running through the train station, looking for a shop that sells beer. We make it back to the platform just in time.

In a small town called Königs Wusterhausen, we need to get off the train and catch a bus. There are buses everywhere, so of course in our confusion, we miss the one we need. We ask a local, pointing to another bus, "Can we just take this bus to get to Lübben?"

She looks at it, looks at us, "*Nein.*"

I guess we're staying in Königs Wusterhausen. What does Königs Wusterhausen have? Why, Königs Wusterhausen is a thriving metropolis of about seven people! There is an Asian restaurant that does not appear to be Zagat-rated, a basket shop, and a couple Jehovah's Witnesses with a stand on the corner. Oh. *Good.*

We stumble upon a beer garden with a lovely view overlooking a small river embroidered with outstretched, blooming weeping willows. We stay for five hours. I realize that once again, I have met another amazing, motherless woman as Steph and I sip German beer and exchange life stories, a few laughs, and even a few tears. We clink our glasses and decide that our road trip to Königs Wusterhausen has been very successful indeed.

Back in Berlin, as we walk down the steps exiting the train station, an old man leans over the railing above and blows raspberries at us. We actually have to move over to get out of the line of fire of rapidly falling spit. We hunch over the railing in hysterics. How incredibly fitting for a city like Berlin.

That night, disappointed and pouting, Steph and I say our goodbyes. I hate this part. I meet the greatest people and, within days, we have to separate to continue on our journeys. It's always such a downer. The best we can do is promise to keep in touch and hope to see each other again.

My last full day in Berlin is sunny and seventy degrees. Under strong recommendations from Steph and Chris, I join Fat Tire, a bike tour that takes tourists around the city while explaining its history. Our guide is from Ireland and is incredibly good at what he does, which is ideal because our small group of twenty spends the next six hours with him. We stop at all the major sites, some of which are just a lawn now because the building was bombed—twice. And then the city rebuilt it and then tore it down just to start rebuilding it again. No wonder Berlin—not Germany—but the city of Berlin is 63 billion euros in debt! When others aren't destroying it, it destroys itself.

We go to historic buildings and learn their usually dark histories and—wait, this building isn't old! Turns out they built it twenty years ago and burned it with torches to make it appear like it did before it was bombed. Very few of Berlin's "old" buildings are actually old—they haven't had enough time without turmoil and war to become old.

We visit the site where the Nazis burned twenty thousand books written by authors such as Einstein, Hemingway, and Helen Keller. A memorial sits in the middle of the large open square, under the ground and covered by a thick piece of glass. Beneath the glass is a room filled with enough empty bookshelves to house twenty thousand books, representing the presence of absence. There is a plaque in the ground next to the glass with a quote inscribed, "That was only a prelude; where they burn books, they will also in the end burn people," written over a hundred years prior to the event by Heinrich Heine, a Jew by birth whose literary works were also burned.

We bike to a plain gravel parking lot covered with random weeds and small stones. There is nothing here to tell you this is the site of Hitler's bunker where he spent his last days, swallowed a cyanide tablet, shot himself in the head, and had his associates burn his body beyond recognition. He did this last part because he was afraid people would do to him what they'd done to Mussolini: cut off his testicles, shove them in his mouth, drag him around the city, and hang his naked body in front of city hall for all to see. The only reason why they even know the charred remains were Hitler's was through his dental records. They then reburned what was left, a piece of his arm and a chunk of his jaw, and threw them into the river. He got the same disrespect he paid to the millions he murdered: no funeral, no grave, nothing. His memorial was the hatred and pain of the millions he directly affected, and the billions upon billions of people in the world whose history books will forever speak of him as one of the most evil men to have ever lived.

Looking back, I can see how Berlin may not sound like a destination as buoyant or beautiful as, say, Cinque Terre or Nice, but please, don't take it out on Berlin. Every country at some point in time has had its dark moments and dark rulers.

Berlin is raw, with a ferociousness of extremes and a continued striving for peace despite the scars of many lifetimes of war. It's passionate and strong and real. With its graffiti and leather, its vigilance and audacity, Berlin shocked and amazed me. It was everything I'd hoped for, yet nothing I expected. I don't know how else to explain it. Come and see for yourself.

But please don't be surprised that if you do, Berlin will sneak in and steal your heart.

And it will not apologize.

Kraków, Poland

I AM SO BORED.

Officially, I think I am on the train to nowhere. The countryside of Poland isn't the prettiest I've seen on this trip. Actually, it may be the ugliest countryside I have ever laid eyes upon. Imagine a normal countryside with fields and trees—boring. Now throw in a couple 150-year-old homes with no shutters, flowers, or colors and take a chisel and hammer to each home and its roof. Now add in a handful of completely worn-down, abandoned buildings with broken-out or boarded-up windows, and then cover the ground with weeds. Slap some "dreary gray" paint across the whole thing, and you've got Poland. It is the epitome of run-down and dreary. In America, we can't even get our haunted houses to look this scary.

My train ride from Berlin to Kraków is supposed to take ten hours, but a few times during the journey, we stop. The train turns completely off, and we sit on the tracks, in the woods, in the middle of nowhere. At one point I rummage through my bags and shove my credit cards, passport, and money into my coat pockets in case we are being hijacked.

Why in the hell are we just sitting here? I remove my headphones and walk to the window to look around. Nothing. We are surrounded by nothing. Every time we stop I do this, and every time I get the same result—nothing.

Needless to say, the train conductor eventually finds the "on" button again, and the train humbly resumes its course. We end up being one and a half hours late, spending a grand total of eleven and a half hours on this damn train in the middle of Europe's version of Gary, Indiana. I tried rolling around in my car, kicking and screaming out my frustration, but it was empty, so all I got was an old piece of Wiener Schnitzel stuck in my hair.

I arrive in Kraków like a death row inmate given a pardon. With only one eye cracked open, I take a deep breath and hesitantly crawl out of the safety of my train. At first my walk is a brisk, stiff version of my normal pace, packed with double checks behind me while white-knuckling my handbag. I have no idea what to expect, so I expect the worst given the train ride in. The farther I walk into town, however, the more my shoulders release their tension and I realize Kraków isn't at all what I anticipated.

Kraków is like a breath of fresh air. There are lit candles in every picture window, nuns and horse-drawn carriages sprinkling the streets, lavish parks in every direction, gorgeous old churches, and a castle in the center of town. It feels like I've stepped into the world of 1876. It is the embodiment of old-world charm. Looking around, I feel so grateful that I came here. I don't know any other time in my life when it'd be likely that I'd find myself in Poland. The town has essentially everything within walking distance, and the food is delightful! The soups and dumplings Poland is famous for are like Grandma's home cooking, which I especially love after all the fried food and potato chips I've had this past month of traveling.

My hostel is small and somewhat cliquey. It's always

uncomfortable showing up in a new city or country not knowing a soul, and I've quickly found that the people I share a roof with can either make or break that discomfort. This hostel is indifferent to my presence and doesn't make much of an effort to be friendly. To be fair, I don't make any attempt to introduce myself either. I am exhausted from my long and tedious train ride in and know I need my sleep. Tomorrow I go to Auschwitz, which may be one of the most emotionally draining days of my life.

Auschwitz

Walking along the barbed-wire fence,
I can't even begin to imagine the tortured souls it has contained.
The trees here
must be among the saddest trees in the world.
They stand proud—strong
but inside,
they must be forever weeping.

Every step I take,
I fight teardrops, and my heart,
my heart is just aching.

The oxygen here
is a different sort of air.
It's heavy—chilling,
there is no movement.

It's so thick,
as if all the cries
of the 1,100,000 people viciously murdered here
are still stuck in midair.
Everywhere I move,
I have to push through their sadness.

Today, I walk on eggshells,
hoping my presence won't wake them,
because as I walk,
I am stepping through their tomb.

Throughout my four-and-a-half-hour tour, I take diligent notes.
I listen to account after account of horrific tragedies,
fact after fact,
number after number;
I walk through room after room filled with
baby shoes,
empty suitcases,
glasses,
even a room with two tons of hair.
I planned on relaying this information so that you could
*   experience it with me.*

But I am not going to do that today.

I just can't.

The accounts of life in Auschwitz are among the most monstrous
*   stories I have ever heard.*
The photos are haunting.
To document my afternoon at Auschwitz is just too much for
*   me to handle.*

So replacing my words
will be a moment of silence,
silence that I felt walking the halls and barracks of Auschwitz,
and the silence that has tortured God,
since the day he went without
eleven million of his beloved children's heartbeats.

When I arrive back in Kraków, it takes a couple hours to work off my Auschwitz depression. I wander the streets in a murky daze, my eyes glazed over, my mind swirling in complete bewilderment and a bitter despair. I feel heartbroken.

I settle on a park bench among some old trees and skateboarders or, more accurately, I crumble in a heap and let myself quiver in misery for a while. Eventually, I find the strength to peel myself off the slivered wood into an upright position, write down my arduous emotions, and then store it all in a safe place within my memory as one of the most moving and significant places I have ever been. And then I let it be.

I leave the park and begin what is my favorite part of the traveling experience—wandering. I amble through the city and its myriad of pigeons, kebab joints, and exuberant shops of amber jewelry and think often as I walk of the history this place holds. I slowly meander through the Jewish Ghetto of World War II and its ghostly skeletons of burned brick with Stars of David and scars of conflict. This is an area of the city originally built to house about three thousand people, but seventeen thousand souls were locked within its parameters until the Germans started shipping them in droves to extermination camps.

Some buildings are profiles of crumbling bricks and broken glass, untouched since those frightful days back in the 1940s. It's chilling.

I head across town to Schindler's old factory. Its outside walls look the same as they did in 1939, but the inside is now an incredibly interactive and well-put-together museum that tells of the sad and haunting history of Poland before, during, and after the invasion of the Nazis. I learn about the

Polish people who died in Auschwitz and other camps just for staying out past curfew or for teaching their students at underground schools. They were murdered for teaching literature. I never knew.

I feel ashamed as I walk back to my hostel. I came into this country not knowing a thing. I judged and labeled its bruises. I turned my eyes from its scars. But Poland deserves more than that. These are a people who have been oppressed for decades. Through invasion and communism and lies these people have fought for simple civil rights and liberties that many take for granted. Poland lost 1.6 million people over twenty years through forced labor camps. Before that, six million perished during World War II, a majority of those deaths being nonmilitary. Millions not being executed during that time were risking death every day by saving the Jews.

I didn't know *any* of this. I didn't know when I packaged up and labeled Poland's façade that I was looking at ruins and wounds from decades of struggle and hostility. There is a reason why some of their country appears so beat up; it has only been since 1990 that Poles have been able to walk the streets in freedom.

Despite Kraków's antique-like charm, my days here remind me of my time spent in Paris; my hostel is small and unfriendly, the weather mostly dreary, and my days lonely. My slumber comes to me in fits and stages; my dreams are anxious and scared. This comes as no surprise, a common side effect of Auschwitz, I'm sure.

Kraków isn't the most exciting or welcoming city I have ever been in, but its enchanting, old-world allure and incredibly fascinating history have made these last three days some of the most transformative of my life. As I head out of town, I rock back and forth to the motion of the train and thank God in repeated whispers for my *freedom.* I have changed. Something inside of me has shifted. You can't explore a part of history like Kraków's, or walk through the quarters of Auschwitz, without it changing the lenses through which you view life, ever-changing, ever-present, ever-fragile life.

Prague, Czech Republic

"OH, AND I HAVE GOOD NEWS!" Anthony, my chubby and somewhat awkwardly hairy hostel clerk, exclaims as he pecks away at his keyboard. "You are the only person booked in your room for your entire stay!"

"Shut up!" I gasp.

Oh! The gods are smiling on me today!

I walk up three flights of stairs to my ten-person room in pure ecstasy. *Oh, the privacy! The calm! The quiet! All the sleeping in I will do!*

My "room" ends up resembling more of an apartment with my very own bathroom, a small kitchen, and a dining room table with four chairs. I don't know a soul in this country who will sit at those chairs with me, but the opportunities are endless! I walk around my huge, two-bedroom loft space just beaming. I have three whole days with no snoring, no earplugs or stinky boys…three whole days— *alone.* Perfect.

On my good-luck high, I run downstairs and meet up with Matt, a twenty-five-year-old from San Francisco whom I met at a tram stop outside the train station. After spending at least ten minutes staring at a large, unmarked, orange metal box with about twenty random silver buttons on its face, we finally figured out how to purchase a ticket. I'm not sure how, and I wouldn't be able to ever duplicate it—I find later—but in that moment we each had one ticket granting us access to the tram.

We head around the corner from our hostel, where we both happen to be staying, and enjoy a locally brewed beer costing us the equivalent of one euro each. I love Prague!

After a relatively inexpensive dinner of chicken schnitzel and frites with the company of a relatively nice guy, I eagerly head back to the hostel for a long and quiet evening catching up on my reading and my sleep.

As I breeze through the door of my room, I'm immediately shocked at the temperature. It's *freezing* in here. Taken aback, I slowly walk to the windows lining one wall to see if anything has been left open. Since it's only about sixty degrees outside, I automatically assume this must be the cause. Nothing.

It's *so cold* in here and—something else. There is something else—something strange. I'm on edge, afraid actually. I'm incredibly afraid. I look around the room and it appears different...scary. I turn on all the lights and continue to look around, my heart pounding. I don't like it. There is something here; I *know* it, I can feel it. Chills race up and down my body. I quickly unpack my bag and layer on my socks and fleece jacket. Then, grabbing three comforters from the empty bunks lining the room, I crawl into bed.

My toes feel like ice. I leave every single light on and lie as still as I can with eyes wide open, drawn for some reason to one specific corner of the room. I am more scared than the time I was eight years old and had thoroughly convinced myself a three-headed monster lived under my bed.

Now, I know after childhood, you should leave all that ghost stuff behind, and I have—no problem. But tonight, the fact that there is a presence in my room is undeniable. I can't move. I give myself a little pep talk. *Jill, seriously. There isn't anything here. Just go to sleep. If there is a ghost in here, he'll let you know, okay?*

I manage to eventually fall asleep but am awakened after an hour by the sharp, throbbing pain in my frozen toes. I curl into a ball for warmth and look around. It's still here, hovering in the corner of the room in complete animosity and indignation.

I don't know what to do. Reception downstairs is closed, and there is no one else in my room. The entire hostel is quiet and apparently sleeping. I seriously consider packing up my belongings and leaving to find a hotel, but it's one o'clock in the morning, not exactly ideal for walking around a strange town by myself looking for a place to sleep.

As I lie bundled in a bounty of blankets and layers of every article of clothing I own, I suddenly hear breathing. I sit straight up in a fury that can only accompany pure dread and scan the beds. Did someone check into my room while I was sleeping? I see no one.

That's it! I haul ass out of bed and run out of the room, letting the door slam loudly behind me. I find one Australian guy wearing a T-shirt downstairs in the kitchen. I ask him how to turn the heat on, too embarrassed to tell him Casper has checked into my room. He has no idea. He shrugs his shoulders with a bewildered expression at my condition of slight hysteria and hypothermia.

The hostel is dead; everyone else is tucked away behind closed doors sleeping. There is nothing else I can do. Feeling defeated, I slowly make my way back up to my room.

I creep back through my door, hoping not to make any sound to alert *it* that I am back. I look around. *Nothing.* There is nothing here. Instantly, the room is warmer— brighter. It's as if a dense fog has cleared away, like a veil has been lifted. It feels suddenly...*empty.*

Still freaked out, I crawl back into bed in my layers of clothing with every light on in my multiple rooms. I'm confused. *What in the hell is going on?* It was scary, now it's fine. Not only do I have to deal with a ghost tonight, but apparently he's confused or suffering from bipolar disorder.

Along with the sudden shift in mood, the temperature in my room has become inviting as well. Within thirty seconds of crawling under the covers, I am toasty warm. I'm so warm, in fact, that I wake up constantly throughout the night to shed more and more layers, starting with my socks and followed shortly thereafter by my fleece and a multitude of blankets.

The next morning I awaken quite comfortably in shorts and a T-shirt. Blankets are thrown in piles everywhere. My room is still quiet and apparently empty, but I am tired. I didn't sleep well, and I'm worried—*what if it comes back?* I've never experienced anything like that before, and even in the light of day, I can't shake it.

I head out to spend the day exploring and meet Salim and Osman, two men from Germany, at the tram stop down the road. The orange box has a red flashing light on top—out of order maybe? None of us can tell. We share a laugh over our misfortune and try to figure out another way to get our tickets. Osman thinks he remembers seeing signs in tobacco stores advertising tram tickets. As we walk, they ask if I'll be their tour guide for the day. After they accept that I'm just as lost as they are in our new surroundings, I happily accept my assignment.

We purchase tickets at a tobacco store around the corner, then head off on the tram to the heart of Old Town, where a large square is surrounded by castle-like churches and an old clock tower.

As we walk through the narrow streets, we can't believe our eyes. We quickly come to a unanimous agreement that Prague is by far one of the cleanest European cities any of us have ever seen. The streets are well kept, sprinkled with old gas lamps, castle-like structures, and shops selling stringed puppets, all prostituting themselves with bright eyes and painted smiles in the crowded picture windows facing the streets.

The architecture is immaculate; the carvings and moldings appear freshly painted and look as if a crew of cleaners with toothbrushes has just swept through. The buildings are painted pastel colors ranging from peach to yellow, lime green to rose, with bright reddish-orange tiled roofs capping the delicately toned buildings. There are no shutters here, because they would cover the intricate detailing of the white wooden carvings and moldings around each window.

As we approach the square, the old clock tower starts to ring its bells, chiming one o'clock. As this happens, swarms of people from all across the square start to run toward it. The three of us smile at each other, too cool to run like all those "dumb tourists." It doesn't take us but ten more seconds to realize that whatever they are running toward, we are missing. We run.

The show the clock tower puts on at the beginning of each hour from 8:00 a.m. to 9:00 p.m. is a must-see. But our hesitation this afternoon costs us the 1:00 p.m. show.

As we continue through Prague, cameras snapping shots in all directions, we find ourselves at the entrance of the Charles Bridge. The bridge is world famous, adorned on each side with thirty assorted statues and monuments. Every day, throngs of tourists make their way across the bridge to touch the different fixtures on each statue for luck, smiling and posing for pictures as they do. The bridge is also peppered with people selling trinkets ranging from oil paintings to jewelry to caricatures.

In the middle of the bridge, a band, creatively named Bridge Band, plays tunes that remind me of America's jazzy, old-school music of the Roaring Twenties. The main singer—an older gentleman with a white beard and clean-cut hair—puts what looks like a beat-up horn to his mouth and sings into it, transforming his voice into a loud, raspy sound. He sings tunes that make me want to sit on a back porch with ice tea and catch fireflies. I tell this to Salim. He laughs at me and shakes his head.

We stop and buy some *trdelniks*, the Czech version of crepes made up of large tubes of flakey crust with giant sugar crystals on top and Nutella layered in the middle. Salim and Osman need to check into their hotel, so we exchange information and plan to meet again later. Unfortunately, despite them texting me every night, this never happens.

Later on in the evening, I head back to the Old Town square to meet up with Brandon, a thirty-something man from Oklahoma who works on a base in Afghanistan as a fireman. He was in the Air Force for four years and then started working as a civilian in Afghanistan in 2008. We were on the same train car from Kraków to Prague, smiling bashfully at each other as we passed for bathroom breaks. We formally met at the currency exchange in the train station, as we both needed to exchange our euros for the Czech koruna. You can use the euro at this point in Prague, but it tends to be cheaper to use the koruna.

We meet in the square at 8:00 p.m. and walk around the city for a while, talking and getting to know each other while looking for a restaurant. He points to an establishment that he thinks looks good.

"Brandon," I say disapprovingly, "there are Coca-Cola signs on the umbrellas. No. It screams 'tourist!'"

"Okay." He laughs. "You pick then."

After wandering for a while and our indecisiveness getting the best of us, he mentions a sushi restaurant next to his hotel, which ends up being Buddha Bar, exactly the same as in Paris. Not exactly a local specialty, but why not? I loved the one in Paris, so I'm sure I'll love this one, too.

I'm right. It's huge, with another overwhelming two-story Buddha inside, Asian-inspired techno music, and such low lighting that the waitress has to give each of us a flashlight to read our menus. Brandon has a good laugh over this.

"This is a little out of my league," he says as he squints at his menu, adding that he's always been a pretty laid-back guy. "Doesn't take much to make me happy."

I look around, delighted, remembering all my dinners out in Chicago with my girlfriends. "This is right up my alley."

We feast tonight, with edamame and roll after delectable roll of raw and tempura'd delights, and Brandon tells me about being in the Air Force and his life in Afghanistan. It is his goal to be out of there within the next year.

"Because after three years," he says humbly, "it starts to slowly change you for the worse. There are men that have been out there six years, and they're different now—bitter. I don't want to be that person, too."

I listen to his stories and ask lots of questions. The life he leads is one most people will never know. He seems like a good man. I don't know if I will ever see him again after this, so I try to stay present and enjoy his company while I have it. I am also trying to keep my mind off the fact that I will be returning to a possibly haunted room tonight, and this scares the shit out of me. Thankfully though, whatever it was in my room never returns again, but I don't sleep well my entire stay.

∼

Brandon and I meet again the next day in the square. I leave twenty minutes early, determined to see the show at the clock tower at 11:00 a.m. I am a couple minutes early and join the large crowd already congregated in front of the incredibly ancient clock, thought to have been built back in 1410.

The first bell rings. *BOOOONG!* We all look up, and cameras in hands shoot above the sea of heads. Two small doors open above the clock and a parade of puppets representing the Twelve Apostles take turns peeping their heads out and greeting us. Four automated puppets representing Vanity, Greed, Death, and Pleasure surround the large clock and dance away, mechanically moving heads and limbs as

the bells continue their monstrous roar. *BONG! BONG!*
BONG! The skeleton, representing death, sits to the right
of the clock, holding tightly to a string, and rings his own
little bell, smiling away as if he were creating all that racket.
And here we are, a crowd of hundreds ranging in age from
five to ninety-five, completely amused and mesmerized like
little schoolchildren.

At the end of the show, a man pops his head out of a
window at the very top, dressed in a red and yellow robe
with long flowing sleeves, and plays his trumpet victoriously.
He bows and disappears behind the faded brick. The crowd
bursts into whistles and claps.

I meet up with Brandon and together we head off across
the Charles Bridge toward the other side of the city to
see the famous Prague Castle. The day is incredible, the
castle breathtaking, the company wonderful. We weave
through the narrow streets as we brush pass bodies of locals
and bodies of tourists, observed ever so faithfully by the
painted eyes of the city's puppets hanging in windows and
swinging off door handles—Prague's own secret society
of benefactors.

As the sun sets deeper into the afternoon sky, my body
starts to slump forward and my head and joints begin to
ache. A bad cold I caught back in Kraków is at its worst
today, and my lack of sleep due to my unexpected houseg-
uest hasn't helped. I am exhausted. I end my last night in
Prague by heading to bed at dusk.

As I wave goodbye to Brandon through the glass window
of my tram, I can't help but wonder, had I been healthy and
somewhat rested, if anything would have transpired between
us…or Matt, Salim, Osman, and let's just throw in Casper

for good measure. It's like Prague gave me a bunch of mini-dates, and a couple longer ones too. No kisses though, no flings to report either, just a couple of really cute men, a couple more puppets, and one *really* angry ghost.

I crawl into bed, exhausted and sick, leaving all the lights on again—just in case. Tomorrow I head to Rome, my first European love. It really is too bad I've been ill this past week, but not surprising considering the rate at which I've been traveling.

The next morning, thankfully, I start to feel better. I send sweet kisses to Prague and even wish my ghost happy haunting.

I'm off to Italy for an incredibly quick twenty-four hours. I don't need to sightsee this time. I just need to send a very special thank you to a very special someone who never gave up on me.

Chicago, Illinois

Who are you?
What do you want from me?

You are a quiet calling, a soft whisper I can't ignore.

When my feet become settled, my body comfortable in warmth,
my heart flutters anxiously,
the ears of my intuition tweak,
and I hear you once again.

Visions of faraway places,
open fields, colorful cultures,
grand schemes and surpassing love…
wisdom,
strength.

Darker voices rebel in fear.
Fear.
Fear.

"What if…"
  "I can't…"
  "I shouldn't…"

I know better.
Some distant part comforts me,
in knowing those darker voices aren't true
…it wouldn't be that way.

But it's all I can think.
More fear.
The strength of which suffocates my dreams.

Until the next quiet hour,
when sweet whispers sing soft melodies
of thick accents and salty ocean air…far away.

Someday, my desire will continue to grow,
like fire in the abundance of oxygen.
It will roar and with a burning strength I shall step into the
unknown.

But if it should reverse,
have pity on me, dear friend.
For then I will have neglected my heart,
my one true love,
quieted those true voices.
Something within me will have died.

And I would have allowed it.

Fear is a dangerous enemy.

Rome, Italy

TWENTY-FOUR HOURS. Twenty-four hours is not enough. Twenty-four hours is like taking the first bite of gelato on a hot, summer day—and the cone falling to the sizzling cement. Twenty-four hours is like touching your lips to your lover's after being away for so long, only to wake up a moment later and realize it was just a dream. It's not enough. You find yourself more heartbroken after one second in heaven than you were before with nothing at all. Twenty-four hours is not enough.

I came to Rome last year with a couple friends from Chicago and fell in love. It's not the most beautiful (although it is incredibly beautiful) or cleanest city in the world, but I am wholeheartedly and unconditionally in love with it. I can't explain how or why—I just know. Rome has consumed me. I knew from the moment I walked its streets and breathed its air. Twenty-four hours here is just not enough.

Why, oh *why* did I only book one night? Now I remember why I left last year wanting to live here. It is such a romantic and vibrant city. Its energy just screams, "Life! Love! Adventure!" It is because of this city that I'm living this adventure today. And for this one and only reason, I have made the journey back to Rome.

I have come to say thank you.

My hostel seems decent enough, just blocks away from Rome's major train station and equipped with a bar inside selling cheap beer. I drop off my stuff and meet my new roommate, Gary, a married guy in his early forties from Georgia. Talking to him brings me comfort. He has a thick Southern accent and is effortlessly kind. I help him out with some questions on his Eurail pass, and then I book it downstairs to get outside. I don't want to waste another second behind closed doors.

I open the large, classic Roman doors to the streets and am met with a wall of water. It is *pouring*. The rain is hitting the cement so hard that it appears like it's coming down from the sky and up from the ground at the same time. Okay then, off to the bar.

I order a beer and sit alone at a long wooden table with benches on either side to watch European football blasting on the big-screen TVs lining the room. Instantly, I am brought back to a day in Chicago when I went to a bar on a Sunday afternoon, just like this, for the first time alone. I was so nervous! I stood in front of the glass doors for a couple of awkward minutes, playing out ridiculous scenarios in my head. I felt so self-conscious, but I went inside anyway. I was testing myself, testing how I'd do in an uncomfortable situation alone.

Now, I had gone to movies alone and lived alone, and not only did I do fine, I enjoyed it. But being in a *social* situation is completely different; bars and restaurants are made for people to gather and be together. When you're not accustomed to approaching this situation alone, you can expect a certain amount of unease.

Long story short, I did just fine. No one talked to me, and

I did the same. And this was okay. Baby steps are sometimes required the first time you touch your toes to the chilly waters below. For me, it was a couple baby steps and then one large, earth-shattering cannonball, and apparently that was all that was needed to get me here. Luckily there isn't a barometer to measure your courage or ability to handle certain situations under pressure. It all comes down to really knowing yourself and understanding your innate intuition. Hopefully, after years of practice, being true to yourself becomes second nature. And now here I sit, alone at a bar in Rome, as if it were the most natural thing in the world.

If there is one thing I have learned so far on this trip, it's that there is a learning curve to facing your fears. Traveling alone has made this journey what it is. Being alone has allowed me to reflect and write and grow and has given me the opportunity to meet new people everywhere I go. There have been amazing moments and not-so-amazing moments. But if facing your fears and living your dreams were a walk in the park, there would be no triumphant glory in the end, no pride, no obstacles to overcome. Prince Charming didn't just walk up and ring a doorbell to rescue his princess. No, he had to fight through haunted forests, conquer dragons, and break evil spells to find his one true love. This is kind of like conquering your fears: it's never easy, but it sure is worth it.

~

The next morning I cram my stuff in storage at the hostel and take the Rome Metro to the *Colesseo* stop. As I climb up the subway's cracked cement stairs around 9:45 a.m., I am met with the intense, ancient structure of the Colosseum standing strong against the deep blue sky. I am wearing dark sunglasses, which is less out of necessity and more to hide my tears. I can't believe I am here; I am back in Rome. There is no feeling like it. I have dreamed of these days, and this one day in particular. To be breathing this air and standing here is the biggest dream come true. I have come full circle. I have come back to this city that has found me in my dreams.

Last Christmas I thought I had finally made up my mind; I wasn't going to go on this trip. Now, this wasn't the first time I'd "made up my mind" to not go, but looking back, I can see it was officially the last. I was going to stay in Chicago and live my life that I had fought so hard to create, because that's what you do. At twenty-six, you're not supposed to give up everything you've spent your entire life building up and spend your life savings to travel the world. No, you're supposed to be settled, responsible, and conventional...and just like everybody else.

At the time, little did I understand that although I was slowly overcoming my fears about this trip, each time I changed my mind about going was also because I was invalidating my intuition—ignoring my heart. To ignore your heart is the worst sin against yourself. When asked the question, "What would you do if you knew you could not fail?" I *knew* the answer. I knew. It just took me a while to listen.

So last Christmas, I turned off my heart—or at least attempted to—exclaiming, "I must not know how to be content. So I'm staying." A dear friend of mine who always patiently listened to my confusing rants back and forth simply smiled and stated, "Good for you. I'm happy for you." I took a deep breath. *Yes, okay. Good. I can be normal and lead a normal, safe life. Yes. Okay, good.*

A couple nights later, I fell asleep not thinking of anything in particular, with no notion whatsoever that my entire world was about to change.

I dreamed I was on a hop-on hop-off bus tour in Rome. It was warm, sunny, and early in the morning. There were people everywhere, and I was alone. I was on this trip, the one I am on right now, and was filled with a peace I had never before felt. I wandered through the streets and found myself in the Jewish Ghetto, in front of an old ruin I had visited on my initial trip to Rome. I knelt down in front of the battered structure and said a heartfelt prayer. I had no idea when I awoke what I'd said, but I remembered finishing my whispers by blowing a kiss toward the heavens and then walking away smiling.

I awoke after this incredibly vibrant and lifelike dream completely heartbroken. That was where I should have been, and now I wasn't going. This was wrong, and I knew instantly.

From that moment forward, I knew I was going and that this trip was meant to be. It's almost as if I never really had a choice in the matter—this was my destiny, written on the walls of my heart. This one seemingly simple dream allowed me to finally *see*, and in that moment, I surrendered.

I didn't tell anyone at first about my change of heart. My faith in myself was somewhat weak after spending three years on a self-imposed fence. After a couple months though, little by little, I filled in loved ones and friends of my swiftly approaching plans. Most smiled and gave me their well wishes, probably hopeful for me but rightfully doubtful as well. It wasn't until we approached my departure date and my tickets and backpack had been bought that most finally took notice.

"You're really doing this?" they would ask, bemused.

I could only respond with a smile. "Yes. I am really doing it."

Today, as I make my way through the familiar streets of Rome, I rarely have to consult a map. It was late when we visited this ruin, but I remember where it is. I walk along the Tiber River and keep my focus fixed on the unfolding scenery across the street. I know it's close, but I'm not sure how close. A couple minutes and a couple blocks later, I see it—the building from my dreams.

As I cross over and slowly move toward it, I'm slightly taken aback at its size; it's a good deal smaller than I remember. I stand for a while in front of its faded columns and decaying arches. It's almost exactly 10:30 a.m., on a beautiful, sunny Monday. *Just like my dream.*

There are no rainbows or cherubs or signs from the heavens. Nothing spectacular happens. Nothing happens, *because it is already happening.* I whisper as many prayers of gratitude as my lips will allow, and just like my dream, I blow a kiss up to the sky. As I look up at the ruin, I notice a heart has formed at the tip of the building from the paint chipping away.

I smile and let Rome's sun wash over me.

Athens, Greece

I ARRIVE AT Athens International Airport increasingly giddy as I see Greek lettering stretching across signs and billboards. I've had an odd fascination with Greece for about six years now, so it feels incredibly fulfilling to finally be here.

After spending a majority of my high school and college years looking at travel photos and daydreaming of endless possibilities, it feels a little euphoric to see that these places I've torn out of magazines and taped to my walls actually exist. It feels like I've stepped into the pages of a storybook; places that once only belonged in my overactive imagination, I now experience in my everyday life.

I take the Metro to meet Kim, a friend from Chicago who is working in Athens as a teacher for the next two years. We spot each other at the same time and almost run to greet each other, elated to see a familiar face so far from home. Kim graciously invited me to stay with her while I'm in Greece, and I accepted in a heartbeat.

As we walk along her neighborhood roads that wind and curve in their own stubborn ways, the narrow and overcrowded sidewalks force us to walk in the streets and practically brush shoulders with the impatient cars rushing by.

"Okay, Jill, remember this corner, we turn left here. Okay, now this street curves to the right, so make sure you turn left here at the park. Look around, okay? Remember to turn here..." Kim patiently schools me.

"Okay, got it. Sure, the park...got it." I say, making mental notes as we go.

Kim lives about a twenty-minute walk from the Metro station and has a couple very long days of work ahead of her, so I'll be on my own for the most part. She gives me a map of Athens as well, which becomes priceless the next couple days as I make my way into and out of her complicated and somewhat puzzling classic Greek neighborhood.

That night we stick to Kim's district, a chic and trendy area full of restaurants and bars. We pick an outdoor café, where I eat my first traditional Greek meal as we catch up on each other's new lives.

As we stuff our faces with feta and lamb, tzatziki and onion, I fill Kim in on my travels and the inevitable adventures that have followed, and she tells me about her new Greek life: the stubborn students at her school, the culture shock of living in a new country, and horror of all horrors— despite being here for months now, she has yet to meet a beautiful, chiseled, young Greek descendant of the gods.

"No hot men? Not even one?" I'm horrified.

"Not even one..." She sniffles.

~

The next day is my only full twenty-four hours in Athens, so I try to take advantage of it as best I can. As I merge onto the streets from the Metro station below, I am greeted by the Acropolis seated high upon a hill overlooking the city. I spend the afternoon walking around Athens's famous

Plaka or old neighborhoods-turned-flea-markets, eating ice cream and browsing the cheap touristy trinkets. It is here that I buy my first souvenir of this trip, a keychain of all things, a mosaic painting of Christ, classic and small, perfect to tag along with me for the rest of my travels.

As I stare up at the Acropolis standing triumphantly on its bed of rock, I realize I have absolutely no idea how to get to it. My stomach begins its usual parade of whines for more food, and I can't in this moment seem to think of anything more appropriate on such a scorching hot day than to have more ice cream for lunch. As I wait in line, I ask the couple in front of me if they have any clue as to how I can reach the Acropolis.

"Oh, okay. Uh, well…" The wife hesitates as she squints down the road.

They painfully look at each other. The husband intercedes. "Follow this road all the way around until it dead-ends, make a right, follow that road for a couple of blocks, and when you see the sign, make a left."

I follow their directions exactly, and when I get to the sign reading "Acropoli," there is an arrow to the left and another pointing to the right. I stare at it, irritated. I go to the left. This is not the first sign in Athens that has multiple arrows for the same place pointing in opposite directions, and also true to Athens, I go up, then left, then right, up, then right again only to hit a dead end, turn around, and do it all over again. But at the end of my whirlwind tour through Athens's endless streets, I see it: the entrance.

It's quiet up here, away from the city streets. Old, twisting olive trees sit peacefully among the cicadas, with flat, white marble stones forming a pathway winding up the hill to the ticket office. It's relatively empty as well, speckled with tourists but thankfully not packed.

As I make my way up the steps, both the sun and wind pick up in intensity. It feels like a sauna is blowing against my face, but I don't care. After five weeks and eight countries, I've become pretty laid-back. Not a whole lot bothers me nowadays. I'm hungry? Okay. I'm roasting hot? All right. I'm tired and have blisters all over my feet? Fine. It is what it is. If I don't like it, I'll fix it or get over it. Nothing lasts forever. I'm pretty content being what I am where I am, and if I'm not, I'll get over it. It's actually quite a lovely way to exist, but I suppose I had to experience this life first to learn this.

The Parthenon is glorious, thousands of years old with bright white marble columns on a hill overlooking Athens—there really is no other word that comes to mind but *glorious*. Completed in 432 BC, the temple was originally built as a dedication to the Greek goddess Athena, the goddess of wisdom, courage, and strength, among other attributes, and whom the 3,400-year-old city (one of the world's oldest) is named after.

High above Athens on a mountain reserved for a god, the view is not only breathtaking but humbling as well. The city looks like a sea of little white boxes, all lying down in reverence to their grand successor.

The sun continues its sweltering barrage of heat as the hot air whips and blows around me. I take a seat under the cool shade of the ancient structures along with throngs of other overheated tourists resting from the midday sun and fanning themselves while chugging ice-cold bottled water from the vending machines by the ticket office, a slightly conspicuous reminder that maybe these grounds are not meant for mere mortals. I think this to myself as sweat forms a current down the middle of my back.

I meet a small group of solo travelers who have recently pieced themselves together here in Athens, and they invite me to join them for the afternoon. I politely decline. I have one thing on my mind at this point in the day: home, shower, bed. Okay, so more than one thing, but one general idea. I need rest. Tonight is a girls' night out on the town, and my feet need...well, actually I just need entirely new feet. I have at least three painful blisters on each foot, and *they are screaming at me.*

Kim's home is like an oasis: quiet, spacious, and surrounded by large decks off open glass doors with views of the city and the neighboring mountains. The doors and windows are always left open, allowing a cool breeze to flow through the rooms. The only thing disrupting our peace is the occasional child's laughter from below and the slam of a door from the breeze wind-tunneling through the rooms, a small price to pay for fresh air. And no mosquitoes! Let me repeat. There. Are. No. Mosquitoes. What a glorious way to live!

Later on that evening, Kim and I meet up with a couple of her coworkers and head to a restaurant in the city center with a rooftop terrace overlooking Athens and the Acropolis.

As the sun dips below the edges of Aegaleo Mountain, the temperature soon follows suit, leaving us with the perfect evening breeze to complement our perfect bottle of red. The mood is set: our lighting supplied by candles and the moon; our music by a man playing the bouzouki, filling the night air with classic Greek tunes; and the Acropolis in the background, lit up like a palace. We eat Greek-style, sharing eight different delectable dishes, including stuffed eggplant, saganaki, and Greek salad. It is the perfect ending to my last night in Greece.

I wrap my scarf around my bare shoulders and listen to the girls talk about what I suppose any group of young women with three carafes of wine would: what guy hasn't called yet, what coworker is driving who crazy, and who drank the last of the milk without telling anyone. No life-altering revelations are revealed tonight, no "aha" moments either. Despite our exotic locale and the unconventional lives we are living, life is still...life. Whether I find myself in Athens, Paris, or Chicago, people are still people. The food on the menu may be different, and I may find myself saying "*efharisto*" instead of "thank you," but as I look around, I see a couple canoodling in the corner, a young child pouting because he hasn't eaten his vegetables, and an older Greek man winking at me (you'll find them everywhere). It is in these quiet moments between what we call "normal life," if you stay open long enough, the world can sweep you up and make maddening love to you.

I suppose we may experience that more when we are out in the unexpected—your mind can't package everything up according to some past module of experience. You have to inhabit every second with eyes wide open, which is why I suppose I am so addicted to traveling; it is the only time in my life when I feel truly alive.

I feel this tonight, possibly a little more than these women who are living here now, paying rent and holding down steady jobs. It's the way life goes, I suppose, so I'm grateful that I'm not living life in any sort of "normal" way, but also that I get the opportunity to experience a little "normal" here amid the locals. So I cheers these women tonight, for inviting me in and then letting me go.

Tomorrow is my last day in Europe; then the real stuff begins. I am off to Egypt.

Electricity is beating through my veins. My arms are in the air and my voice carries in song as I dance around my apartment. I have my ticket! I have the ticket that will fly me around the world!

And the most exciting part is that now I am also going to Egypt, a place I have never even considered before. This fact brings me great comfort in who I am, because when offered a chance of a lifetime, to explore Egypt for a mere forty dollars more, not only did I take it, but I took it with grand excitement. I educated myself on the country's safety for a whole five minutes and then didn't waste a second in calling my ticket broker back with a holy "Yes!"

I then called some of my closest friends.

*"I'm going to Egypt, I'm going to Egypt. Holy crap, I'm going to Egypt! Do you even know where that is? It's in **Africa!**" I felt drunk and dizzy in my excitement. I was then met with a quieted and calm "Cool."*

*Of course this is their reaction. This is not their trip. One friend even responded with, "I thought you were already going to Cambodia." **Awkward.** But how could I expect any different? I was looking for a fever that would match my own and was met with a cool indifference. And this is okay. This is another quiet lesson and reminder that this is not their trip. This isn't their dream. It's mine. This is my sacred* *journey. I will be seeing these things on my own, so I need to remember that no one will ever truly understand. This might take me a while.*

Today I came across a quote by Mark Jenkins that struck me deeply:

"Adventure is a path. Real adventure—self-determined, self-motivated, often risky—forces you to have firsthand encounters with the world. The world the way it is, not the way you imagine it. Your body will collide with the earth and you will bear witness. In this way you will be compelled to grapple with the limitless kindness and bottomless cruelty of humankind—and perhaps realize that you yourself are capable of both. This will change you. Nothing will ever again be black and white."

*I read this, chills running down my body, and I start to cry. I don't well up in tears like I usually do when something touches my heart. I start **bawling**.*

Then, with my head in my hands, body trembling, and tears forcing themselves between the crevices of my fingers, I cry even harder. Years of prayers violently flood my memory:

"Please help me."

"Don't let me let go of this."

"Help me find my way."

"Lord, let me fly."

"Please help me fly."

"Give me the wisdom to see past this fear."

I see myself as a seventeen-year-old dreaming about living abroad, then again as a twenty-year-old wanting to start a dental hygiene movement in Greece, and then as a twenty-three-year-old dreaming of dancing on the shores of Australia. I see all of my younger selves who prayed and desperately held on to this fate that seemed more like a fantasy. I hold these memories in this moment and cry with gratefulness.

Then, in the midst of my sobbing, I start to laugh. My brain, sitting back and watching all this, sends some warning messages that I may actually be going crazy. I laugh even harder.

Today, today is a good day. Today is the first day of the rest of my life. I tried, and I didn't give up, and now I am going. Life is a grand adventure, and I intend on living it.

I can hear inside me, somewhere deep inside me, an ecstatic young girl kicking up her feet with a triumphant fist in the air, screaming, "Yes! I knew I'd make it one day..."

Africa

Cairo, Egypt

I ALWAYS ASSUMED I would need a Xanax on the flight connecting Athens and Egypt. I figured I'd be nervous and scared to end my "comfortable and easy" travel and begin the "real and somewhat uncomfortable" leg of my journey.

I was wrong.

The past thirty-seven days backpacking Europe alone has changed me in ways I could have never imagined. As we shuffle single file off the plane at Cairo International Airport, I am absolutely *thrilled*. I crouch down to view the surroundings out the small rectangular windows and am met with endless desert and sand. The plane's speakers are blasting Bollywood-type Arabian music while, as if I'm about to board a rollercoaster, my mind is screaming on repeat, "Oh, my God. Oh my God. OhmyGod."

As I walk out of the airport, crowds of tall dark men are holding up signs with names scribbled on them. I spot "Jillian" on a sign toward the end of the line. I smile and greet my driver, Mohammed, who kindly offers to carry my bags for me. As he throws my pack over his shoulders, he grunts a little from the weight and I bow my head in sympathy.

Walking with Mohammed through the muggy parking lot with my dark sunglasses on, I kind of feel like royalty. Just having someone carry my bags and personally drive me to my hotel is a luxury I haven't experienced yet on this trip, and I can't say I have any need to complain.

The city of Cairo is huge. No, actually, it's *huge*. I put my seatbelt on and Mohammed looks at me disapprovingly. "No, no." He points his finger at me as he shakes his head. I laugh.

"Oh yes, Mohammed. Yes." I click it shut.

The entire forty-five-minute drive is cutting cars off, being cut off, and honking. They honk constantly. Because there are no apparent rules of the road, it's like they are reminding each other, "Hi, I'm here next to you. Hey, next to you, you ass. Hey! Hey! Hey! Hey! HEY!"

The car behind us continually taps his horn for minutes. *Beep, beep, beep. Beep, beep, beep, beep. Beep. Beep. Beep. Beep. Beep. Beep.* On and on he goes. I can't for the life of me figure out why he is beeping constantly, but Mohammed isn't fazed. He explains the different sights to me as we pass and even puts my visor down when the sun gets in my eyes.

This city is unbelievable. It's authentic, real, beat-up, and chaotic. I stare out my window to see Muslim women walking the streets with their traditional Al-Amira hijabs wrapped neatly around their heads and flowing gracefully over their shoulders. The traffic and honking are unrelenting, and trash litters the corners and crevices of this city like glue in a jigsaw puzzle. It's pure chaos. Oh, and my driver's car has fake fur all over the dash. Sweet.

The towering buildings are made up of generic cement and covered in dirt and grime—they all look like mud. Some have awnings or signs that look like they used to have color, but after years of abuse from the pollution and sun, they too are mud brown.

A thick haze of smog lies over the metropolis, so much so that I don't need to squint in the midday sun. Over the tops of the skyline, dome-shaped mosques with full or half-crescent moon-tipped poles ascend into the heavens. I think it may be safe to say I'm not in Europe anymore.

My hotel is top-rated, but when I show up, I can't help but wonder why. It appears to be an abandoned warehouse. I hesitantly make my way up the dingy, dirty, low-lit stairs. Five flights and a few stray cats later, *voila!* My hotel. I am greeted by a wave of smiling, enthusiastic men.

"Hello! Jillian!" They jump up to grab my bags. "Welcome! Sit down! Relax! I give you best room!"

Everyone is smoking inside, a pet peeve of mine that I've given up since traveling. I sit in the common room with the owner, Moustafa, his family of employees, and a few other travelers. It is the most hospitable and welcoming place I have stayed at so far.

"Sit! Have some food, have a cigarette!" Moustafa jumps up to hand me a beer.

"Wow. Thank you." I sit back in disbelief.

The receptionist strings some Egyptian flowers for me that smell like hyacinths. His name is Nael. He is an older man with incredibly kind eyes, who I quickly adopt as my "Egyptian Grandfather."

There is nothing grand about this place. It's actually kind of shitty, but it's clean—definitely mid-renovation though, with not-so-gently used mix-and-match furniture—but I love it anyway, which makes them love me.

"You are so happy," they say. "Your eyes just sparkle."

This is no lie. I am happy. I wave my notepad in front of my face, as it is very hot, and someone jumps up to point a fan at me. I enjoy my time here so much that instead of going out, I sit in the common room with the family and enjoy a couple Egyptian beers. So far, Egypt has surpassed all of my expectations, and I haven't even stepped outside my hotel.

That night, in my silk sleep sheet, with the light above me flickering on randomly, I hang my string of flowers next to my head. My life may not seem like a bed of roses, but right now, all I can smell are flowers.

~

The next day my rose-colored glasses are still on but getting slightly dusty. It's early afternoon and I still haven't gone exploring. This is unlike me, but I am afraid. Being a lone female walking the streets in the Middle East can be a frightening thing. One woman at the hotel has been in Cairo for a month now and says she's "over it"—it doesn't faze her. Not this Midwestern girl. Ring or no ring, scarf or no scarf, I stand out—*bad*. Large groups of men sit around in open-air coffee shops and smoke shisha and stare. Then come the comments and the hissing and the waving. This is my ninth country on this trip, and nothing—nothing—has kept me inside. Italy and Greece are known to have some of the more aggressive men—didn't faze me. The Italian men are actually quite adorable and harmless in my experience. Not here. *Not* here.

Moustafa marches into the common room and tells me to grab my things. He is taking me to a coffee shop to have tea and smoke shisha. So off we go, out into the jungle.

As I walk alongside this older Egyptian man, it's like I have a force field. Oh, they still stare, but that's it. I finally feel free and able to experience this incredibly old Middle Eastern city and not fear for my safety. Of course, I never feel like I am in any *immediate* danger out on my own, but I don't enjoy a second of it. Only one time do I step outside my hotel alone during my stay in Egypt, and that is to run to an ATM.

Moustafa takes me to a dingy alley off a side street, where a coffee shop has placed its outdoor seating. We grab a spot in the corner and sit at a small plastic table surrounded by various plastic chairs and *teeming* with flies. I am a little apprehensive at first, but this is nothing compared to my reaction when using the coffee shop's bathroom. I stand in the open doorway with flies swarming around my face and turn right back around. I just can't. I hold it.

I order fresh mango juice, eat my shawarma and baba ghanoush that we picked up on the way, and wait for our apple shisha to come. Moustafa shows me how to smoke it, which is exactly the same as a hookah. He inhales deeply from the mouthpiece as smoke fills the clear hose extending off the shisha. He is slightly hunched over, and I watch in amazement as his slicked back hair doesn't move and two tunnels of smoke stream out his nostrils. He hands the hose over to me. I inhale the apple-flavored tobacco and exhale the thick smoke. Moustafa looks at me proudly.

"Yes, yes. Nice? Okay?"

It's nice, but I'm not so sure what all the fuss is about.

"Yes, very nice," I say with a smile.

I wonder, while we sit there and smoke, why this man is being so nice. Honestly, I bet sixty-five percent of it is genuine, and the other thirty-five percent? Meet another Mohammed, who joins us for tea. He is another middle-aged Egyptian man who "just happens" to own the perfume shop across the alley. Moustafa "just happens" to know people all over town, and he loves to show me their businesses. Ah, I kind of knew this was coming. This is the way life works in much of the world, so I don't fret. Peer pressure never did much for me, and I have no problem telling them kindly that I am not interested in buying anything. So I guess Moustafa and I are both guilty of doing the same thing—using each other. He gets commission by bringing me by his friends' shops, and I get a free guide and man-protector for the day. Works for me.

Later that evening, my driver (another Mohammed), picks me up to go to a dinner cruise on the Nile. Moustafa comes as well, as we are meeting five other people on the boat who he has previously corralled. As we wait at the site for the gates to open, the evening prayer call fills the air, echoing off the water and surrounding buildings.

It's almost eerie in a fascinating way to sit back and listen to the man's voice outpour and flow throughout the city. I ask a local man selling toasted nuts from a small cart on the sidewalk what the song is saying. He is delighted to tell me and paraphrases in English as the prayer continues: "God is greatest…There is no God except Allah…Mohammed is God's messenger…Come to prayer…God is great."

It is dusk now. I sit against an old, rusted railing along the Nile and listen to the song-like prayers as cars incessantly honk their horns. I feel like I'm really out in the world now.

The group of five ends up being a fantastic group of Australians who join us just as we are boarding the boat. We get along instantly and are all bummed when we discover we can't sit together. They are seated at one table in the middle of the restaurant while Moustafa and I are at a table for two in the corner. *Great.* My prayer-call high and rose-colored glasses are fading fast.

Do you want to know my definition of hell? A dinner cruise on the Nile. It's two hours of karaoke-style Arabian techno music with strobe lights, cold buffet food, over-priced water and about two hundred people over the age of seventy-five. I order four tequila shots for myself and am told with a somewhat judgmental tone that alcohol isn't allowed. I slump farther into my chair.

"Fine. I'll have a water on the rocks," I say without looking up.

The server walks away confused.

Moustafa stays outside for most of the dinner, which is good because he reeks of BO and cigarettes. So I sit at my table, alone and feeling very close to sticking my plastic spork into my eye.

At the end of the cruise, I stand on the rooftop deck talking to the Australians as the elderly push and shove their way off the boat. We are giving it a minute to clear out because most of the world apparently has no concept of the meaning of personal space. Many times now while waiting in line, I've found that if people aren't cutting, they are practically sitting on my shoulders. In the customs line at the airport, the short old lady behind me was so close, if she would have licked her lips, she would have licked the back of my arm. The hairs on my arm were swaying to the rhythm of her breathing. I'm not exactly used to these new rules of the line, so it takes all the patience I can muster to not turn around and kung fu the shit out of someone.

Back to the Elderly Express, as I am talking to the Australians, Mohammed the cab driver grabs my wrists and vigorously shakes me back and forth. I stumble back, stunned. Conversation screeches to a halt. Irritated, he shakes his fists in front of my face and says, "Please, please let's go!" One of the women in the group breaks the awkward silence and kindly gathers me into her arms.

"Yes, okay," she says quickly. "Let's get out of here."

She walks me toward the stairs. It takes my brain another minute to catch up to the reality of what has just occurred, and when it does, my blood begins to *boil*. I grab Moustafa downstairs and tell him how his cabbie "handled" the situation upstairs. He hesitates. "You know, it is the Egyptian way. Maybe…maybe he thought you were falling."

"Oh, give me a break!" I say through gritted teeth. "This is completely unacceptable and very offensive. No one has ever manhandled me that way, and I'm certainly not going to take it from some random cab driver on the other side of the world!"

Moustafa pulls the cabbie aside and starts to yell at him in Arabic. He yells at him the entire drive home. This is normally not my way—to cause a scene—but my defense is up in this city of smog and dirtballs, and you bet your ass I'm not going to let some man grab me like that. Mohammed apologizes again. There is nothing left to do but go back to the hotel and forget about it.

~

On my third day in Egypt everything is rosy again. Rita and Brian, a young married couple staying at my hotel, have joined me to go to the desert near Giza to see the pyramids. We split the cost of our driver (Mohammed *again*) and a charismatic and knowledgeable Egyptologist named Gad.

As we make our thirty-minute drive toward the only remaining Ancient Wonder of the World, Gad tells us about Egypt's history and kings, so that we may better understand the 4,500-year-old structures we are about to see. Turned toward us in his seat up front, he whips out a full presentation laminated in his three-ring binder, equipped with figures, facts, and timelines. I'm impressed.

We stop first in a poor stable town just outside the gates of the pyramids. Rita wants to ride horses after hearing a couple horror stories of riding camels in the desert, so after haggling with the manager for what seems like hours, we finally agree on a price that doesn't feel like an incredibly enormous rip-off.

A happy young boy takes our reins and leads our horses to the entrance of the pyramids. We are going the back way, since we are on horses, which is an area that the tour buses never see. The entrance is not grand, just metal gating with guards and piles of trash *everywhere*.

We slowly make our way through the desert to the pyramids, which doesn't take long because they are so close. We stop and take numerous photos, all at the direction of our tour guide, who happens to know of an assortment of poses for us to try, including the ever-so-tacky arms-stretched-out-to-each-side-illusion-of-touching-the-pyramid-tips pose.

Then we meet an old man who insists that we get on his decked-out camel, Michael, and take pictures (for money of course). He whips the back of the camel's curved neck with a wooden rod to get him to his knees so I can climb on top. A harsh, low gargle bubbles up from his long neck, a camel version of a growl, I can only assume. "I'm sorry, Michael," I whisper as I climb between his furry humps.

On the ride over, Gad warns us that people will put trinkets or assorted drinks into our hands and then charge us a steep fee. We aren't hassled too much, although one guy walks up to me mumbling only, "Very hot," and proceeds to place a cloth on my head. Determined, he fastens the white cotton with a band as I reiterate like an echo, "What are you doing? I'm not paying for this. I'm not paying for this. I'm not paying for this." Rita and Brian stand back and laugh. There is another clown at the Sphinx who tells me if I don't buy his light-up pyramid, he will go home and kill himself. It's a desperate move, but I can't really blame him considering how desperately hot it is today under this African desert sun.

As we make our way past the Sphinx, we continue to receive the unending beatings and pleadings from trinket sellers and food stall vendors. After a quick bathroom break, we get into our air-conditioned car and head toward Memphis, an old village that used to be the thriving capital of Egypt back when kings ruled. We also stop by the Stepped Pyramid of Djoser, the world's first pyramid, built back in 2648 BC.

The villages we drive through make me feel like we are in India. Poor, dirty, and trash-filled, these towns bordering the outskirts of Cairo are filled with tuk-tuks, donkeys, and children playing barefoot in the dirt roads. Women here are wearing the niqab, a black headdress that covers absolutely everything but the eyes. It is Friday, the day of prayer, so the song-like prayer calls are on loudspeakers all over the villages. The entire time I am glued to my window.

That night, Rita, Brian, and I treat ourselves by going to the very top of the Grand Hyatt Hotel located next to the Nile for a fancy dinner in their rotating restaurant. The restaurant moves almost unnoticeably slow, so it takes drinks, soup, dinner, and coffee for us to go full circle. The city from way up here looks sweet, almost calm and inviting. The cars below float through streams of streetlights while the lit windows of the high-rise buildings around us almost twinkle like stars in the night.

But I know this is not the reality of the world below me. The walk over here was like being between a rock and a hard place; from the constant bickering of Rita and Brian over which direction to go, to the unending honking and breathing in clouds of dust and exhaust fumes, I can't decide which was more unnerving. But up here in the clouds, I let all that fade away and ignore the fact that I will return to that world once again in the not-so-distant future. I enjoy my overpriced meal, piece by delectable piece, and the privilege of pretending I belong up here in this succulent and glittering world high above the manic city below.

~

My last afternoon in Cairo, Moustafa and Nael throw me a going-away party. The tables in the common area are filled with food: stuffed eggplant, koshari (a chili-like dish), and spicy potatoes with Stella beers to wash it all down. We also have coffee and tea, and Moustafa refuses to let me help pay for the food.

Despite the harsh tones and raw sharpness of this city, the hospitality of a few locals offsets my aggravation and leaves a bittersweet taste in my mouth for Cairo. Unfortunately, because of my fear, I wasn't able to wander the streets, markets, or mosques this time around, but this gives me an excuse to return someday—hopefully a little more traveled and much more prepared.

Moustafa has been asking me for days to extend my stay in Cairo. But I am ready to go. I am off to Bangkok tonight and after Cairo, I feel I am definitely ready.

Southeast Asia

Bangkok, Thailand

A DROP OF WATER BURSTS against the tip of my nose. *Splat!* And another, breaking loudly against my shoulder. This is our only warning, and within seconds Bangkok's sky opens up into a ferocious downpour. We have just left the gates of the Grand Palace and are now running through the streets frantically searching for cover from the monsoon-like waves of water falling from the sky.

Standing under the umbrellas of the city's unfazed street vendors, we look around at each other and laugh. Being in Southeast Asia during its wet season is so authentically exhilarating. When it rains here, it *really* rains. And it's never happy with just that—the rain is always accompanied by an intense, crashing thunderstorm. It really feels like we are in the tropics now. Tuk-tuks splash by as street vendors rush to cover their goods with plastic. We decide to wait it out while having lunch at a small, family-owned restaurant. We are the only foreigners here.

I order a noodle soup with vegetables by pointing to each item on a cart hugging the entrance to the restaurant. I watch as the plump, middle-aged Thai woman grabs handfuls of noodles and large, homemade croutons and combines them all into a bowl. Using an old metal ladle, she pours in the broth from a steaming bucket, throws in handfuls of colorful spices, and finishes with a dab of a bright pink goop that I can only assume is a sweet-and-sour mix. It's actually quite delicious.

~

When first arriving in Bangkok, I take an express bus from the airport into the city. After the driver drops me off, I stand on the curb with my backpack strapped to me, confused and disoriented. This corner doesn't look at all like what the hostel said it would.

"Do you have any idea where to go?" comes a voice from behind me. I turn around and meet Ellie, a solo backpacker from England with a petite frame and fierce red hair, who also happens to be going to the same hostel I am. I love when this happens. And she has a map! I gratefully explain to her that she must be my guardian angel as she confidently guides us through the narrow streets to the stop where the bus driver was *supposed* to drop us off.

We approach a busy street we must cross in order to get to our smaller, quaint neighborhood streets, but to do this we must first play our own little death-defying version of leapfrog. The road has multiple lanes of traffic traveling in opposite directions with no lights or crosswalks. We are both prepared for this, as we have been properly schooled by previous travelers to Thailand, so, hesitantly, we walk out into oncoming traffic and pray they stop. This is the only way to cross. The trick is to not stop and stutter but to walk confidently with a steady, predictable pace as your life flashes before your eyes. Buses and cabs tend to stop for us while the parade of motorbikes whiz around us. Slowly but surely we make it across, laughing and possibly peeing ourselves the entire time.

It's still too early to check into our hostel, so we head out for lunch on the notorious Khao San Road just two blocks away. As we turn the corner, we are met with countless neon billboards and signs, layered on top of each other and stretched out in every direction, waving desperately for our attention—almost as desperately as the people working the street. Every crack, corner, nook, and cranny of this stretch of road has some sort of business crammed in: vendors and restaurants, food stalls, fruit stands, fake ID printers, T-shirt makers, tuk-tuk drivers, and massage parlors, all simultaneously vying for our attention.

"You want Thai massage? Massage? I give you good price!" yells the lady next to her parlor, with a lineup of smiling faces awaiting our arrival.

"Where you go? Where you go? Ten baht!" insists the tuk-tuk driver.

Beggars with deformed limbs humbly bow next to their tin cans on the street, causing my heart to wince a little as we shuffle past.

∼

Later on that evening, Ellie and I meet in the common room of our hostel before heading out for dinner and a Ping-Pong show. Within the period of thirty minutes and one beer, our group has grown to nine people. I meet Amira, a young woman from Switzerland with a strong English accent. She is beautiful, with long, thick brown hair and hazel eyes, a fierce attitude, and an incredibly kind spirit.

Within the course of the evening, we learn we are both traveling the same route from northern Thailand through Laos and then Cambodia.

Amira practically jumps at the opportunity to travel together. Having already been traveling the world alone for six months now, she recognizes our chance meeting as an ideal situation for a travel mate. I, however, am not so sure. After traveling for two months now with only six days on a beach, I'm pretty set on heading south to the islands before starting my northern trek.

"You should really consider skipping the south for now and go north with me," Amira states as a matter of fact. "It's a perfect scenario, and I think we'd have a lovely time."

"Yeah…" I hesitate. "I don't know."

Ellie starts corralling the group to leave, and I hope as we head out that our change of scenery will bring about a change of subject as well.

Like a small herd of confused cattle, our group heads to Khao San Road in search of dinner. No one has any idea where to go, so we stumble into the first establishment that looks somewhat inviting. Amira and I split a dish of green curry and vegetables with rice. This is my first time trying curry, and it tastes like an explosion of flavors with the coconut milk, lemon grass, chilies, and ginger. I am delighted, as sweat drips down my temples and my mouth burns from the spices, with each mouthwatering spoonful.

It ends up being too late for Ping-Pong, so we save it for another night. A small group of us girls breaks off from the herd and ends up at a bar with a cover band playing the likes of Johnny Cash, The Eagles, and Oasis. We drink Tiger and Chang beers while singing along to our favorite songs, and fill each other in on the lives we've abandoned and the lives we're living now.

There is something magical about Thailand, its ambiance and energy. It's Third World, to be sure. Some of the buildings are crumbling with dirt and pollution smearing down their faces, and the street corners are packed with trash, but the atmosphere here is unlike anything I've ever experienced. I love it. As I walk down Bangkok's crammed and chaotic roads, aromas from street vendors selling local curries and soups rise up into the air. Dimly lit lanterns hang from building to building, tuk-tuks and motorbikes fly by, and Asian-inspired music travels along the muggy streets, vibrating off puddles and ponds with lotus flowers and lily pads.

One traveler I met in Rome called Southeast Asia "Neverland," and I couldn't agree more. It's like a parallel universe, where you can roam free and be a kid again. Throughout Thailand, Laos, Cambodia, and Vietnam, I will be exploring the cities, riding tuk-tuks, jumping off waterfalls, sleeping with geckos, and swimming with elephants. On top of all this, the travelers who walk these streets alongside me are an incredibly diverse group of friendly and intriguing people from all over the world.

∼

My second day in Bangkok (the day we are stuck in the monsoon by the Grand Palace), we decide to spend the day "wat hopping" and take my first tuk-tuk ride to the palace. Here we begin to experience the first of what seems like *endless* occurrences of deceit in the name of money.

To enter the palace, you must have both your shoulders and knees covered. I have a shawl with me, but this is not considered to be a proper amount of cover. As soon as my foot steps off the tuk-tuk, I am approached by an older Thai woman informing me that I need to rent a shirt from her for 200 baht (about seven U.S. dollars). I look at the table of used and faded T-shirts and seriously consider, but I decide I can come back if this is really necessary.

As we walk across the street to the palace, a guy standing outside the entrance asks us if we are in a group. After we respond that we are, he directs us down the road to buy tickets. When we get to the next entrance, the guy working this corner tells us that the palace is only open to monks and Thais for the next hour and a half for prayer. But if we would like, "We can take you around in a tuk-tuk to see the other sights of the city for only fifty baht each until the palace reopens." The girls agree and ask me what I think. I am hesitant. I don't know why I feel unsure, as it sounds likely that a place of this importance would actually be closed for prayer for a short time, but it doesn't feel right.

"I don't know," I whisper while eyeing the smiling man waiting beside his tuk-tuk. "I heard people will tell you places are closed so you'll go with them instead and they can make commission off you. Let's just go back to the first entrance and check it out."

Turns out it was a scam, and a very clever scam at that because of a foreigner's vulnerability in not knowing the local customs. This isn't the last time we are misled about Bangkok's wats being closed and unfortunately, Bangkok isn't the only place in Thailand where we experience it either. It's all part of an intricately set up "gem scam" that

I am not fully aware of until about a year and a half after returning from my trip. I only know at the time that if a tuk-tuk driver tells you a place is closed, confirm with a second source.

As we walk through the open gates of the Grand Palace, we tread lightly with our heads down, expecting at any minute to be stopped and yelled at for trying to enter such a religious and prestigious place during a time when foreigners are not allowed. Nothing happens. To top it all off, I am given a free shirt to wear while I am there.

The Grand Palace is a beautiful place with expansive courtyards full of temples and monuments, curling tails of burning incense, and the Emerald Buddha made completely out of jade.

After our visit, the monsoon, and lunch, we head to the famous Reclining Buddha in a temple known as Wat Pho. Here I use my shawl to cover my shoulders, line my shoes with the others outside the temple, and walk right in. He's absolutely stunning and *enormous*. Housed in one of the largest wats in Bangkok, the golden Buddha measures 141 feet in length, stands fifty feet high, and symbolizes the passing of the Buddha into nirvana. The wat also holds a staggering amount of Buddha images, over one thousand in total, as well as a library and university. We slowly tour the temple and take photos while gawking at the intricate detailing of these holy monuments.

We spend the entire day doing this, wandering in and out of wats, through busy city streets and markets, and end our excursion with a climb up the stairs of one of Bangkok's oldest temples, Wat Arun, or the Temple of Dawn. The stairs are among the steepest I've climbed, so,

using the railing like a rope, we pull ourselves up onto
each of the narrow steps like babies learning to crawl. As
we ascend higher and higher, I notice the entire surface
of the wat is covered in colorful flowers made out of
broken china. Reaching the top, we take a much-needed
rest and gaze at panoramic views of the city unfolding
in every direction.

That night, after my second cold shower of the day, we
all try for round two of going to a Ping-Pong show. Amira
and I head off first to get street food, green curry again for
me and a coconut milk soup for her, then meet the others
back at the hostel for some drinks before we head out, as
we are told drinking is absolutely necessary before a show.
Our group fills up two tuk-tuks, and we end up racing neck
and neck down the streets of Bangkok.

In the neighborhood of Patpong, the streets are filled
to the brim with food vendors and night markets selling
knock-off brands of sunglasses, jewelry, and purses. All
the while, men litter every corner, advertising for shows.
Everywhere we walk men try to stop us. "Ping-Pong show.
You want Ping-Pong show? Ping-Pong show?"

Now, I'd never heard of one until I went on this trip,
and despite it sounding incredibly offensive, my curiosity
got the best of me. A Ping-Pong show can be found in
strip clubs throughout Bangkok, where women entertain
crowds by doing very unconventional and unsettling tricks
with their vaginas. Unfortunately, travelers from all over
the world go to see it, and unfortunately, I was told it was
a "must" when I was in Bangkok.

Walking into the dingy, low-lit club, I am horrified to
see a kaleidoscopic stage filled with young, naked Thai

women in heels. They shift their weight from heel to heel, twirl around the stripper poles, and look into dark corners filled with callous men with dying eyes. I stand, appalled and motionless in the middle of the room as aggravated patrons are forced to walk around me.

I thought I knew what I was getting myself into. I expected dingy. I expected dirty. But there is something about these women—something void in their gaze, like the heavy black smoke from the endless burning cigarettes has filled their bodies and now swirls in layers behind their eyes. It's as if the life has been sucked right out of them.

We cram into a booth and order a round of beers. I am uncomfortable. More than uncomfortable—I am overwhelmingly disturbed. One woman looks directly at me and holds up a sign to tip.

I realize right then, as our eyes meet, what I am finding so disturbing: with the absence of hope lies the epitome of despair, and these women wear it on their faces like captives.

Just then, the birthday song starts, and all but one woman clear the stage. A cake with a dozen candles is brought out, and she is handed a straw. Lying on her back, she inserts the straw into her vagina and proceeds to blow out each candle. She is followed by a woman who inserts a dart gun to pop balloons, a woman who inserts a cigarette and smokes it, and last but not least, a woman who shoots out Ping-Pong balls at our group.

Ducking for cover and laughing nervously, we unfortunately appear to be entertained while the woman with the sign to tip still stares at me. I consider giving her money but feel trapped by my own confusion. I want to help, but how could I possibly be helping anything by tipping? I don't know what to do, so I end up doing nothing.

We don't stay for long before our group agrees that this is not a place we'd like to spend any more time in. As we exit the building, I hesitate at the back door and take one last look at the world I hope to never see again. I wish I could bundle the girls up and take them with me, far, far away from this life. I am disgusted that I supported this establishment tonight. Absolutely disgusted.

~

I spend the next couple days wandering the steaming hot and overcrowded streets of Bangkok, going out with new friends, and solidifying my newly formed friendship with Amira. I am still absolutely thrilled to be here and easily find more and more to love about Asia each day. My tongue has canker sores from all the spicy food, but eating it makes my mouth feel alive…and makes all the food I used to eat back home seem bland. When I say this to other travelers, they laugh.

"How long have you been in Asia?" they ask curiously.

"Only a couple days…" I reply sheepishly.

More laughs.

"Give it a month."

~

On a slightly daunting tuk-tuk ride through a maze of motorbikes, Amira has had enough of my ho-hum indecisiveness. "You're coming north with me," she yells over the loud humming of the tuk-tuk motor and smiles. I stare at her as our hair whips and snaps around us. *Who does this broad think she is?* I laugh. I'm going to the warm and sunny paradise of *southern* Thailand, and I'm going to bum around for weeks. I don't give in to peer pressure! *Puh,* little does she know.

The next morning Amira and I pack our bags and catch a bus headed for northern Thailand.

One Year Pre-Trip
Chicago, Illinois

*I'm afraid my entire life will pass me by and I'll miss it because I am **so tired**. I feel lifeless. I feel stifled.*

I don't want to run for the wrong reasons if I can find my happiness in Chicago. I keep going back and forth because I keep thinking I should be able to be happy right here and now. I should be able to breathe the life back into myself without spending thousands of dollars and leaving the country.

At the same time, I don't understand why I keep fighting myself. If I'm meant to go, this dream will bother me every day, which it has been doing for years. So why do I keep fighting it?

I believe in something bigger than myself; I believe there is more to life than this. I just don't know how to find it…and until I do, I feel like I am dying inside.

I feel like I could be talented at writing, at taking photos, at finding the beauty of life.

*So maybe the life I am supposed to find can only be **found** when I remove myself from all this and give myself the time and space to stretch my soul.*

God, help me find the faith to believe in my vision, despite everything I know telling me that it's not logical—or safe. It's huge and risky and scary. God, give me the strength to believe in this…I'm sick of going back and forth. Please, help me have faith.

Chiang Mai, Thailand

IT'S PEACEFULLY QUIET TONIGHT, and cooler too, in this village high up in the mountains in northern Thailand. We are in Chiang Mai, a modest little city about 360 miles north of Bangkok, and an adventure-sports lover's dream. This doesn't come as a surprise, considering the *natural* excitement level of Chiang Mai is about the equivalent of a crocheting club at your local retirement home. It's beautiful and calm, but the city doesn't have a whole lot to offer besides a cooking class or two, a night market, and a few bored prostitutes.

So, being the resourceful people they are, the Thais *gave* it something to offer—adrenaline. You can do anything in Chiang Mai: zip-lining, trekking, mountain biking, four-wheeling, white-water rafting, bungee jumping, motor-biking, and the list continues. Best of all, you can stay in a village in the mountains and go through mahout training, or learning to ride and care for your own elephant. Almost all these activities are located just outside the city, which becomes painfully obvious as the sun goes down and the only stimulation is a single puppy chasing its tail on an empty street corner.

Thankfully though, this is no matter because, despite my stubborn pigheadedness, I am not alone. After spending a couple days with Amira in Bangkok, it dawns on me one night that companionship with another traveler whom I enjoy spending time with *and* has the same itinerary as I do is a fantastic opportunity. I was so set on going south that I forgot to open my eyes and see what was actually happening—I have found a new friend.

Within twenty-four hours of traveling north, we run into Jess, a loud and spunky Australian woman Amira met while traveling in South America a couple months ago. We meet her on our first morning in Chiang Mai in our hostel common room when Amira recognizes a large straw hat on top of a mop of wavy blond hair. Forty-eight hours later, the three of us are off on the first of many adventures together, and all because of a "chance" encounter that I almost let slip between my fingers.

Nam, our primary guide and caretaker at mahout training for the next couple days, picks us up in Chiang Mai early in the morning. He smiles often, spouts off jokes, and makes sure we are safe and happy and comfortable…well, as comfortable as we can be staying in a bamboo hut on stilts in a small village in the mountains—with no electricity.

We arrive after about an hour of traveling in the back of a pickup truck with benches bolted down in the back. It's quite a bumpy ride as we wind up dirt roads with large divots missing deep in their paths. We hold on for dear life in the back, laughing and bracing ourselves as we fly off our benches and into each other like freshly popped popcorn.

The village is a collection of six bamboo huts folded between a handful of mountains. After we arrive, we walk past a couple large elephants just outside our hut, happily ripping leaves and branches off the jungle floor and chomping away. Tea awaits us on the picnic table, along with sets of worn, denim uniforms we'll be wearing for the next two days to save our clothes from the mud, wear, and tear.

Our hut is a single room on stilts with a giant log as a step from the porch. The floor is made up of various sizes of bamboo, which are not exactly packed together, as I can clearly see green foliage and clucking chickens beneath us. A handful of Thai women carry in some weathered cushions to fashion a bed for us. They tie a large mosquito net onto the ceiling of our hut and tuck it underneath the mats. We all nod our heads and smile of course, as this is the "land of smiles," and say thank you in Thai, "*Khob khun ka!*" They smile and nod back.

We relax on an old picnic table outside our hut and enjoy our tea, breathing in the fresh mountain air and watching the roosters and chickens around us pick at the ground for food. Nam shuffles up with a slightly toothless grin; it is time to meet our elephants.

As I walk up to Mateo, I am slightly intimidated by her size, but she is a calm elephant, so I am told, and the grandmother of the elephants we are to be caring for. She looks me over with her big brown eyes with lashes the length of fingers. She is beautiful. I start to giggle as she lifts her trunk to smell me, which is her way of getting to know me. Our other guides and their assistants then attempt to teach us some of the commands and body language to communicate with our elephants.

We will be riding the elephants bareback, so we are given a wooden handle with a dull hook at the end. If we want our elephant to go right, we hold the wooden device in our right hand and touch the left side of their head, squeezing our legs as we straddle their necks, and yell, "*Bpai! Bpai!*" (Go! Go!) We also learn how to touch their legs so they'll lift them as we grab hold of their ears and climb on top. They ask for a volunteer to go first. Jess and Amira hesitate, so I raise my hand like I'm eight years old again. "Oh! Oh me! I will!"

As Mateo lifts her leg, it almost seems impossible for me to bridge the distance between the ground and her neck. I grab the top of her freckled ear, stepping onto her lifted knee and stretching my other leg across her neck so she can lift me high enough to mount her.

It's amazing being on top of a creature this size with nothing between us. The top of her head is covered in dry clay and dirt, with ants tracing a path between the short, coarse hairs sporadically extending from her enormous head. As I wrap my legs tightly around her neck, her big ears flap back and forth to fan herself.

I like Mateo. She's so relaxed that I easily relax as well and go with the flow of her motions. I have a bunch of bananas with me, so I lean across her giant skull and touch the front of her forehead with them, yelling, "*Gin! Gin!*" Her trunk lifts up and searches for the food right in front of my face, blowing hot air so forcefully that my hair flies back. I hand her a couple bananas and watch the tip of her trunk wrap around them and bring them back down to her mouth. Now knowing I have food, she barely has time to swallow before she lifts her trunk up again and stubbornly holds it there until I give her more. The bananas don't last long.

On our elephants the three of us head out into the jungle with our guides walking by our sides. We have a good laugh as we watch Jess and her guide fight like hell to get control of her naughty young elephant, Camnoi. These incredible creatures with their own personalities and intense intelligence live to be as old as most humans, around seventy to eighty years. My elephant is a grandmother at forty years old with an obvious maternal instinct about her. She patiently waits for Jess's elephant if she gets too far behind, and if my legs even slightly release their grip around her neck, her ears fly straight back to press me firmly against her body.

Jess's elephant is a mere ten years old and basically couldn't care less about continuing on the path. Still growing, she wants to eat constantly, so our lineup halts often and we watch, amused, as Jess and her guide try to get Camnoi to stop eating long enough to walk five feet.

We ride for over an hour, passing huts and fields of bright green rice paddies in a backdrop of lush jungle mountains. Thais living in the surrounding villages run up to greet us with warm smiles and hellos, waving the whole time. We all smile and wave back, high on top of our elephants. "Hello! *Sawasdee ka!*"

Life in these villages is a simple one. Nam explains to us that time doesn't exist here. If you make an appointment, it's, "Tomorrow, early." How early, you ask? "Second rooster." The roosters, I learn firsthand, start crowing quite loudly at 3:30 a.m. and then every hour on the hour after that. Okay then, second rooster. These birds are like family in these villages, walking freely in and around the huts. They become so attuned with their people, Nam says, that if the villagers run out of food and have to kill a rooster, they know. "Next morning," he says somberly, "they no crow. They know."

At the end of our trek, we stop by a large, mud-brown river and watch as the elephants happily submerge themselves. Mateo playfully sticks her trunk in the current and sprays out water, as Camnoi twists and turns beneath the river, pulling out roots and weeds from underneath. With buckets and scrub brushes in hand, Jess and Amira join the enormous creatures in the cool water, scrubbing their skin and using the buckets to rinse off the layers of mud and clay. I join the guides sitting along the shore and laugh as the girls climb on top of the elephants and receive a continued barrage of water streaming from their trunks.

A truck stops on the street alongside the river to pick us up. It's time to let the elephants go back into the jungle. We pile in the back of the pickup. Mot, our younger male guide at about nineteen years old with hipster-tight jeans and Bob-Marley-style Afro hair, is to lead the trio of elephants back up the road and into the jungle. Before waving goodbye, Mot leans into me and whispers, "You are beautiful."

"Oh…" I smile awkwardly as Jess and Amira look at us with curious eyes. "Okay," I say. "Thanks."

He gives me one last sultry look before he and our elephants walk away. "Where are the elephants going?" I ask the older guide, hoping he didn't catch our little dialogue. Oblivious to Mot's and my exchange of words, he informs us that it is our job as mahouts to rise early tomorrow morning and find them.

Sitting in the back of the truck, we endure a silence with the tension of a pin to a balloon. Amira breaks it first. "So, Jillian, I hear Thailand is a fantastic place to raise children."

Laughter erupts.

"Ha." I look at them, unimpressed. "*Ha ha.*"

There is more laughter, which I can't help but join, in spite of myself.

We stop by an open-air shack on the side of a dirt road that ends up being a convenience store and pick up some Chang beer before heading back to our huts. After changing into dry clothes, we relax at our table outside our hut and enjoy our beers while they're still cold. Nam wanders up a couple times and asks if we are ready to make dinner, and every time we respond with a "maybe later." It is just too easy to do nothing.

As the breeze picks up and weaves through the branches above us, the chickens peck away at the ground and a rooster crows in the distance. My eyes scan the canvas of jungle surrounding us and catch a slow movement unfolding behind the trees across the gorge.

"Are those our elephants?" I ask in disbelief.

Amira and Jess snap out of their lazy fog and scan the trees.

Looking slightly defeated, Nam approaches us again and reminds us that if it becomes too late, dinner will be difficult as the sun goes down around 6:00 p.m. and there is no electricity. Oh, we have forgotten this!

As we walk over to the kitchen hut, I ask Nam if the elephants we see in the tree line are ours. He nods happily.

The other hut has a gas stove on a table with piles of meat and vegetables already cut into pieces. We set up candles and grab flashlights to see better, as it is now dusk, and prepare a green curry dish, chop suey, and a soup with cabbage and fish balls, which are essentially white golf-ball-looking chunks of minced fish. They sound and look awful but end up tasting quite delicious. I unfortunately pay for this meal the next day, which hasn't been too unusual in Asia for me. My body isn't used to the mix of spices and bacteria in this part of the world yet, so I continue to cross my fingers that I adapt sooner rather than later.

The toilet situation is another fun part of this adventure. Besides the general "hole in the ground" type of toilets where you squat and hope not to splatter your shoes, at least half the toilets I've encountered also don't flush. A large bucket of water sits next to the toilet, with a smaller bucket inside that you fill with water and pour in the toilet. The pressure of the water being poured pushes the waste through and essentially flushes the toilet.

With no toilet paper in the stalls and soap a rare find, my purse is always equipped with hand sanitizer and a bag of tissues—which have to be thrown into a wastebasket next to the toilet because the drainage system can't handle the paper. If you have forgotten toilet paper, don't worry. There is normally a spray nozzle attached to a hose on the wall that you can use to wash yourself.

Being a woman in Southeast Asia is also a hoot, with no soap, toilet paper, or tampons with applicators. This little number goes something like this: walk into a stall with sanitizer in pocket and bag of toilet paper held in teeth. Sanitize hands, remove toilet paper from bag, ration out a couple snips, replace remaining back into bag, and replace back in between teeth. Squat. Don't let anything—pants, underwear, etc.—touch the wet ground (remember hose?), pull out of pocket teeny-tiny applicator-less tampon and insert with sanitized finger (now unsanitized again).

Resanitize when done, throw tissues and tampon wrapper in the wastepaper basket, and flush the toilet with the bucket. Wash hands when done, the whole time with toilet paper bag in between teeth, and repeat for days. If you're a man? Whip it out. Pee. Flush.

Yeah, *a real hoot.*

~

After dinner we make our way with our guides and candlesticks through the dark back to our hut. Pouring the melted wax pooled on top of our candles onto the picnic table, we follow Nam's direction and stick our candles in, allowing the drying wax to be our base. Mot makes an appearance in his hipster jeans again with a black sleeveless shirt. Together, we all spend the evening sitting around our candlelit table, singing songs and playing puzzles with sticks. Mot breaks apart the small sticks and forms a picture of an object, giving us the assignment of forming another picture by only moving two sticks.

Throughout the course of the evening and the consumption of more than a couple lukewarm beers, our group has dwindled down to Jess, Amira, and me…and Mot. The distance between Mot and me has disappeared as well; I can feel his leg against mine under the table, and he has taken it upon himself to position his arm along the ledge behind me. At first I think it's possibly a coincidence and reposition my body just a little away from his—naturally, of course—so that we are no longer touching from shoulders to feet. But it doesn't last long before Romeo slithers right back to my side again.

It actually feels kind of nice to be touched. It's not something I've really thought about until now, but as a lone traveler, I don't get touched often. It's odd, really, to consider the last time I've been hugged, but it's been a while. So I let Mot's body rest against mine, and I don't flinch when his arm moves off its ledge and onto my shoulder. Jess and Amira, getting bored, start prepping for bed and head off to the outhouse with their flashlights dancing and bobbing farther and farther away, leaving Mot and me—*alone*.

The candle has dwindled to almost nothing. Mot looks at me, eyebrows lifting up and down—another attempt at a sultry look, I'm sure. I look around anxiously. *What is happening right now?* I'm not sure what to say. I've given up with the small talk, as his English is elementary at best. He knows what he considers to be the essentials, which makes conversation with him sputter and pause when attempted. His hand wanders to rest on my thigh. *Oh God.* The girls make their way back, quickly excusing themselves into the hut when they approach, but not without highly amused laughter trailing behind them.

Our candle burns out, with more hysterical laughter from inside the hut. I can feel his breath on my face. He leans in farther and kisses me, a young kiss—sloppy, impatient. I find myself kissing back, intrigued yet hesitant. I'm not so sure about this; the boy is practically a zygote. Nothing about this feels sexy. It actually feels more like an opportunity for a young man to try to appease some wet dream he had after watching *American Pie* with subtitles. I push him away. He leans in again.

"No, please. Please don't stop," he whispers, searching once again in the dark for my lips.

Like I said about his English—only the essentials.

"I'm sorry," I whisper back. "I can't. Goodnight."

I leave Mot in the dark and stumble into the hut. Both the girls are wide-awake and incredibly curious.

"Where's your jungle boy?" Jess prods.

"Ugh," I grumble as I climb under our mosquito net. "I sent him back to the village people."

~

In the pitch-black early morning hours, I awake to a chorus of jungle noises and an intense need to pee. I grab my flashlight (or torch, as the ladies call it) and walk outside our hut. As I stumble out from underneath our porch cover of dried leaves, I gasp out loud. The stars—there are thousands of them. I turn off my light and stand alone in the dark, head tipped back in awe of the twinkling light show above me. I could stay for hours, but common sense reminds me that I am deep in a jungle and have the handicap of not being able to see two feet in front of me.

The next morning we wake early to find our elephants. It's quite the trek deep into the jungle, but following the broken tree branches, muddy elephant tracks, and elephant droppings, we eventually find our trio. Actually, we sit below as Mot climbs even higher onto the side of the mountain and brings them down for us. We have already been hiking for hours in the rising heat and humidity—as well as tension between Mot and me—and we're exhausted.

Mot and I politely said our acknowledgments earlier this morning, conscious to be nonchalant, as the older guides are present once more. He remains a perfect gentleman and attempts nothing further with me besides the occasional "beautiful" comment.

He is now being closely watched, I learn, as Nam approaches me and apologizes for Mot's behavior. Nam reminds me that it is his responsibility to take care of me and make sure I am safe, and it is unacceptable if Mot has encroached upon that. *Busted.* I feel like I'm in seventh grade again, getting caught making out behind the pine trees at school.

I assure him all is well and as Nam walks away, I catch him shoot Mot another look of disapproval. He is to cease and desist, from what I gather, and this I am okay with. Last night was definitely an odd one in my list of experiences, kissing a nineteen-year-old in the middle of a jungle, and I don't feel the need to repeat it. It's not like I broke any laws last night, but there was nothing sexy about it.

We spend our last afternoon on another trek with our elephants. Halfway through, I need to get down and walk. My inner thighs and butt are so sore and raw from the past day that it has become highly uncomfortable to ride any longer. I walk alongside Mateo, running my fingers over her rough, corrugated skin, and feed her bananas while taking in the rich jungle scenery and the occasional glance from Mot.

I am astounded at how extraordinary Mateo is, with her enormous ears flapping and trunk swinging, deep breaths forcing themselves out of her long nose as tears stream from the inner corners of her eyes to keep them lubricated. She is truly an amazing and intelligent creation.

I am overwhelmed with gratefulness in this moment. It still hits me, as if for the first time on this trip, the reality of my life right now. I am in northern Thailand, walking through the jungle with elephants. Amira tilts her head back from on top of her elephant and asks me how I'm doing. All I can do is smile.

We head back to our hut to pack up our things and say our goodbyes. I feed Mateo the last remaining banana as I stroke her face and wish her a long and happy life. We thank our guides as well, and Mot and I wave farewell from a distance.

～

The past couple days weren't exactly what I expected, I think to myself as I ricochet around the back of our battered old truck, and this too, I am okay with. I didn't leave home to find mediocrity. I left home to find an adventure—and that's exactly what I've done.

And when I least expect it, a little adventure sometimes finds me.

In Transition

Thailand to Laos

THE JOURNEY TO CROSS THE BORDER into Laos isn't as easy as we'd hoped, but Amira and I do find a way that suits us. After spending a blissfully chilled-out week doing nothing in the hippie haven known as Pai in northern Thailand, we part ways with Jess until Vietnam and make the journey back to Chiang Mai to head toward the border.

As we reach our destination, our driver pulls into a fancy, overpriced hotel and turns the vehicle off. Confused, we watch as he unloads all our bags onto the curb, tells us, "Last stop," and orders us off the van.

"Excuse me?" Amira asks. "Are we at the border to Laos?"

He shakes his head yes and points down the road. "Border right there."

Okay, not what we had in mind, but we're unprepared to argue. He drives off, leaving nine of us travelers on a curb, scratching our heads. A hotel employee guides us in the right direction. "Straight, then at road go left, ten-minute walk."

Annoyed, we throw on our packs and begin our "ten-minute walk." Fifteen minutes into our hike, sweat is dripping down my back, my neck, and off the tip of my nose. A local points down the road from the shaded front porch of a street-side business. "Border! Six hundred meters!" He rocks back into his chair and laughs.

My head snaps up. In my misery, I had been concentrating on putting one foot in front of the other. "Six hundred meters? How far is that?"

"Well." Amira pauses. "It's not far, but it's not close either. We're only about halfway."

"What the *hell.*" I yell out loud. "We're walking along a paved road that he easily could have driven us down, but no, he had to collect his 400 baht (about twelve U.S. dollars) from each of us and his commission by cheating and dropping us off at a hotel instead of at the border. This is *bullshit!*"

At this point, as we have walked almost a mile in the midday heat, my love of Southeast Asia is faltering a bit from having to deal almost daily with flat-out, complete, and wholehearted *lies.* "It's how they survive," I'd justify. "It's how they feed their families." *Blah blah blah.* It gets old.

Now, every time someone smiles and tells us they can help, Amira and I say no thanks. Unfortunately, especially in the touristy areas, we've learned from experience that few are to be trusted. When trying to take a tuk-tuk up a mountain to a wat, the driver says, "No, no. Wat closed. Close at five p.m." I look him in the eye and announce that I don't believe him and walk straight into a tourist center. It doesn't close until 7:30 p.m. Lies, I tell you, all lies.

As I walk the road to the Thailand/Laos border, I resort to a coping mechanism I used back in college every time I pulled into the parking lot of my early-morning waitressing job: "This will all be over with soon."

Just like all moments in life, the good, the bad, and the ugly, one day or even a moment later, it will be over.

Back in Pai, riding my motorbike along the narrow mountain roads, I thought of this often. I was frustrated. I had been walking through the city's street markets looking for some sort of souvenir to remember Pai with, but I couldn't find what I was looking for. I asked myself then, "What exactly do you want out of this trip? What sort of trinket will give you the satisfaction of 'taking away' a memory? No matter how many stories you accumulate, how many photos you take or souvenirs you buy, nothing can replace this gift of living *this moment.*" The best gift I can give myself is to live this *now*—even if I don't always like it.

Amira and I eventually cross the border by taking a wooden boat across the Mekong River, and we stay in a very small village called Huay Xai in Laos. We spend one night there in a guesthouse overlooking the Mekong River with Thailand just across the water. We pay two dollars each.

~

We spend the next two days on a slow boat cruising along the majestic Mekong River through the jungles of Laos. The view is stunning; we are surrounded by dense foliage with mountains in the background cutting through the cloud-dotted sky. The wide, mud-brown river weaves through the land while we relax under the boat's patched roof among rows of old minivan seats placed inside. We are on our way to Luang Prabang, a UNESCO Protected World Heritage City in Laos known for its beauty and friendliness.

I think often during this boat ride about how, "This too shall pass," and I am grateful in this moment that time seems to move a little slower here. Despite some of my harder moments on this trip, and there have been many, I still take a moment each day to whisper prayers of gratitude into the cloud-speckled blue skies. A moment like this, floating along the Mekong River in Laos, is just one moment of many—good and bad—that I will never forget. It is part of something a trinket could never give, and lies could never take away, this dear, sweet, sacred journey of mine.

Luang Prabang, Laos

I'M OFTEN REMINDED during my travels of that Mark Jenkins quote about experiencing the world, "the way it is, *not the way you imagine it.*" I think of this quote often in moments when I am so amazed by the world that I can feel the experiences of my life slowly sift through me as they change me to my core.

I also think of Jenkins's words frequently in moments when I am shocked and angered by the world, which to be truthful, can be quite often. I think of it this morning, as we awake by alarm at 6:00 a.m. to begin our last day of our delightfully peaceful stay in Luang Prabang. I hit the snooze on my phone at least three times, giving Amira and me about seven minutes to brush our teeth and head out into the early morning air to watch the procession of the monks.

Every morning in this UNESCO World Heritage City, the locals line up along the streets with gifts and food, kneeling on mats as monks pass by and collect gifts. This is done out of respect, as you are not supposed to be "higher" than the monks and they are not supposed to "ask" for food.

As we step out onto the street, a small group of enthu-siastic local women greet us, smiling and inviting us to join them in giving to the monks.

"Come! Come!" they say. "Feed monks!" they invite as they fill our hands with baskets of sticky rice and banana leaves full of food.

"Uh…" I hesitate in my early morning haze. "We pay?" No response. I ask again, "We pay for this?"

Ignoring me, they continue to smile and pull us to the next street, where the monks are already starting to pass. They unroll a large bamboo mat on the street and guide us further.

"Come! Sit!" they insist as they open the baskets and grab more handfuls of rice to put in our hands. I kneel down, nervous, as I have no idea what I'm doing, and hope by my ignorance I don't offend the monks that are seconds from passing by.

The monks, young and old, shuffle past in their bright orange robes wrapped neatly around them and open their metal containers for me to place the wrapped banana leaves and sticky rice inside.

After a couple dozen pass, each with overflowing pots by the time they reach me, the parade is over. Smiling from ear to ear, I look up, saying, "Wow, that was amaz…" and am met with four women, no longer smiling, rubbing their fingertips together.

"Money. Money," they say. "You pay!"

I sigh in annoyance. "Of course you do." I say, pulling myself to my feet.

We glance at each other. "Well," we agree, "guess we should pay the women."

They each want 30,000 kip (about three U.S. dollars).

"We don't have that much cash on us," I protest. "We didn't know we had to pay you, and we never agreed on a price. We only have enough to give you 10,000 kip each."

"You pay! You pay!" they say as they stand about an inch away from our faces. This continues on for a couple minutes before I hear Amira's flustered voice coming from behind me saying, "Yeah, yeah, *just hold on!*"

As we walk away completely aggravated, one woman follows us and persists that we pay her.

"We gave you all 10,000 kip each! Now please stop. Go away!" Amira yells at her.

"You pay! You pay!" she insists.

Amira and I frantically search our bags and hand over our last combined 10,000 kip.

Now, 10,000 kip isn't a lot of money, but it's not the money we are aggravated about; it's the constant, unending trickery that has happened from day one in Asia. All we wanted to do this morning was to see the locals giving to the monks. The women seemed genuine, like they wanted us to join them in their traditions, and had we been awake for more than ten minutes, someone probably would have questioned it longer... *I* would have questioned it longer. To have your guard up every second of every day is exhausting. The world has continued to shock and amaze me—all at once.

~

The French used to control a lot of this region, and their influence is *everywhere.* Luang Prabang is another small town with crumbling French mansions and international cuisine, surrounded by jagged green mountains with the Nam Khan and Mekong rivers on each side. Amira met an English couple, Reese and Laura, in South America a couple months back who happen to be in Luang Prabang the same time as us. Together, we wander the old French-influenced streets and night markets as the sun sets behind the backdrop of mountains.

After a couple somewhat lazy days of wandering and eating, we decide to kick our existence up a notch and head to the other side of town to see the area's famously beautiful waterfalls. We are dropped off at a small, dirt-road village on the Mekong River and from there hire a man in a long wooden boat to take us to the waterfalls.

When we arrive, we are met with not just one waterfall, but many, compiled with a myriad of large, white boulders with rushing turquoise-blue water cascading down into a variety of pools—with waterfalls in opposite directions forming from those pools and falling into more pools of water below. We play for hours.

I find a rope tied to a tree with an old tire swing attached. I climb up the slippery mud, grabbing bamboo and roots as I crawl up the side of the tree. I walk across two bamboo trunks tied together with a slightly unraveling rope to the small V in the tree to jump off. My heart is pounding. Everyone is watching. I wrap my hands around the tire, pull myself back, and fling myself off the tree into midair. Screams fly out of my mouth as I plunge into the icy-cold water below.

As I reach the surface, laughter flies out of my mouth that I almost don't recognize. It's a childlike laughter, accompanied by an emotional glee I haven't felt in years. A handful of young men who were watching from a distance all bolt for the tree. I jump a couple times, just to feel the splendor of flying again, but even more to hear that somewhat foreign but illuminating laughter that flows through me every time.

∽

Since I will be in Vietnam in about a month, I spend an entire afternoon on the Internet researching the Vietnam War and the ways it has affected not only Vietnam but Laos as well.

For eight years during the war, the U.S. carpet-bombed Laos because of the Vietnamese presence in the country. For eight long years, we bombed the hell out of a country that was initially neutral in the war, dropping *two million tons* of bombs costing us $2.2 million *a day*. One-third of the bombs failed to detonate, leaving this beautiful land littered with unexploded ordinance or "UXO." It is estimated that four hundred to six hundred people in Laos die every year from bombs we dropped over forty years ago.

I read an article in the paper about how farmers have unused land that could help the country with food and finances, but it can't be touched because it's full of UXO. A group began clearance work throughout the country sixteen years ago, using metal detectors supplied by the United States, and has so far removed about a quarter of a million pieces. My Lonely Planet guidebook and the newspaper both state that at this rate, it will take another century to make Laos safe. Missions and programs have been put into place to help those with missing limbs and dead loved ones cope. Now, I know it takes two to have a war, and there are a lot of opinions about a sensitive subject like the Vietnam War, but it's incredibly shocking to be here and see still, after forty years, the aftermath of a tragedy for all parties involved.

"You…will collide with the earth and you will bear witness. … This will change you. Nothing will ever again be black and white" (Mark Jenkins). In this new life of mine I walk side-by-side with the world's people, experiencing a life I never knew existed. I continue to feel a kaleidoscope of emotions, from anger and discouragement to joy and gratefulness, leaving me feeling more alive than ever. I have learned how to laugh like a child again. I think of home fondly and often, remembering the laughter and the faces and comforts, not wanting to leave here, but comforted in the day we will be reunited again. This journey I am on has taken years to get to, years of insecurities and fears so great that I'd close my eyes at night and pray to forget. This voyage across lands and time and cultures—that initially scared me to death—has brought me back to life.

Vang Vieng, Laos

"AND WE'VE GOT A COCKROACH in the room!" Amira yells from the bedroom.

"Oh yeah?" my voice echoes from inside the bathroom. "Well, I'm having quite the party in here with a couple slugs in the sink!"

"Great!" Amira yells sarcastically. "Let's just invite the whole damn jungle inside our hut!"

We have just arrived in Vang Vieng, Laos, a hustle and bustle town on the Nam Song River with about six streets and no stoplights. We went straight to Lonely Planet's pick of "Best Guesthouse," which I think, as I watch a line of ants pass a couple gecko droppings on the floor, is a little dated.

We are staying in a hut on the river with panoramic views of the surrounding mountains and quite possibly as many creatures on the inside as there are out. We have in total: one cockroach, one snail, one leach, one large wasp, two slugs, apparently a gecko or two, and a village of ants. One large cricket sits on the outside of our door like a watchdog and is literally the size of my outstretched hand. I don't like crickets, grasshoppers…anything that can jump. Every time I walk past it I whisper pleadings. "Don't move. Please don't move. Please don't move…"

After hanging our mosquito nets and tucking them neatly beneath our mattresses, we run to a large, open-air common area of the guesthouse covered by an awning of dry, threaded leaves. Here the owner and a few travelers have cracked open some beers and are watching the swiftly approaching thunderstorm. We take our seats just as the rain starts to pour and the thunder and lightning pick up intensity.

As we start swapping the usual questions of, "What's your name, where are you from, where have you been, and where are you going?" some of the guesthouse kittens have decided to seek shelter from the storm on my lap. There is nothing left to do but huddle together and wait it out.

The weather at this point is raging. We watch in excitement from under the open-air porch as a flash of lightning and large boom of thunder take out the entire village's source of electricity. We cheer and laugh as we sit in the black of night, our only source of light coming from the flashes of lightning bouncing off the surrounding trees and water.

"Oh my God, the tubers are still on the river!" I cry out.

"Yessshh." Our slightly drunk guesthouse owner bobs his head. "They'll be okay."

∾

Vang Vieng has gotten itself on the list of "must-sees" for travelers not so much for its culture or charm, but for its river. The only reason you go to Vang Vieng is for the tubing. Other than that, it's a small village of guesthouses, restaurants, and bars with the exact same menu and TVs playing *Family Guy* or *Friends* (which can actually be quite nice when you are hungover).

The seating areas that fill each establishment are collectively raised platforms with bench-like backing and tables just tall enough to sit at comfortably with a cushion or two beneath you. After leaving your shoes on the floor below, you climb up and make yourself comfortable, order food, and sit for hours. Not exactly a cultural wonderland, but a nice taste of home on a lazy day.

The next day, with electricity returned and life resuming normal activities, Amira and I pack up and head down the half-dirt, half-paved road for a little less eco-friendly accommodations. We land a brand new guesthouse with air-conditioning, a balcony, and windows wrapping two of the four walls overlooking, again, the river and mountains. We pay a whopping four dollars a night each.

We meet up with a group of friends Amira met in Vietnam, namely Stacey and Leam, two men from England, and their posse of friends at what we call "the breakfast place." There is a running joke between us "falangs" (white people) about a phrase you'll find all over Southeast Asia used to describe a vast assortment of things such as guesthouses, restaurants, buses, food, and vendors: "same same but different."

Me: "What's the difference between this boat or that boat?"

Asian man: "No, no. Same same."

Okay then.

The restaurants in Vang Vieng are—you guessed it—same same but different. But not different, just same same. This forces our small group to meet at the same same places during our stay. We try to agree on a day to all go tubing together, which ends up being three days after we arrive because of hangovers and a mysterious flu-like sickness that hits a couple of the travelers. We spend the first three days doing strenuous activities such as reading, writing, eating, drinking, and watching hours and hours of *Friends*.

In the evenings we head to Bucket Bar, the big daddy of bars in Vang Vieng across the river with layers of outdoor seating, hammocks, and dance floors under the stars. The establishment follows the Southeast Asian trend by serving us large buckets of the local whiskey and Coke as we dance the night away and try our attempts at fire limbo.

Many backpackers generally stick to the same tourist trail, so we frequently run into the same same people throughout the different towns in Laos, making it incredibly easy to see a smiling, familiar face everywhere we go.

One night at Bucket Bar we meet Rusty, a hyper little man from Australia that I think…may have a drinking problem. He goes tubing every single day (which always involves a copious amount of alcohol) and parties out at Bucket Bar every night. He invites himself to join us for tubing and meets us the next morning at the breakfast place. He brands our upper arms with his trademark *R*, which isn't a big deal as we have been told spray-painting your body is part of the tubing experience.

The local tubing company loads us up into tuk-tuks with stacks of tubes tied on top, after, of course, we sign waivers accepting how many opportunities there are to get hurt. Comforting. Our group has dwindled down to Amira, Stacey, Rusty, and me.

As the tuk-tuk pulls down the dirt road to the first bar on the river, sounds of techno music and screaming people hit us in waves. We put our tubes with the others in a giant pile next to the river as I smile at Amira. "Here we go!"

Beautiful Laotian women greet us with smiles as we

walk up. "*Sabai dii!*" they sing and hand us yellow strips of fabric with "I love Laos" and "I love Vang Vieng" painted on them. We instantly tie them across our foreheads Rambo style. Rusty is already up on the wooden platform of the bar, bouncing around and taking a multitude of free shots.

Another smiling woman approaches us, holding a tray of whiskey shots and a bottle of Laotian whiskey filled with dead wasps. We clink our shot glasses together, repeating in unison, "Here we go!" then spray-paint our bodies in bright neon designs like we are ready for a hippie war.

The Nam Song River that curves around Vang Vieng is peppered with an assortment of bars along each side. The only way to reach each bar is by floating on inner tubes down the river. When you decide on a bar to stop at, you paddle over to the side of the river as several men throw ropes with plastic bottles attached to reel you in. The current is quite strong at times, so we hold on to each other and the rope and pray for our dear lives that our fisherman doesn't let go. Almost every bar has free shots to greet you and incredibly elevated zip-line swings for you to propel your slightly inebriated self into the rushing water below. I pass on the first couple swings as I observe some graceful and other not-so-graceful jumps into the water.

At the third bar, I finally pick my swing. It's one of the highest, but I pick this one because I know if I don't do it now, I'll never do it. I take mental notes of other people's mistakes, the biggest one being where to let go. If I release my grip anywhere in the middle of the river, I'll either hit rocks at the bottom and say goodbye to some precious pieces of my legs or get swept away by the current.

During my mental schooling, I have watched a couple girls who were unable to work through the current get swept down the river. One girl had friends run out with tubes to swim after her, and the other eventually swam to a bank down the river and had to walk back.

I'm scared to the point of shaking. My brain is screaming warning signals to me as I feel the whiskey coursing through my veins. This is not my smartest decision.

"Jill. Stacey is a lifeguard and we'll swim in after you. Don't worry, okay? You can do it! Woooo!" Amira cheers.

I half smile. "That was a *terrible* pep talk."

I climb up the wooden ladder on the somewhat wobbly structure to the certain death awaiting me. My heart is pounding. A Canadian with "Eh?" painted on his back is behind me. Both our teams of comrades are cheering us on below.

"I'm really scared," I allege quietly.

"Me too." He inhales deeply. "Want me to go first?" he asks, clearly feeling obligated.

"Yes." I don't hesitate a second.

"Really? Oh...okay..." He slides past me to the man holding the zip-line swing.

He jumps off the multiple story platform, swings into the river, and pulls himself out—alive. That happened way too fast.

The worker holding on to the trapeze bar coaxes me forward as profanities effortlessly slip from my mouth.

I lift my feet, jump off the platform, and fly over the podium of spectators. The inertia of the fall robs the screams from my mouth as I feel my heavy body being pulled to the earth. The swing flings me upward. Once I swing back the screams find their way out—laugher too—as I hold on for dear life.

Now, most people let go after one full swing. Not me. I swing back and forth, back and forth, and back and forth again. Three full swings trying to convince myself to let go. Finally, I aim for the side of the river and, somehow releasing my death grip from the bar, I plunge into the waters below.

Even on the side, the current is strong. It carries me to the base of the wooden structure I jumped off, and I hold on until I make a plan to beeline for the rocks on the shore. The Canadian is waiting to help pull me out. What a gentleman.

I climb onto the rocks with my knees knocking together, and I drag myself onto dry land. It takes me at least twenty minutes to stop shaking, but I'm happy that I faced my fear and did it.

The next five hours involve barhopping, tubing, mud, and buckets. It's a hilarious show of falangs having the time of our lives and Laotian workers shoving shots in our faces.

Dusk quickly approaches as we stumble around the last bar, covered in mud and soaked to the bone. We have been warned by others to above all, "get out of the river at the bridge before dark."

There are no signs telling you when to get out, so people before us have just continued floating until it was pitch-black and had no idea where they were. When they were finally able to pull themselves up the muddy banks, they had to walk, dragging their tubes through the dark of night, and ask locals how to get back into town. One group was chased by stray dogs and then fell into a basement of a house being built. They had to scream until locals heard them and helped them out. All this was during the huge storm that cut the power on the first night we arrived.

"Get off at the bridge." *Don't have to tell me twice.*

A couple minutes after floating from the last bar, we see the bridge. One by one, people in our group hold on to the bamboo framework, not an easy task, as the current is deceptively strong at this point. My tube builds speed as I am approaching. Amira holds out her leg and screams for me to hold on. My wet hands reach out and grab hold of her foot, but I quickly slip away. My tube and I continue on.

I am alone. I watch as the bridge forever falls from my grasp. I keep thinking about the girl's story: "There is nothing but pitch black after the bridge." It's almost completely dark at this point. I start to panic.

I cruise underneath a low-hanging tree and grab hold of a vine. All my strength in every muscle of every finger is desperately holding on to this one vine, while my legs wrap around my tube beneath me.

The water is almost white in its intensity, angrily pulling on my tube. I'm finding it hard to breathe as my anxiety and fear reach almost unmanageable levels.

"Jill! *Jill!*" I can hear Amira's voice screaming through the dark from the bridge.

"I'm here!" My voice cracks as I breathlessly yell back.

As I continue gripping the vine, I look around for options. I cannot continue on this river—this cannot happen. The edge of the river isn't too far; it's just the thought of getting to the bank without being swept away that's knocking the wind out of me.

"Okay, Jill," I say out loud. "Deep breaths. Everything is

okay. You can do this. You're not going to die. The worst that may happen is you get swept away by the current and float down the river a little farther—that's all—in the dark... alone. Then you'll get lost and wander the jungle alone, get chased by rabid dogs, and *then* you'll die. Okay, not helping. The bank is *right there*. You can do this. You can do this."

I finally manage to calm myself down a little, take a few deep breaths, and prepare to swim. Still holding the vine, I lower my legs into the middle of my inner tube. As my lower half sinks into the river and my tube rises around my chest, I create an even larger resistance to the strong current, making it impossible to hold on any longer.

"Oh! Oh, God..." I whimper as I watch the vine burn and slide ever so slowly out of my white-knuckled hands.

I don't know what happens next. If I have to guess, I would say I probably use all limbs and flail around like a panic-stricken maniac until I make it over to the rocks on the riverbank. I'm not sure, but I do know that I make it, and not too far down from the vine I held on to.

"*Jill!* JILL!" Amira is screaming from a distance.

On all fours, I do not have the energy to scream back.

"It's okay, I think I see her over on the riverbank." A fellow tuber's voice comes in.

I pull myself to my feet and humbly walk to the bridge.

Amira grabs my shoulders. "Are you okay? We thought we lost you."

"I'm okay." I mumble. "I'm okay," I repeat again in reassurance to myself, "but I'm not so sure about my hands."

We both look down and inspect my hands. Little pieces of skin are missing along every finger and my palm, right where the vine slid through. Small sacrifice.

Later that night at dinner, with our Laotian whiskey buzzes officially worn off, exhaustion kicks in. "We have free buckets at Bucket Bar waiting for us," Amira says, smiling. I smile back. We continue eating. No one says a word. We both know the only thing we'll be slamming tonight is into a pillow.

Back at the guesthouse, I hesitate to write home about my experience. It was dangerous and we all knew it, which I suppose is what made it that much more exciting. We were doing everything we knew we shouldn't, but it was okay, because we were doing it together.

A couple years later, I read on the Internet that the whole tubing operation was almost completely shut down. Most of the swings, slides, and bars were torn to the ground, the serving of alcohol banned, and the drop in the numbers of tourists completely devastated the town. Because it was so dangerous people died. Many people. Young people. What a *tragedy*. We all just wanted to have fun, but the cost was too high, and like the article declared, "the party's over."

≈

The next day we return to our lazy routine of eating and watching *Friends*. With full bellies, we shuffle back to our guesthouse and sit around on our balcony, looking out onto the Nam Song River and questioning our goals after this trip. I sit back on my wooden chair and think, but only for a second and I already know the answer.

"Nothing."

"Nothing?" Amira replies.

I smile. "Nothing. Of course, I'll always have goals," I add.

"I'll continue to travel, probably much smaller trips. I'll take classes because I love to learn, whether that be yoga, salsa, or learning Italian. But I've had goals my entire life. As a young girl, I would lie on my bed and dream. I wanted to go to college and graduate with honors. I did that. I wanted to move to a big city, live in a high-rise and 'live it up.' I did that. I wanted to travel the world and live abroad. I'm doing that. I wanted to do it all independently, and for *me*. And I had to work, *hard*, for every single one of those dreams. The plan now is to have no plan. Spend time with my friends and family, travel, work, write, cook, get a dog...*live*. Put my feet up, for the first time in my entire life, and just *be*."

I've always known what I wanted, and realistically, I suppose that could change, as life always does. Walking through a street market earlier, I was feeling a little disconnected, so I asked myself a familiar question that always brings me back to myself: "What do I know?" and a familiar voice from deep inside whispered, "I am living my destiny."

That's all I need to know. My life is exactly as it should be. Gazing into the skies here in Laos, I've noticed that the moon looks different. Here on the other side of the world, it almost looks like the moon has been flipped around; the curve of the crescent is underneath instead of being in its normal crease shaping the side. Or maybe it's looked like that all along, but I've never been present enough to notice it. But I'm present now, appreciating the life I live instead of fearing it. I would have never seen the moon this way, or the world this way, had I never followed my heart.

"I am living my destiny."

I look up into the evening sky and smile, and for the first time in my life, the moon actually smiles back.

Vientiane, Laos

MY INITIAL THOUGHTS OF VIENTIANE: "It is the capital of Laos. The food is disappointing, at best. They love karaoke. The bars are swarming with prostitutes and lady-boys. They barbecue dried squid in the street, giving Vientiane an inescapable putrid smell. The end."

All in all, I'm not impressed with Vientiane. No, okay, I flat-out don't like it. Somehow, we manage to spend five days here, and the last forty-eight hours change everything; we meet Melody and go to a Buddhist festival.

~

Melody is a young Laotian woman in her late twenties, born and raised in Paris. Having moved to Vientiane less than six months ago, she works at our guesthouse and offers warm hospitality and invaluable advice on where to go. On this particular Friday morning, over tea and yawning, we tell her of our plans to leave in the evening.

"Oh, no! No, you should not leave now. Our festival starts today. Stay! We have a barbecue tonight and celebrations all weekend. I'll take you out. You should stay."

And so we stay, and that makes all the difference.

Later that evening, as the sun sets below the horizon, the city is immersed in alternating hues of deep orange and dark shadows from the crowded Parisian buildings. Loud Laotian music clashes in the air from the surrounding parties, street firecrackers fire off randomly, and children run giggling through the streets.

We sit, like all neighboring parties, outside and half into the street. The owner's wife crouches on the ground and flips a questionable-looking meat for the twentieth time on a small, charcoal grill made from cement cylinders and wire. The meat we eat, true to all the meat I've had in Laos, takes at least ten minutes to chew; "chewy" would be an understatement.

The men across the street have pulled out their karaoke machine and are entertaining their family and friends by belting off-key notes to the music of synthesizers and cowbells. I giggle to myself and ask if anyone is familiar with the *Saturday Night Live* skit of Will Ferrell with his cowbell. No one knows what I'm talking about.

"No?"

Silence.

"I need more cowbell!" I shout.

My laughing stops abruptly as I notice I am the only one amused.

More silence.

Melody grabs a chair next to me and smiles as she passes me another plate of meat. I quickly hand it off to my neighbor, relieved when she takes it immediately and in doing so, saves my jaw another painful bout with TMJ.

Melody leans in to reveal to me that a couple guests at our barbecue happen to be cops by day and prostitutes by night.

"I have a lot of friends that are prostitutes," she whispers as she eyes a young woman eating across from us. "It's not legal, so I have to be discreet."

She leans in closer as she divulges the lives of the women sitting just a few feet away. Their English is limited and the music is loud, so we are safe in our conversation.

I ask her many questions, as I am curious about the lives of these women who hide behind smiles. Amira and I have frequented a handful of bars in this town, and the prostitution is inescapable. Just getting a beer involves an unending show of mostly middle-aged Western men—*shopping*. The men I don't really wonder about, except maybe who they are on Christmas and if they have wives, children, and grandchildren—which I'm sure some do—but I suppose that is their business and not mine. But who are the women?

Without specifics, Melody tells me they are mostly young, single mothers who are doing the best they can to provide for their families. Laos is the poorest country in Southeast Asia, and the secret jobs these women hold when the sun goes down provide not only for their children, but for their families out in the countryside as well. This way of life is so foreign to me…in my eyes, compassion—not judgment—is the only way to see this world; otherwise it will break your heart.

After our friendly dinner of rawhide and gossip, Melody takes us to her favorite bar, where she seems to know everyone. Within fifteen minutes, our table is surrounded by the smiling faces of young, beautiful prostitutes. They introduce themselves and laugh and dance, and then go about the bar for business. Amira and I smile and drink our beers, but it doesn't take long to realize that this isn't our scene. Interesting? Yes. Out of the ordinary? Definitely. But we are ready to go. Tomorrow, we have a festival to attend.

∾

As we walk down the streets of Vientiane, I am reminded of the Fourth of July. Fireworks and firecrackers crackle and pop along the roads, filling the night with glitter and light. Whole roads are blocked off as the streets fill up with families and friends eating, drinking, and singing karaoke to music five times over the legal sound limit.

We are making our way down to the Mekong River, where the official festivities are being held. To get to the entrance, however, we must walk along the main street running parallel to the river, which is packed on both sides with booths and their workers screaming for your attention. Because the herd of people walking this street is shuffling shoulder to shoulder at about an inch an hour, the only way for vendors to be heard over their neighbors is by standing on makeshift stages with large-scale sound systems and microphones, barking out their business.

With my heels beat to hell and my toes throbbing from being stepped on, I can't help but laugh as I watch the sea of black heads below me. If I've ever stood out from the crowd, tonight is the ultimate experience in doing so. Not only is my hair/skin/eye color combo doing a number, but I am at least six inches taller than the throngs of people surrounding me.

When we finally make it across the street, we find ourselves following the mass of people down to the Mekong

River. It is the official celebration for the end of the Buddhist Lent. I try getting more information from a young woman with her child and husband, but all I get is "three month," "Buddha," and "monkeys" (monks).

We stop and buy a small boat made of flowers and banana leaves with a candle and stick of incense inside. Amira and I each write on a piece of paper something we'd like to let go of—whether that be a habit, grudge, or belief—and place these folded papers inside the boat.

Climbing down a hill of boulders to the Mekong, we see before us hundreds of little boats with candles lit and prayers of letting go already slowly floating down the river. It is a magical sight. As fireworks explode among the stars, red and white lanterns float serenely in a lineup toward the moon while the Mekong does its best to mirror the sky, with its floating candles twinkling like starlight.

With the help of a young boy by the river, we contribute to the ambiance and bid our regrets farewell as he sets our boat into the current.

As I watch our boat join the rest, I can't help but wonder, *where do they all go?* I guess to the place where forgiveness is born.

Making the unsteady climb back up the random jumble of boulders, we find a spot to sit and watch the crowd light their paper lanterns for a very important second half of the festival. This is a celebration after all, and in the name of equality we must fill the hole left by letting go with something positive.

After buying our red paper lantern, we open it and attach a cube the size of our palms to a large wire ring forming the base of the lantern. Amira and I take out our other pieces of paper and wrap them around the metal—our hopes for the next year. I made only one wish. I kept it simple.

With Amira holding the lantern upright and open, I hold a match to the cube until it catches fire, and I quickly join her in holding the lantern upright. Smoke continues to fill the lantern until it's so full it starts to tug a little at our fingertips. We then let go, watching it float up into the midnight sky to join the hundreds of other lanterns.

As I watch our lantern float away, I have only one thought in my head, a smile across my lips, and a sense of peace in my heart. If there has been one truly spiritual and magical moment in my trip, I'm convinced tonight will hold that honor.

When I used to wander the travel section in bookstores—oh, hours and hours I would spend—I came across a Lonely Planet guidebook about Asia with a cover photo of a lit lantern being released into the sky. I have no idea now what country it was for and had no idea when I saw it what it was about, but I yearned for that experience. I remember thinking, "I want to do that…"

This celebration was unknown to me and completely unplanned up until about twenty-four hours ago. It only happens once a year. I sit back and laugh out loud as I realize:

I am living a dream I forgot I even had.

I look up into the sky of lanterns, wondering where they'll go. I think, maybe, to the place where whispered prayers are heard. One thing I know in this moment is if I'm right, then the lanterns in the sky are headed in the right direction.

Si Phan Don, Laos

MY EYES GLAZE OVER as I watch a lone fly work his way around my plate. His mouthpiece lowers and suctions the stagnant juice from my leftover watermelon. He then wanders in circles before pausing to rub his front legs together.

I look around to find the only waitress working this place is now sleeping in a hammock in the middle of the restaurant. A random longboat cruises down the river. A stray dog sleeps under my wobbly wooden chair as a chicken clucks at Amira's feet. It's *quiet*. We are eating lunch at a restaurant at the end of the main dirt path around the island of Don Det. I'm not sure the path even has a name. It doesn't need a name—there aren't enough roads for it to matter.

This town is almost too quiet—slightly numbing actually after all the karaoke and cowbells in Vientiane. We are in Si Phan Don, also known as Four Thousand Islands, located at the southernmost border of Laos. This collection of islands, sandbars, and rocky mounds jutting out of the Mekong River is about thirty miles long with only a couple islands large enough to house locals and the especially chilled-out tourists.

With Cambodia only three miles south, and not a whole lot else in the other directions, Si Phan Don is by far the most complacent and carefree piece of land I have ever set foot on.

We are staying on Don Det, with one main dirt path that runs around the perimeter of the island and a couple offshoot roads that cut through to the other side. The islands have just been equipped with electricity two years ago, although it isn't everywhere, so we need to carry our flashlights to get home at night. Si Phan Don is also known for the Irrawaddy dolphin, a rare and elusive freshwater dolphin that spends most of its time by one of the larger islands next to ours called Don Khon.

Guesthouse prices on our island range from one to eight U.S. dollars a night, and you get what you pay for. Amira and I rent one of the most expensive bungalows at eight U.S. dollars a night, split between the two of us, with our own front porch, hammock, fan, a private bathroom, and two beds (with white sheets! Rare!).

The one-dollar bungalow down the road is a pieced-together, old wooden shack with no fan or air-conditioning and a communal outhouse for a bathroom, and the bed is a wooden slat with a mattress that is essentially a sewn-together sheet filled with chunks of cotton. Oh, and the sheets have a faded Mickey Mouse design with "Merry Christmas!" printed on them.

I'll pay four dollars a night, thank you.

The island has an assortment of restaurants serving mostly Western and Asian dishes that taste like they were poured out of a Lean Cuisine box. Only two restaurants, one Indian and another Western, serve relatively tasty dishes, and that's it for the entire island.

What is there to do in Si Phan Don? Well...nothing actually. Our daily goals involve getting out of the hut by noon, having a cup of tea, and greeting our friendly pack of stray dogs that hang around the guesthouse. We then pick a restaurant on the main path to eat breakfast and play cards, write, and read. Then it's time to eat again and repeat.

We soon meet Tim and Anna, a couple from England whom we run into every single night somewhere—mainly at the Indian restaurant that has an adorable little lady-boy as its only server. Tim and Anna are a fun-loving couple with fascinating stories usually involving an adventure and a foreigner, or better yet, having an adventure while *being* a foreigner. Each night we end up shutting down the restaurant of choice, laughing and talking incessantly about any random subject that comes up.

The island shuts down around 10:00 or 11:00 p.m. With the shortage of electricity we have a few lights at best to lead us home and a backdrop chorus of frogs and crickets to sing us to sleep. That is until 3:00 a.m., when the lineup of competing roosters around the island begins their defiant act of rebellion against anything resembling silence. So I guess despite the general "quiet" of life here in southern Laos, I am still obliged to wear my earplugs.

All in all, it is a somewhat charming place to unwind and do nothing. Even the workers in general can't be bothered to work, giving actually the whole of Laos the least attentive service imaginable. Welcome to my daily life as an islander. Welcome to Si Phan Don.

~

After a few lazy days, Amira and I decide to explore a little farther and see Southeast Asia's largest waterfall, located on our neighboring island. Perched on our somewhat rusty bicycles with bells that ring over every rock and pebble, we head down the bumpy dirt path that cuts through Don Det to the next island over, Don Khon.

As we cross the bridge, we unknowingly pass the small road to the right that leads to the waterfall. So after another hour of bumpy, off-road cycling, we find ourselves on the other side of the island—sans waterfall. Not exactly a successful day. So in typical islander style, we shrug our shoulders, plop down at another empty family-run restaurant, and order a beer.

The next morning, we take a lesson from the first attempt and ride our bikes down the scenic, less-bumpy dirt path along the Mekong to the bridge connecting Don Det and Don Khon. Crossing over, we ask a tired, half-snoozing local sitting by the bridge for directions and take the first right. Smart girls we are.

We wind through expansive fields of bright green rice paddies and old, wooden huts, lazy water buffalo bathing in the mud, and a legion of stray dogs. As the path narrows and the brush thickens, crashing sounds of water echo in the distance. We are getting close.

Cruising faster now across small bamboo bridges and tunnels of overgrown branches, we follow the sounds of water. A clearing opens ahead with a large cloud of mist hanging in the air like fog. We have arrived.

Swimming today is not an option. This is not one waterfall. I stand on the cliff and count one, two, three…at least twelve different waterfalls merging together with large clashes of water fiercely raging against the side of the cliffs. I can't see where one waterfall begins and another ends. A jagged old piece of a wooden bridge once allowing access to the other side now lies torn and beaten, half gasping for air outside the shallower waters below. "DANGER!" signs plastering the cliff warn the less faint of heart against climbing the rocks around the water: "Don't take the risk."

After breathing the air and taking in the sights, Amira and I stop for some coconut water at one of the local stands before continuing on. Our next stop, the Irrawaddy dolphins.

The ride from the east side of Don Khon to the west side is breathtakingly scenic. At times, the path is so narrow that the jungle leaves and brush cover our bodies head to toe as our bicycle wheels roll us along. The only sounds are those of birds above and frogs and bugs below. The air is cool, the intense sun blocked by the nurturing cover of large leaves and domineering trees.

We pass a small herd of water buffalo chomping away at the foliage along the confined path and unintentionally scare the baby away from its mother. As the baby panics, it runs in front of me and has nowhere to go but forward. I have nowhere to go either, making it appear to Mom that I am pursuing her baby. Immediately I hear Mom groan and her feet pound the ground directly behind me. She is charging.

My heart catches in my throat as I pedal faster, picking up my pace as much as possible. Getting attacked by an angry water buffalo—not top on my list of priorities. The baby runs off the path and I continue on around the next corner. I stop and turn to face Amira, who is right behind me with no angry mother in sight.

"Yikes! Did you see that?" I shriek.

"Yeah, thankfully the mom was tied up, and I had a little space behind you to speed up myself!"

Turning off the smaller jungle path onto a larger dirt road, we are almost to the dolphins. Up above us, a small herd of a different sort is making its way down the path. Children.

As we approach on our bikes, the brood turns around and starts yelling and pointing. We slowly cycle past while hordes of children about the age of five start running alongside us. They are laughing and grabbing hold of anything they can: our clothes, seats, and handlebars. With them not knowing English and us not speaking Laotian, we can only assume they want money. I laugh along with them and kindly repeat "No" until they eventually let go and give up—on me.

As I continue on, I look back and see Amira still behind with the children. I stop to take a photo, and as I do, those persistent young ones see this as a perfect opportunity to come after me once again.

Turns out they just want to ride on the back of our bikes. With a little girl attached to Amira and a young boy on the back of my bike, we race down the road neck and neck, with gaggles of giggling children running behind us.

It is nearly 3:00 p.m. now, perfect timing, as the dolphins are most active at sunrise and sunset. With two hours until dusk, we have just enough time to head out for a one-hour cruise and still get back before dark. We negotiate a price for a longboat and driver of 60,000 kip (about six U.S. dollars), which includes one hour of sitting on the Mekong to watch for the freshwater dolphins.

Before the observing begins, however, we have to take the boat to the police on the other side of the river to pay our "donation to the dolphins" of one U.S. dollar each. The land we pull up to is Cambodia. We are paying not for the dolphins' well-being so much as paying off the police for allowing us to cross into their borders. But our guidebooks have prepared us for this, so we go along with smiles and "donate" to the dolphins.

Sitting in the middle of the Mekong, true to southern Laos, it's serenely quiet. This is perfect for us to spot dolphins, as it allows us to hear them as they come up for air. As my rear throbs from the hard wooden bench below me and my eyes scan the water in front of me, I hear a loud rush of air to my left, and there they are: two Irrawaddy dolphins coming up for air. Never in the same place twice, the loud rush of air gives us our only chance of seeing these elusive creatures.

I rush to grab my camera to snap some photos, even just a bluish-silvery fin along the water's edge if anything, but the glimpses of them are just that—momentary glimpses. There are maybe a dozen or more, and I realize after a few failed attempts that this is one of those moments I do not want to experience through the lens of a camera.

On the bike ride back, with the sun softly setting along the horizon, locals and their families are getting ready for the night. Next to dragonflies, fireflies, and water buffalo, groups of children and adults alike bathe and brush their teeth in the Mekong River. I watch in admiration as the kids dip their brushes in the river and put them back in their mouths. If my toothbrush even *looked* at the Mekong River, I'd probably grow purple spots and drop dead in an instant.

Passing by another local's home, we notice a crowd of screaming and cheering men tightly packed in a circle. As we park our bikes and walk up, I look to my right at a

protesting rooster stuck under a wicker cage and realize
suddenly in horror what we are about to view. I look behind
me to Amira.

"What is it?" Amira asks.

"A cockfight. Do you want to see?"

"Not really."

My curiosity overtakes me. My heart pounds at the
thought of what I'm about to witness. It's like turning
away from a car wreck—you know it's bad to stare, but
you can't help it.

As I peer over the heads of the half-crouching men,
I look into a makeshift cardboard ring with two roosters
inside. One quickly jabs at the other's neck. The men roar
in cheers. I wince and close my eyes. When I open them
again and really look at the birds, they surprisingly appear
mostly unharmed. The opposing rooster jabs back, followed
by more clamor. As I am about to walk away, the birds close
in on each other. One swoops his head in close and holds
his neck to the other's, forming a cross. The birds don't
move. The fight is over. The men disperse and the owners
collect their birds and winnings.

Whew. I got away with that one. It was incredibly stupid
to walk up to that situation and hope not to see anything
horrific, and I was only so lucky. I won't tempt fate again.

∼

Despite the distinct indulgence of doing absolutely nothing,
our week in Si Phan Don seems to pass rather quickly. It's
surprising how natural it feels to just…exist. We spend
our last evening at the Indian restaurant with Tim, Anna,

and our favorite lady-boy server. The chicken tikka masala may be getting a little old, but enjoying decent food is not.

While traveling New Zealand, Amira ate at a burger joint called Murder Burger that is famous not only for its delicious collection of carnivorous concoctions but also for its nutty, original atmosphere. She walked away with a set of "rating" cards for food, scoring 1–10, with an entertaining description under each rank.

My experience with the food in Laos can be consistently rated as, "mediocre," slipping steadily into "constant disappointment." The food is never what its description promises and never seems to taste how you'd expect it to taste, which if you enjoy food the way I do, can get a little depressing. Now, I can promise you that after traveling Southeast Asia for almost six weeks, my expectations are not that high. But when you order a flatbread pizza with cream cheese and capers and instead receive tomato sauce and onions, it gets a little frustrating.

Even Laos's famous dish, Laap, with its enticing mix of rice, meat, herbs, and cilantro, is served at a cool room temperature, which comes as a shock when you are eating meat and rice. Quite often, when asked how my meal is, I've grown accustomed to replying with, "*Eh*, it's okay."

So you can imagine the elation and shock that shakes Amira and me when, taking a break from our usual Indian cuisine, we sit down at another generic family-owned restaurant on "Main Street" and order a chicken Caesar salad and a burger to split and get a chicken Caesar salad and a burger that tastes—dare I say—delicious. I have tears in my eyes. My cheeks hurt from smiling. I call the owner/server/cook over and thank her repeatedly. She seems a little apprehensive at first, but soon she is nodding with palms pressed together in thanks to us.

But, all in all, I'm afraid to tell you, Laos, that I give your food a "5." And the 5 card reads as follows: "Yet another for the festering mud pit of mediocrity. Never before has the term 'ho-hum' been more apt."—Murder Burger, New Zealand.

Ouch. The world is a harsh place, and being hungry doesn't make it any better.

Siem Reap, Cambodia

T HE COUNTRIES I'VE BEEN TO SO FAR in Southeast Asia
have been "same same but different." As you cross into
a new country, you know you are still in Asia: the people are
still...well, Asian; motorbikes, tuk-tuks, geckos, and ants
are still ubiquitous; they've still yet to master how to put
together a sink or toilet that doesn't leak; and the children
are still beautiful. On the other hand, Thailand, Laos, and
Cambodia are completely different when it comes to prices,
food, language, currency, begging, scenery, temples, attrac-
tions, and even smells. I think I know what I am getting
myself into when I enter Cambodia.

I am wrong.

First arriving in Siem Reap, I am impressed by the tuk-
tuks. So well put together! So smooth! No rust! No rope
tying it all together! Now this is luxury. Then we pass by
Pub Street, marking the beginning of a district filled with
upscale bars and restaurants, spas and markets—essentially
every Westerner's dream. Being away from home and backpacking a couple different continents, sometimes a little
luxury and charm can go a long way.

After settling into our guesthouse, Amira and I head
into town to check out our new surroundings. As soon as
we turn the corner onto Pub Street, the circus begins, and
it doesn't end until we leave Cambodia.

An average five minutes walking through or to any tourist venue:

"*Hello*! LADY! You want cold drink? Only one dollar!"

"Okay? Hello? Lady, hello? Where you from? Where you from?"

"America."

"America U.S. Barack Obama. Capital: Washington D.C. Yes? Okay? You buy cold drink! Only one dollar!"

"No, thank you." Keep walking. They follow, in crowds.

"Okay? Madam? Two for one dollar! I give you best price! Where you from? You want postcard? You can send home to your mom or dad? Okay? Only one dollar! Okay? Lady?"

"No, thank you." Keep walking. They follow, in crowds.

"Okay, you want magnet? I give you good price. You can hang on your fridge, only one dollar!"

"No, thank you."

"Okay, I ask you first. Don't buy from other girl, you buy from me, okay?"

"Yes, okay."

Now enter the children, on average under the age of ten, holding real babies under the age of six months. There are no parents in sight, but they are watching. Oh, they are watching.

"Please, madam? I need milk for my brother…okay? Madam? Please, I need milk for my brother."

They tug and hit and pull on your arms; they plead and they beg, any time of day, any time of night. I even get a couple "Fuck you, lady" comments when I don't give. The droves of young ones are in exceptionally high numbers after 1:00 a.m. (Mom knows drunks are much more likely to give.) At one point I look down at a girl about the age of eight, holding her two-month-old brother at

1:30 a.m., and ask, "Why aren't you in bed? You should be
sleeping." Like a well-trained puppet, she only responds
with, "Okay? Please, my brother need milk. Okay? Please,
my brother..."

Tuk-tuk drivers:

"Hello! *Hello!* LADY! You want TUK-TUK? Tuk-Tuk?
Tuk-Tuk? Tuk-Tuk? TUK-TUK!?"

"NO! I DON'T NEED A DAMN TUK-TUK!"

"Okay, weed? Meth? Ecstasy? Cocaine? You want cocaine?"

"NO!"

And the circus continues.

On top of all this are the mine victims—children and
adults—missing anywhere from one to all four limbs, selling books or sunglasses. Cambodia is littered with mines
from decades of war, giving it one of the highest casualty
rates in the world along with one of the highest ratios of
amputees—1 in 290 people affected. Being in a country
with one of the most disabled populations on earth, it
comes as no surprise that you will be approached at every
opportunity to invest in their daily salary. Like I've said,
this world will break your heart.

After a while, the relentless round-the-clock pleading
starts to wear on me. Sometimes we give or buy, but when
you buy from one, at least a dozen will spot your transaction
and will swarm you with deals and appeals. It never stops.
And the children, the beautiful little children.

∾

Halloween quickly approaches, and Siem Reap is prepared.
Bars, fully equipped with decorations and specials, proudly

advertise and await the throngs of creatively costumed Westerners. The night before, I pep talk a group of people we met on our bus ride from Laos to dress up with us for Halloween. Our group consists of a Dutch couple, one American, one Swiss, and one Englishman. I am the only one who has ever celebrated Halloween.

By 8:00 p.m., we now have a maid, a cook, a cat, a masked bandit, and a cowboy. Not bad for not having a single Halloween store in town. With only black eyeliner as my prop, I draw whiskers and a nose on my face, pin my hair up to make ears, and *presto!* You have a cat. And a cat I obviously am walking the streets of Siem Reap tonight; large groups of full-grown men (mostly tuk-tuk drivers) all turn around and *meow*. I even get a few, "I love you" comments thrown my way. A little uncomfortable and strange to say the least, but entertaining. And I thought I'd have to go without Halloween this year.

Despite all the fun to be had on Pub Street, the real reason we are here is for Angkor Wat—a collection of eight-hundred-year-old ruins from the ancient Angkorian Empire, which ruled for over six hundred years back in 802 AD. It also contains the largest religious building in the world and is sometimes referred to as the Eighth Wonder of the World—in a nutshell. We buy a three-day pass and arrange for our own tuk-tuk driver to take us to and from Angkor Wat along with transportation throughout the different temples each day.

Temple after temple, stone after crumbling stone, my three days at Angkor Wat are quietly explosive. With the crumbling architecture and jungle vines curling deeply around every curve, arch, and stone, proud godlike faces looking deep into my eyes, and sunsets painting the horizon and ghostlike abandoned city of worship a deep red, it is a place of profound mystery and awe-inspiring majesty. Angkor Wat is the imagination of the gods.

∼

Twenty-four hours prior to falling into the grasp of a sickness I could never prepare for, I am spending my last couple hours at Angkor Wat. I am tired. I am hungry. The fatigue never stops. I go to bed at eight thirty that night and don't rise until ten thirty the next morning.

Still exhausted, I attribute my lethargy to too much sleep and go about my day in Siem Reap. I return some long overdue emails and even stick my feet into a large tank of hundreds of fish and watch as they eat off all the dead skin. By 2:00 p.m., only four hours after waking up, I am exhausted. I slowly stumble back to my bed, aware that I may be headed for some trouble.

It's over eighty degrees outside and we have no air-conditioning, which we're unfazed by at this point. Under the covers, chills race up and down my body. I close my eyes and fall fast asleep.

Two hours later, I am awakened by a deep, mind-numbing ache. My entire body hurts—every joint and every muscle. I'm freezing cold and miserable. I know at this point I have a fever, but to what extent? Amira has gone museum hopping for the day. Struggling, I drag myself out of bed and hobble into town for some 7-Up and a thermometer.

As I shuffle along the muggy dirt roads and through the clouds of dust, I become slightly delirious and lost in my own world of hurt. But if there's one thing you quickly realize when traveling alone, it's how much you pull through for yourself when there is no one else.

Back in my room, I unwrap my thermometer from the pharmacy and take my temperature. What...*this is in Celsius.* I have no clue what temperature this is. After a few sympathy tears, I push down my misery and leave my room *again* in search of the Internet. Thankfully there is a computer downstairs, so I don't have to travel far.

One hundred and three degrees Fahrenheit. Damn. I must have the flu. I crawl back under the covers, too exhausted to dig through my backpack for my Tylenol, and cry myself to sleep.

Amira comes in a couple hours later.

"I think I'm sick," I mumble as she closes the door behind her.

Her face concerned, she examines the scene laid out before her: a pale and sickly roommate, curled into a ball and shaking under the sheets. "What's wrong?" she asks without moving.

"I have a fever. Everything hurts...*bad.*"

She heads straight to her backpack and pulls out her Lonely Planet guidebook on Southeast Asia. "Could be malaria, Jill. You should go to the hospital."

"Really? I was just going to wait it out twenty-four hours," I mutter, worried, as tears start to surface.

"If it's malaria, twenty-four hours is pushing it. It says here to get to the hospital as soon as possible at the onset of *any* fever."

I force myself up with the help of a dear friend who has cared for me more than once, and together we head for

The Royal Angkor International Hospital in Siem Reap. Two hundred and twenty dollars and one blood test later, I am told I have dengue fever. Not malaria, but still not great news.

Dengue fever is caused by a virus transmitted through the bite of a mosquito. It's common in tropical areas but is considered "low risk" (*puh!*) to travelers except during an epidemic, aka right after the wet season. And right after the wet season equals *right now*.

There is no medicine or cure except rest and fluids. It is also known as breakbone fever because of the extensive pain and aching you experience in your muscles. There are multiple strains of the virus, four of which can cause a hemorrhagic fever that can cause you to go into shock and die, especially if you have been previously infected, or are female or Caucasian.

Out of my obvious misfortune, I am at the *very least* relieved to know my pain has a name and therefore what to expect. I will be severely ill for "seven days," according to my doctor, with an undeniable loss of appetite and thirst.

"You *must* eat and you *must* drink. You won't want to, but you must. If no," he warns sternly, "you must come back so we give you IV. You also must come back in two days for blood test, so we make sure you don't bleed to death."

"Well, how much is that going to cost? I don't have very much money."

"Same," he replies.

"I can't afford that. Do I have to come back?"

The doctor sighs. "If you bleed from eyeballs or nose, you come back right away because you have strain that make you bleed to death."

And I cry for days.

Amira comes in and out throughout the days, checking on me and rubbing tiger balm, a 1,500-year-old Chinese concoction (think Vicks VapoRub) used to treat pain and inflammation, on my aching back. If I'm not sitting on the toilet or crouching over it, I am in bed, huddled into a ball and rocking myself back and forth as I moan. The doctor gave me packets of electrolytes to add to my water to help with dehydration, but just looking at the sweetened orange fluid makes me want to vomit…again.

Amira comes in with what used to be my favorite Vietnamese soup, pho. I shoot up in bed as the smell hits me.

"Get that out of here!" I screech.

"Jill, please." Amira inches forward. "Please drink it. We'll take all the food out of it, but please drink the broth…"

My stomach twists into itself. I start salivating, as my internal plumbing is about to hit the reverse button once more.

"Amira, I'm not joking with you. Please, please get that away from me."

Instead of smelling delicious and hearty, the aroma wafting from Amira's soup is the equivalent of a rotting corpse. I want nothing to do with it, just like the doctor warned. I'm not sure what is happening; maybe it's the body's way of killing the host of the virus—*me*—but the mere thought of ingesting food or fluids is the equivalent of eating feces.

Amira attempts to reason with me. "Jill, listen to me. I'm worried about you. You have barely touched your water, and you haven't eaten in days. I'm going to have to take you to the hospital if you don't get something in you. Please, just drink this."

At this point I'm sobbing. I feel hopeless and lost. *What is happening to me right now?*

"I'm trying!" I wail. "I'm trying…"

Amira holds my head in her lap and strokes my hair. "I know you are, sweetie. I know."

I pull my strength together and sip the soup. I manage to keep it down for about a half hour. Amira returns to the room after a tea and cigarette break as I am coughing and heaving into the toilet. I have not had pho since.

My fatigue and aching last about five days, but it is about nine or ten until I feel somewhat normal again. My first trip downstairs to the guesthouse lobby for tea involves multiple breaks where I lean against the wall or crouch on a step to gather my strength. In the period of five days, I manage to keep down two apples and a fraction of my ingested fluids.

I don't know what I would have done without Amira. I suppose I would have pulled through for myself, as would most people when you have no one, but it would have been dangerous, extremely dangerous. I don't even want to think about it. She coaxed me to drink more, held my hair back as I crouched over a foreign toilet, and fed me pain relievers when I didn't have the strength to get them myself. Amira was my angel, and I'll never forget it. I have never been so sick in my life, and still, so far from home, I was taken care of.

～

Our original plan was to be in Siem Reap for four to five days. We were there eleven. With different plans after the next town, Amira and I only had a couple days left together when I got sick, but she put everything on hold to look after me. I guess, "It was the best of times, it was the worst of times" may accurately describe my days in Siem Reap. It was one hell of a ride.

Phnom Penh, Cambodia

IN 1975, THE LEADER of a rebellious communist movement in Cambodia, Pol Pot, took over the Cambodian
government and ordered a "cleansing" of the country. This
resulted in the deaths of over two million people (almost
a quarter of the population, although the numbers are still
not exactly known). He forced all uneducated people to the
countryside to work in forced labor camps so that Cambodia
could be a self-sufficient country, while anyone who was
educated or held any position of power was tortured and
murdered along with their entire family. The government
made 1975 "year zero" of a new civilization that lasted until
1979, when the Vietnamese army invaded and forced the
new "government" of Cambodia to fall. This is an incredibly
and almost shamefully short version of what happened
only a little over thirty years ago. It is Cambodia's Nazi
Germany; it is this people's Auschwitz.

∼

I'm having déjà vu. I swear I've been here before; I know
I've felt this sadness, this horror before. Hundreds of skulls
stare down at me from inside a glass monument, and I
remember the shame and barbarity of Auschwitz.

The flies are unremitting, which comes as no surprise

considering the amount of atrocious bloodshed that occurred on these grounds. Not much is left here at Cambodia's killing fields, nothing but an immense glass monument filled to the brim with skulls and bones, along with large holes and divots throughout the grounds where mass grave after mass grave has been dug up.

I feel especially speechless when it comes to writing about heart-wrenching and merciless genocide. It's so much like Nazi Germany, but so entirely different. The educated and freethinkers of Cambodia were viciously murdered, not with efficient gas chambers and guns, but with blunt objects, beaten and sometimes buried alive. There are bits of cloth, shoe, bone, and even teeth sticking above the ground. Heavy rains have washed away layers of topsoil, revealing the precious residue of life buried not so far below.

The most unbearable parts, though, are the trees. One, known as the Magic Tree, stands crooked and ashamed, as its prior purpose was to support speakers that played loud music. The noise allowed the soldiers to drown out the screams and groans of their victims as they beat them to death.

Another lone tree with a heavy base, surrounded by mass graves, is almost too unbearable to think about. How can I put this delicately? No, it is not possible to even attempt to protect you from the blow of my words. I'll say it quickly, and I promise to spare many of the details.

It was used to kill babies, held by their ankles, beaten against the tree, and thrown into a pit.

How does this happen? It's happened all throughout history and continues to happen at this very moment in different areas of the world. Have we not evolved past apes? How can human beings be so barbaric?

Unfortunately, I believe it's because of our evolved brains—*thinking*—thinking has caused these murders, these wars, these genocides. Obviously, fear and hatred are the known perpetrators, but those emotions start with a single seed, the most evil thought in the world, the one thought that all harm stems from: that your life is superior to that of another.

Why do people rape, steal, and murder? I think because deep down they believe they deserve more, and others deserve less. They believe themselves to be *entitled.* Throughout all the war memorials and after-effects of war in this world, this one belief I am sure of.

The Khmer Rouge soldiers were children, literally. The rebels trained young, uneducated boys and girls aged nine to twenty to form their army. They were babies with rifles. Their ages made them perfect targets to manipulate and brainwash. Those children were merciless and succeeded in killing off almost a quarter of the population of Cambodia. How could they do this and not think twice? Because they believed the educated and powerful were evil, dangerous, subhuman. They didn't deserve to live, and the soldiers had every right to murder and torture them.

To believe you are superior to another human being is the most dangerous thought in the world.

～

Back in the city, we visit an old school the Khmer Rouge turned into a prison and torture chamber. Here they brought in the educated citizens and government officials to torture them to death. I watch in horror as we walk from room to room, each with a lone, rusted bed above the stained tile floor with one black-and-white photo on the wall. Each room displays a different photo of the murder scene the Vietnamese soldiers walked into when they saved the Cambodians over thirty years ago. I am horrified again as I see some of the rooms weren't cleaned at all and are left to this day with blood stained into the floors.

As the guide takes us through the grounds, he excitedly rushes up to an older gentleman standing alone and introduces us to him. His name is Chum Mey, and he is one of the only seven survivors of the prison. With our guide translating, Chum Mey tells us tales of his life and the tortures he endured. He smiles often and has incredibly kind eyes. He is eighty-four years old, and as we walk away he wishes us a "long and peaceful life."

Toward the end of the memorial museum, we see a faded black-and-white photo of the seven survivors, and it doesn't take long to pick out Mr. Mey. He is thirty years younger, but his tired eyes still speak of strength and compassion.

After thanking our guide, we wander into the school's courtyard and practically fall onto a bench in exhaustion. Amira's eyes fill with tears as she talks of her horror and shock. I am only slightly less upset, being somewhat numb after northern Europe and Auschwitz. We decide it's best to get out of there as soon as possible.

Back in the center of Phnom Penh, we find a quiet restaurant to spend Amira's and my last evening together. Sitting at a table overlooking the Mekong River, we enjoy fireworks marking the beginning of the Khmer Water Festival. Looking back, I am grateful we left when we did, as this was the same festival where only days later, over 340 people were trampled to death when the crowd stampeded. Life is strange in its chance encounters, close calls, and vulnerable fragility.

Early the next morning, Amira and I say our good-byes. We have spent over six weeks together, traveling and exploring northern Thailand, Laos, and Cambodia. We've had quiet conversations and loud adventures. We've shared life stories, Coca-Colas, and hotel rooms. Amira held my head while I cried in misery from dengue fever and held my hand as I learned to travel a part of the world so entirely different from anything I've ever known. Continuing on won't be the same without her.

I travel now with Jess, my Australian friend from northern Thailand, to Vietnam, the last country on my world trip before my new life begins in Australia.

Ho Chi Minh (Saigon), Vietnam

I THINK IT'S SAFE TO SAY I arrive in Vietnam with a bit of a chip on my shoulder. Standing in the near-empty immigration and customs office, I'm getting the sneaking suspicion that I may have been exposed. *What is he doing behind that counter?* A crossword puzzle maybe? Reading *War and Peace?* I sigh heavily as I glare at him. He keeps his head down as another name is called that's not my own.

At this point I have watched about 150 people pass by before me, with names called and visas stamped, so I slump over my only companion at this point—my backpack—and continue to wait. Jess has already gone through and has been waiting for me on our bus for at least an hour.

How predictable.

I know this is happening before it even happens. *That dick is going to make me last* is my initial thought when at least twenty others wait along with me. There were five busloads of people initially crammed into this room, at least two hundred people I would guess. The bus drivers had collected our passports before we arrived and handed them to the immigration officers for us.

First through are the locals—fair enough. Then the foreigners are called. I am still hopeful after they call Jess's name, thinking I should be next, as our passports were handed in at the same time. I look around the room and notice that I am most likely the only American. My mind starts to wander, and it doesn't take long to figure out what may be happening. At first I chastise myself for giving the guy so little credit. So I make myself a deal: if I am wrong, I'll make an even greater effort to give people the benefit of the doubt.

But I'm pretty sure I'm right.

As we whittle down to five people including me, a French guy next to me chuckles and says, "Saving the best for last, yes?" He grins in a flirtatious sort of smirk.

I do not return his smile, saying only, "Oh no, I'll be last."

He laughs.

"No really," I say as a matter of fact. "That man took one look at my passport and said, 'This one can go last.'"

The Frenchman's name is called and passport handed back to him. He disappears from my sight. One by one, names are called as I sit cross-legged on the floor in the middle of the room.

Finally, when I can hear nothing but the sound of my own breathing, the officer throws my passport onto the counter and calls my name.

"Who, *me?*" I squeal with an exaggerated smile. I can't help myself.

I must admit that I am not in the least bit surprised. I have been warned about Vietnam and its memory of our time spent together fifty years ago. Sad to say, until recently I didn't know much about the Vietnam War, or as they rightly call it here, "the American War." I did my research via Internet in my slower days traveling through

Laos and Cambodia, as I traveled with my "neutral" Swiss friend who had more than one opinion about America's red, white, and blue need to involve ourselves in any war we possibly can.

I read about the destruction and the deaths, the massacres and the deceit. I read about when news finally reached America of the reality of the grim situation in Vietnam, and the anger and lack of support for our soldiers when they returned home. They were hated, and many hated themselves. It was an appalling war, and despite the fact that most people have moved on, the ones directly involved have not. And that's tragic.

Jess and I visit the American War Museum in Ho Chi Minh and walk through room after room of shocking, eye-opening, and *biased* exhibitions of the war. I learn that fifty thousand of our soldiers were killed in that war, along with two million innocent Vietnamese civilians. The American soldiers were called "murderous, crazed devils" and the Vietnamese who killed the most Americans were awarded "American Killer Hero" badges.

The museum's photos show a very certain reality of some very unforgivable massacres on America's part, but I also can't help but notice there is rarely a photo of a Vietnamese soldier holding a gun or even participating in the war in the first place. This simply isn't true and leaves me feeling very trapped between compassion and resentment. I need to get the hell out of here.

Traveling the world allows you the opportunity to see countless memorials and the aftermath of countless genocides and wars. After the American War Museum and a guided tour of the Cu Chi Tunnels, including displays of booby traps used to disable, dismember, and destroy our soldiers, I am devastated. As we head back to our hotel, I put my hands in the air and announce, "I'm done." No more death, no more war. I can't take it anymore.

~

With Ho Chi Minh being my first city in Vietnam, I have been previously prepared on the politics involving crossing the road here. "Oh right, yes, well I've been to Thailand, so I understand," I respond with a slightly arrogant tone. But I am reprimanded. Very few places in the world parallel Vietnam when it comes to traffic and crossing the roads. Thailand is child's play.

Nine million people live in Ho Chi Minh with roughly five million motorbikes on the road. There are rarely crosswalks or even lights for that matter. It's pure chaos. I've been told, "To cross the road, just walk out into traffic in a slow and steady manner, and the bikes will just whiz around you. *Do not* stop or hesitate or they'll swerve and people will get hurt." I understand this now as Jess and I stand along the edges of a motorbike highway. I've done this before, in Thailand, but the level of intensity when it comes to sheer numbers of speeding motorbikes packed into each lane of traffic is incomparable. We hesitate in our uncertainty, logic telling us this is suicide, but our stomachs reminding us that food is just a short trek across the road.

Since learning to cross the road as a child, you are engrained with logic stating not to knowingly place yourself into a steady stream of motor vehicles. When crossing the road in front of oncoming traffic, it is only logical to stop, hesitate, and scream. So after days of practice and multiple hesitations followed by swerving and honking, I figure out how to cross a road in Vietnam: *don't look.*

When a slight break in the steady flow of motorbikes opens, I walk. This gives them an opportunity to see that I'm there and to plan a way around me—at least this is the theory. I look straight ahead and put one foot in front of the other in a tense and somewhat miserable manner, whimpering and whining the entire time. Every once in a while a local—usually an old, hunched over, toothless woman—will grab my hand and guide me across four to ten lanes of speeding bikes to the other side. I bow and say, "*Cám on!*" (thank you!) and she normally attempts a smile back. But when the little old ladies aren't around, I cross all by myself, like a big girl.

When we're not spending our time crushing our souls with the aftermath of war, Jess and I wander the city. With vendors and motorbikes surrounding us, cockroaches beneath us, and more power lines than one could possibly imagine tangled above us, we explore the city sights and escape certain death by traffic many times throughout the day. We are staying in the backpacker district, or District 1, which centers around Pham Ngu Lao Street, is known for cheap guesthouses, and is jam-packed with bars and restaurants that we frequent each night.

On one particular rooftop of a four-story restaurant, I sit up at the bar to enjoy a drink while Jess sits at another table and practices her Spanish with some men from Argentina. Both Amira and Jess were in South America months back and learned the language in the process, and Jess will jump at any opportunity to speak Spanish with anyone who is able.

As I perch at the bar, a beautiful young man from Austria slides into the seat next to me and lays on the thickest attempt at seduction I have ever experienced. He leans in real close and puts his hand on my leg, asks me lots of questions, and plays the "we" game the first chance he can. "Oh, you love Italy? Me too. My family has a villa there. *We* could go sometime, and *we* could enjoy fresh wine from my family's vineyards."

I'm slightly entertained by this man's tacky attempt to get laid, and to amuse myself further, I allow it to continue instead of pouring my drink down his shirt. The concoction of bullshit that flies from his mouth sinks from nauseatingly (and deceitfully) sweet to drowning in desperation. I answer his questions and force a sorry excuse for a smile while simultaneously shoving my hand in his face every time he attempts a kiss.

It doesn't take long for this to get old. I just wanted to let loose and go with the flow for once. I'm so damn uptight when it comes to strange men and the possibility of being *used*. Throughout my travels I've been surrounded by both men and women who've experienced the one-night stand more than Tiger Woods at a Vegas strip club, yet I insist on standing in the corner while tightening my chastity belt. Now I'm no virgin, but I can't just go home with a stranger…at least not often. I only want to flirt with this man, but my harmless flirtation practically gives the guy a concussion as he repeatedly runs into the metaphorical brick wall I have placed between us.

Finally, *Rico Suave* throws in his final chip and asks, "So we go to your home for the sex?"

I practically choke on my beer and laugh in his face. "No, buddy, no sex for you tonight."

Annoyed, he chugs his beer and slams it against the counter. "Fine, you are too uptight for me anyway." And he walks away.

This is when I realize a valuable lesson: a bar is a bar is a bar. It doesn't matter where you are in the world—you will never escape the douche bags. The only difference is the accent.

I have to say, I did like Ho Chi Minh, but after three days of war and heat, motorbikes, honking, and cockroaches, I was ready for a beach. Jess and I decided on Mui Ne, an intimate and carefree beach town about five hours north of Ho Chi Minh. Traveling and backpacking can get exhausting, and a holiday from our traveling was in order. Looking back, we couldn't have picked a better place than Mui Ne.

Chicago, Illinois

"I would much rather have regrets about not doing what people said, than regretting not doing what my heart led me to and wondering what my life had been like...if I had just been myself."
—*Brittany Renee*

I didn't know. I could see all my angry and frustrated emotions seeping out at all the wrong times, but I didn't know why. Last night I read my diaries from the past couple years and I saw myself clearly for the first time in a while. I saw all the rationalizations, all the confusion, all the denial—and all at once.

If you were to come up to me and say, "Jillian, you don't celebrate differences..." I would probably laugh in your face. I celebrate differences! I love different people, different cultures, different food. I am ecstatic to be exploring in different cities and surroundings. I celebrate differences—apparently all but my own.

Last night I read my words written to myself, words written in an attempt to figure out who I am and somehow rectify this longing that I couldn't ignore, but couldn't accept either.

All this effort, all this time spent writing about the same things over and over again. For three long years I've written journals denying who I really am, trying to ignore my dreams and find some sort of middle ground that satisfied my longing and felt...safer—more logical.

To my own frustration, I was searching for an answer outside of myself that could not be found. Thinking, thinking, thinking way too much, and ignoring the one and only answer that was inside of me all along by filling my head with one rationalization after the next:

"I must be running."

"I have a thirst for something else."

"Maybe I just want to be married."

"I'm scared."

"I'm scared."

"I'm scared."

"Maybe I should go back to school. Maybe I should move to California. Maybe I should move to Colorado. Maybe I should stay with this guy. Maybe I'm asexual for not wanting this great guy in front of me. What is wrong with me?"

*It's crazy how ignoring **one thing** can upset your life so much. The answer was right in front of me for years and by ignoring it, I created a whirlwind of confusion.*

"I'm doing it. No turning back now! No regrets!"

And then:

"I'm not doing it. It's just habit to think about it. I must not know how to be content. I must be running from something...I can't go. I should stay here because I shouldn't...I can't..."

One journal where I'm trying to convince myself I can't go because this dream is just being used to "complete" me says, "The travel dream pops in my head every single day. But ninety percent of what you think today is habit...just recycled thoughts and connections from yesterday."

I think it comes from being young and wanting to do something so unconventional. I just didn't understand myself. I didn't know why I had this dream and no one else around me did.

The past seven months I have rummaged the pages of Face-
book, judging person after person from my hometown. I saw
face after face of twenty-five-year-olds who are settled and
married with children. I have never felt so alone.

So I judged them for not being like me, and deep down
I judged myself even more harshly for not being like them. I
unknowingly resented my difference. And after looking down
on them for their differences, I would feel awful. It's not in my
nature to criticize like that. I knew from my disappointment
in myself that my judgments were not as they seemed.

Turns out, I wasn't resentful of what I thought was other
people's criticism against me; I was resentful of my own. Now
that I can see what has been happening, I can let it go, and
just like that, the judgments disappear. I can now celebrate
my uniqueness and no longer resent it. I feel like an enormous
weight has been lifted.

When you are confident in who you are, you don't need
to critique others for their life choices. It took me years to see
how much I rejected my differences, but now that I can see the
heartache from my fear, it has disappeared completely.

I've always felt the same way about life, that it is a grand
adventure to be lived. I have a thirst that cannot be denied.
The sad thing is, no one was actually denying it…except me.

Mui Ne, Vietnam

DRIVING ALONG the palm-tree-lined boulevard kissing an ocean of deep blue, I know we have reached our destination. As I gaze out my large bus window, I inwardly curse the intermittent clouds as a threat to my very survival. I am here to lie in the sun and will throw a toddler-like fit if I don't get my way. I have been in Asia for almost two months now and still have not set foot on a beach.

World-known for its kite surfing, mile after mile of beautiful shoreline, and fresh-off-the-boat seafood, Mui Ne is quickly becoming a popular vacation destination for all ages. Thankfully though, for now, its small size and charm remain only lightly affected by the tourism industry. This won't last for long.

After the bus drops us off at our guesthouse, we pick our packs up off the side of the road and take in our new surroundings. Eclectic storefronts spill open to the streets, selling sunglasses and surfboards alongside family-owned restaurants filled with multi-colored plastic chairs and tables. The signs displayed throughout the town advertise in Vietnamese, English, and Russian, as this has been a Russian vacation destination for years. We check into our bungalow just steps away from the Pacific Ocean and unpack our bags. Then with flip-flops in hand we head out to explore.

Our guesthouse is made up of about a dozen bungalows, a pool, and a restaurant with seating overlooking the ocean and a bar-turned-discothèque at night. We have been told this is one of the more "happening" places to stay, which is precisely why we picked it. This guesthouse is also home to one of the town's better-known kite-surfing schools—one of the major reasons most people visit Mui Ne.

The coast is dotted for miles with large kites swaying in the wind. The sun is fierce, the breeze constant. The majority of the people walking this part of the beach are kite surfers, mainly Russians, but some Irish and English speckled into the mix as well. There are fit and toned bodies everywhere, the guys and girls alike in long board-shorts, hair in ponytails and six packs glistening in the sun.

Passing by a few of the ladies, I quickly gather that we may not be making too many female friends in this town. The Russian women are beautiful, incredibly skinny, and cold as ice. There are no smiles, no "good mornings," not even a general nod in our direction. I understand this may be a cultural difference, so I'm okay with this. I have met plenty of amazing women throughout my travels, and I'm sure I'll meet more. It's the amazing men that have not exactly been plentiful.

To be honest, most of my daydreaming before this trip usually involved a great-looking man, always equipped with a beautiful package of a body and an accent that made me swoon. I guess I always assumed that finding love would be part of the deal, that some part of this trip would include meeting my soul mate, who would whisk me away into a new and different life.

Most of the men I come across on this trip do nothing in the way of whisking. Most have dreadlocks and tattered clothing, traveling alongside me as part of the young generation of adventure-seekers and culture junkies. When it comes down to it, none of us are really here for love, besides the sheer love of being here. But I usually have one eye scanning the crowd for that inexplicable familiar face that may just be "the one"—a vacancy often left unfilled, which leaves me feeling slightly…wanting.

~

After a long day of sun soaking and flagging down the Vietnamese women who comb the shore selling passion fruit and mangoes, Jess and I doll up our looks for a night out on the town. Equipped with a handwritten map with the local hot spots from our guesthouse bartender, we decide to do our own version of barhopping, cruising from bar to bar by flagging down a motorbike taxi and hopping on back. We start the night at the farthest bar at the end of the strip, DJ Station.

The establishment carries a chic ambiance with deep red lighting and plush modern couches for seating. We settle in on the large open deck overlooking the ocean, with disappointed faces I'm sure, as the place is completely empty.

"No worries," Jess chimes in, breaking my mental fog of blighted hope. "It's still early in the evening. Let's get some dinner and a drink and see where the night leads."

The only man working the joint approaches our table, and instantly the mood shifts. He is beautiful, and has just moved here from Hungary to help run this joint with a good friend from home, we soon learn.

He is tall, with rich olive skin and deep brown eyes, short brown hair and a sexy five o'clock shadow. His name is Hugo, and I am instantly attracted. He is too, as I soon find out the next day while we sip chilled coffee at the restaurant at my guesthouse.

"You are so beautiful. I hate you, I think you could be my wife."

"Oh…" *Awkward.*

Last night we spent a majority of our evening hanging out with Hugo and his friend, Andras, who soon joined us. Hugo's flirtation went from mild to slightly intense, as he decided that all the "whisking" was being done by *me.* As for myself, I'm not so sure.

He finds me on the beach today and takes me to the restaurant at my guesthouse for a mini-date before he has to open up the bar. I haven't had the coffee yet in Vietnam and am absolutely floored as I take my first sips. Poured over a mountain of ice and condensed sweetened milk, the coffee here is a delightful change from the dried, instant coffee I've grown accustomed to drinking since leaving Europe.

"Wow, this is amazing."

Hugo grabs my hand. "You must know how I feel about you. I really hate you, because you make me fall in love with you."

Oh God. Abort. Abort!

"Well, that's nice. When do you open the bar?" I pull my hand back.

He looks hurt. "You not feel the same?"

"Hugo, we just met. I think you are very nice, and I'm looking forward to seeing you again at your bar tonight. But you are a little intense. You know? Do you understand?"

He looks confused.

"Uh," I hesitate. "Too much! Yes? You and me and love—too much! Okay?"

"Oh." He smiles. "I understand. I will be better, okay?"

"Okay."

Later that evening, in clouds of perfume and hairspray, I have reached the conclusion that my dry streak may be over.

"I think I'm going to sleep with Hugo," I say with another spritz of hairspray.

"Yeah? Do it, Jill, get yours for once," Jess responds as she traces her eye with black liner.

"Yeah, I haven't had sex in at least eight months, and he's beautiful."

"A little intense though. Maybe make sure it's worth it to you before the marriage proposals start."

"Hmm." I hesitate as I step back from the mirror and look myself over. I'm wearing a floor-length black dress with a heart-shaped neckline—the same dress I wore on my first date with Connor in Paris—with deep silver gladiator sandals and my hair back in a bun.

"I kind of feel like I've spent the day talking myself into it." I add with ambivalence, "I'm not really sure I'm making the right decision if I have to work to convince myself."

I turn around for approval from Jess, who, like much of the world, doesn't really find an occasional one-night stand to be a huge deal and may possibly think I'm slightly ridiculous with the intensity of seriousness I tend to apply to all of life.

"Whatever, mate. Do what's right for you." She spritzes on her perfume and with a nod, we head for the door.

We arrive, once again ahead of the crowds so Hugo and Andras can spend a little time with us before the bar gets busy. Hugo and I share a couple kisses while Andras makes up our mojitos. He is a fantastic kisser, soft…attentive. He runs his fingers down my neck and along my collarbone. Right now would be the perfect time. The bar won't fill up for hours, and Jess and Andras are distracted, picking out music to play and having their own little mini-date. I prepare myself as we finish our second drink.

"Is there anywhere we can go to be alone?" I ask with my most seductive smile.

He reads me instantly, and his face lights up.

"Well, I don't have my own place yet, or my own room. I just sleep on couch. But we can go into other room and put blanket on floor?"

Ew. This isn't going as planned.

Seeing me cringe, he adds, "We can go into room with TV? No one there."

"The room that is open to bar guests? No."

"Please, let me touch you. Let me kiss you. Let's go into room. I find lots of blankets. I really think I love you. I hate you for doing this to me. Please."

I'm uncomfortable now.

"Let's just forget it. This should be easy and effortless, and it's not. Let's just have fun and worry about it later."

I have had enough of my own head now, combined with Hugo's begging, to realize I have been listening to everything but my own intuition. I'm not going to talk myself into having sex with this man. It should just be natural. I should have learned this by now. And so I grab his hand and lead him to the bar, doing all I can to let the moment and the possibilities fade into the music.

Hours later, I push myself through the crowds to congratulate Andras on such a successful establishment. The music is pumping, the crowd is young, the location and ambiance dynamic and chic. Hugo is now working behind the bar, dancing and fist-pumping while eyeing me like prey to be conquered. Desperation is in his eyes, a sadness too, as he sees me talking with different men in the room. He's a hopeless romantic to be sure, and I find myself hoping for his sake that he is like this with all women, as his neediness and desperation have suffocated any chances with me. If this is his way, he should have a new "future wife" within days.

As Andras heads to the bar to help Hugo, a young man next to me turns to greet me. He smiles and yells over the music in a thick Irish accent that he couldn't help but notice my American accent.

"Where are you from?" he yells into my ear as he lightly holds the back of my arm.

"Chicago."

He smiles. His name is Ray; he and his brothers are here to teach at one of the kite-surfing schools. He used to live in San Francisco for a couple years before a family emergency sent him back home, also alerting the authorities that he had been in the States for eighteen months past his visa. He is now banned for five years and owes a $7,000 fine. He really loves the U.S. though, and misses it deeply, which is probably the biggest reason my accent drew him to me.

Ray and I talk for hours. I meet his brothers and introduce them to Jess. He is tall, with broad shoulders and short, curly brown hair. He is ruggedly handsome and incredibly kind. Hugo is quick to catch sight of us speaking and laughing and comes to me with a note.

Pulling me aside, he puts a paper in my hand.

"For you," he whispers, a sense of defeat growing behind his eyes, and heads back to the bar.

I look down at the paper, an old flyer used to attract people to the bar. The blank side is now covered in blue ink—a large heart in the middle with, "What I can only this. To Jill and every time kiss 4 U." Ray and his brothers see it as well, the large print being hard to miss.

"I'm sorry," I mumble, embarrassed. "I met him a couple days ago…he's pretty intense."

"Are you with him?"

"No! Well…I kind of liked him when I first met him, but not anymore. He's way too much for me to handle."

"Good."

I look up and we smile. Now *this* is how this is supposed to feel. Effortless.

The next five days Ray and I are inseparable. He grabs hold of my hand and I never want him to let go. We take long walks along the beach and talk about life, go on dinner dates by candlelight, and finish our nights with long kisses under a blanket of midnight stars.

The original plan was to stay in Mui Ne for two nights—we stay for seven. Both Jess and I agree each day to go to the ticket office "tomorrow," a mutual unspoken understanding that we aren't leaving until we've absolutely no choice. Unfortunately, my time in Southeast

Asia is winding down, and we still have the entire coast of Vietnam to explore.

Something else unexpected occurs in Mui Ne as well, something I could never have prepared for—homesickness. Despite the sunshine and romance, I feel a quiet sadness surfacing. I write the following confession in my journal as I watch the kites flutter in the early evening breeze:

"What an amazing adventure I've been on. I know I'll never regret or forget these days I'm living…but it's also a long lesson to learn that there is no place like home. I'm burned out, I'm tired. Living life among strangers, the constant feeling of discomfort, the extremes of love and hate…it's not so easy, this life. I've lost it. I can't see my life so clearly anymore. My purpose for being here has been lost, lost, lost.

"I have forgotten who I am, the passion that drove me to this life. I'm just going through the motions, surviving, tolerating. The beauty has blurred, my purpose smudged into a daily life of sleepwalking through a world full of wonder and beauty. But I don't see it; I don't feel anything. Lost. I've lost it, and I don't know how to get it back.

"When did this start? Maybe in Thailand and Laos, when my travels went from hectic to downright crazy and frustrating at times…or maybe when I didn't really have a moment to be alone and reflect on my experiences. Constantly being with a companion is a blessing and a curse. I can't imagine even for a moment traveling Asia without Amira and Jess, but I do know the constant companionship has been continually drowning out the passion that burned so strongly before. Distracted. I'm so distracted.

"This isn't the thrilling adventure I thought it'd be. There, I said it. I feel so guilty admitting that because not only does

it falsely sound like I'm not grateful to be living this life, but also because I worked so damn hard and gave up everything to be here.

"I'll never regret this, and knowing what I know now, I'd still do it all over again, because despite all the immense lessons and ecstatic joy…this is my sacred, once-in-a-lifetime journey. To always be able to say, 'I did that' and to understand 'there is no place like home' is priceless. I'll never have to wonder, 'What could have been.' Despite the tears of joy and tears of pain—I'll always know I gave it my all, I lived my dreams, I conquered my fears.

"I just had no idea that doing this for so long and alone would feel…like this. I'm so burned out. It's lost, and I don't know how to get it back."

It's excruciating to admit something to yourself that is so wholeheartedly disappointing, but admitting my pain and frustration only makes my journey more real. This is life. There are no fairy tales. There are conquered dreams and painful realities. My painful reality is that conquering my dream involves a certain degree of agony. It's painful to accept this. I have cried countless tears from the elation and pride of realizing my childhood dreams and turned around the very next moment to curse this world and its harsh whirlwind of deceit. Living this dream is not what I thought it would be. It is in Mui Ne that I finally accept this and realize I may not find what I was looking for, but an entirely different reality altogether.

I don't know why I am here. I only know that when I lay my head down at night, I have a peace in my heart that comes from living my truth. I'm just not sure this journey will last as long as I thought, or will lead me to places I had always assumed it would. Only time will tell.

~

We spend our last morning in Mui Ne waiting at a hotel lobby for our bus to come. Ray waits with us and holds my hand as I pout.

"I don't want to leave," I mumble. "This is the only place in my entire trip that I am genuinely sad to leave."

He sighs heavily as he looks into my eyes. We have exchanged phone numbers, emails, and Skype accounts, all in a desperate attempt to plan a time and place to meet again while we are both still in Southeast Asia, but it doesn't look promising.

"If anything, I'll fly you to Ireland and you can meet my family. You'll love them."

I kiss him one last time before stepping up into the bus.

Hanoi, Vietnam

Racing motorbikes, crowded buildings, perpetual honking—Hanoi is Vietnam's New York City. There are some differences, however: bright red flags with one yellow star proudly announce communism's rule; roosters and chickens abound; and the street vendors sell curries and spring rolls instead of hot dogs and pretzels. The little devil scooter may have replaced the big yellow cab, but the chaotic vibrancy is still the same.

Based on the many recommendations of other travelers, Jess and I stay at Hanoi Backpackers and meet up with a good friend, Ivo, whom we met back in Pai in northern Thailand.

As our cab drives frantically through the streets, our driver seems to have little competition racing alongside him. *Where is everyone?* Then I remember, not only does this communist country block Facebook (gasp!), but this city in particular has a curfew of 11:00 p.m.

"Not to worry," Ivo comforts us as we walk through the doors of our hostel. "There are plenty of places that 'appear' closed but are indeed very much open."

The streets of Hanoi after curfew have an eerie, almost apocalyptic feel about them. Stagnant puddles collect along the deserted streets as mist hangs about the streetlamps like half-crooked halos. The three of us walk beside the abandoned, dusty cars lining the street and catch up on each other's adventures since we last met.

Ivo is a journalist from the Netherlands. Tall in stature with light brown hair and complacent blue eyes, he has a soft, almost childlike semblance that displays his kindness across his face. We met in the most random of fashions, at a small farm hidden in the mountains outside Pai, fishing for piranhas. His inviting, warm personality yet dry sense of humor bonded us almost instantly, and Pai being such a small village, it was effortless to cross paths almost every day we were there.

∽

We approach a tall, broad-shouldered Asian man in a dark gray suit standing under a single lightbulb outside a dark building. There are no other lights or people, not even a hint of music coming from inside. He nods at Ivo in a mutual understanding and lifts the heavy metal gating that matches its neighbors, all advertising locked and closed establishments.

As we walk the narrow, low-lit passageway, we follow the increasingly loud yet muffled thumping of techno music. Two heavily insulated doors later and we find ourselves standing at the entrance of a thriving, pumping nightclub.

As the strobe lights paint the bar in glitter and the sea of heads bounces to the bass of clashing electronic tunes, I realize through tears of laughter that Ivo, Jess, and I, oh, we're going to have a *good* time. As the hours increase into the night, so does our consumption of drinks, and before long, we blend into the young, inebriated crowd.

Unfortunately, our social euphoria is cut short when the establishment's bright lights flip on and the music screeches to a halt. Within seconds the room fills up with a barricade of stern-faced Vietnamese cops, pushing through the crowds and glaring at us as we stare back like deer in headlights. *Busted.* Whistles start blowing from every direction, and we are escorted out like a herd of cattle.

Ivo is shaking his head at me as we shuffle out. "See, if you Americans would have bombed this place a little longer, we wouldn't be having this problem."

All I can do is laugh. Rather than become offended, I have *finally* learned to laugh about America and the harassment I receive for our increasingly unpopular reputation.

After the cops clear away, we hear of other clubs throughout the city where the parties are still going strong, but we decide it's best to stumble on home. Tomorrow is an early day, and we've got a boat to catch.

～

Standing on the large upper deck of our two-story ship, it comes as no surprise that Halong Bay is in the running for one of the current "Natural Wonders of the World." As far as the eye can see, hundreds of immense limestone cliffs and islands tower over rich green and turquoise waters where traditional Vietnamese fishing boats coast in opposite directions. It's brilliantly and breathtakingly stunning.

I look to Jess. "So this really does exist."

She doesn't return my gaze, only shakes her head while scanning the horizon.

"Indeed."

The weather isn't ideal. The whole area is shrouded in a dense fog and rainy mist on our first of three days, but we aren't fazed. We just stand and stare, eyes wide and mouths gaping.

We are on the beginning of a two-night, three-day cruise, and unlike my cruise on the Nile, the food is delicious and company hilarious. There are probably fifty of us, with representatives from all over the globe. We spend the afternoon exploring every nook and corner on kayaks, paddling through Halong Bay, its mysterious floating fishing markets, and large, abandoned caves.

Late into the evening, after a large dinner and festive cocktail hour, I find myself on an outer deck wrapping the sides of the boat, exploring Ivo's life as a journalist while the other young men and women on our cruise find dark corners to explore each other's tonsils.

Clasping my hands as I lean over the railing, I sigh deeply and look out into the pitch black. The night is peaceful, the only sign of life coming from the darkness being the red and white lights of fellow boats resting on top of the calm blanket of water. Muffled voices and laughter from inside the boat sporadically echo against the cliffs surrounding us as Ivo casually tilts his head back and exhales a thick stream of cigarette smoke. I watch as the cloud wavers in resolution for a brief moment above him before the light ocean breeze swirls and drags the smoke up into the sky.

"So why all the questions about my job?"

I look at him briefly while clutching my chest like an expectant mother does her belly.

"Because I want to be a writer..." I say softly. I hesitate in my admittance, as my message is fragile. I hold my hand over my heart and feel that same instinctual tug like a kick of reassurance. "I've been writing for years, but I'd love to write a book."

The corners of his lips tug down in an absent "sure, why not" sort of way.

"I've heard that before. You any good?"

"I don't know…I think so. I'm okay."

"Well, Jill, no harm in trying. I say do it."

A few moments pass as I weigh my discontent with his answer. I'm not sure what I was hoping to hear in exchange for my confession, but a shrug and a "why not" wasn't it.

"I will," I reply, gripping the cold metal railing. "I have to." My affirmation quiets to a whisper. "I feel it in my bones. I'm not sure what I'll say, but I feel it will be the reason I'm here."

Ivo doesn't respond. I'm sure he doesn't know what to say. He just stands in the dark and nods his head repeatedly.

There is silence. It seems like our conversation, along with the cigarette smoke, has followed the trail of laughter being carried away by the wind. We sit in silence and stare up at the stars.

~

The next morning we cruise off to Castaway, a private island tucked deep into Halong Bay, to spend our day and evening. The morning is quiet, with collective muffled groanings and deeply groggy eyelids among the faces of the previously intoxicated.

After eggs and coffee, I crawl into a reclined chair along one of the boat's many decks and watch the world pass by as I consider our conversation last night. I haven't told many people about my writing dream; I suppose I was searching for some sort of reassurance. Although Ivo has never read anything I've written, so I'm not sure what he could have told me. It's just sometimes that dream seems farther away than home at this moment, and home seems *very* far away.

∾

I spend my last day back in Hanoi running errands, which can be a little frustrating when there is a language barrier as heavy as there is here. I find when most people don't understand what I am saying, instead of shrugging their shoulders and shaking their head no, they say, "Yes, okay." This is not "okay" when you have a 6:00 a.m. flight the next morning and you drop your laundry off the afternoon before.

Me: "I need this back tonight, yes?"

Woman: "Yes, okay!"

Me: "You drop off at my hostel *tonight*, yes?"

Woman: "Yes! Okay!" Smiles.

Much later that evening I check for my laundry that was to be dropped off at my hostel's front desk. Nothing.

Next thing I know I am running through the streets of Hanoi, getting honked at and responding with my own words of reproach as I make my way back to the Laundromat. It's closed. Of course it's closed. A parade of verbal abuse flows from my mouth as I race back to my hostel.

"Please, what can I do? They said they'd have it back,

they *promised* they'd have it back by tonight! I leave for Thailand tomorrow at 6:00 a.m. and they have most of my clothes in there. What can I do?"

A few frantic calls later and Hanoi Backpackers has gotten ahold of a security guard to let me in. Problem solved. Problem wouldn't have been a problem if the worker wouldn't have responded "*yes, okay*" when she didn't understand me. Now, I don't blame her for not speaking English, it's not like I speak Vietnamese, but "yes, okay" when you don't understand is not *okay*.

Once I have my laundry back, Ivo suggests we take a much-needed break from drinking and spend our last night in Vietnam at the movies. Hanoi is supposed to have a great movie theater that the expats here love. We decide on seeing *Megamind* for three reasons:

1. It looks funny.
2. The selection of movies to choose from is very limited.
3. I've never heard of the other movies.

Traveling for an extensive period of time removes you so far from one reality and throws you face-first into another. Intuition and street smarts become stronger than ever, whereas new music and movies? No idea. The date and day of the week? Clueless. I can't even begin to count how many times I've sat with a group of people and not a single person had a clue as to what day it was. Monday, Tuesday, Friday, Sunday? All the same.

Time is also warped. Four months feels like four years. Every day is something new, and every week you are some *place* new. You do in a couple months what some may never do in a lifetime. I've gone four months in Chicago without seeing the loves of my life in Michigan—no problem. Four months here…feels like a lifetime. I miss them so much it hurts.

It's quite hilarious watching *Megamind* in 3-D, and thankfully it doesn't take long for me to get over the Vietnamese subtitles jumping out and practically punching me in the face. The funniest parts though are when the jokes are obviously lost in translation, and we're the only ones laughing out loud in the entire theater.

As the credits start to roll, I stand, collect my bag, and am instantly hit with an intense pang of disappointment like a punch to the gut. I got lost in the movie and forgot. For a brief moment I forgot where I was and thought I was home. I look at the dimly lit faces surrounding me and realize I'm not home at all. *I'm in Vietnam*. Instead of feeling gratitude, I feel an overwhelming sense of sadness.

I'm burned out. In the four months I've been traveling, I've been to fourteen countries and over forty cities. I've also been repeatedly sick in a short period of time. For the sake of my peace, I think I need to stop soon, even if just for a short while. Wherever that may be, I don't pretend to know. I will continue to follow the whispers of the gods.

I gather my bearings and flash a smile to Ivo and Jess in an attempt to avoid conversation and move on. Yes, move on, move forward—one foot in front of the other. That's all I can tell myself to do in moments like these, moments when life shocks me, surprises me, and saddens me all at once.

Bangkok, Thailand

STARING UP AT THE CEILING of my jail cell of a room, I can't help but think to myself, "How in the hell did I get here?" This place is a total and complete shithole. This, of course, is completely my fault. I can proudly say I've become one of *those* travelers who just wings it when I get into a city. Where am I staying? How will I get there? I don't know. I'll figure it out—I always do. And ninety-nine percent of the time, it's fine.

Here in Bangkok, however, I am stuck in a three-dollar-a-night hotel room that looks more like a prison cell than a warm place to lay my head. I'm on a mattress with the comfort level of a brick, with one fluorescent lightbulb hanging from the bare "white" walls and no air-conditioning. It's over ninety degrees outside. The water sitting in my plastic bottle is actually hot.

I head out to Khao San Road to reunite with Amira and have lunch—chicken fried rice at our favorite street-side restaurant—and catch up a little before our evening plans start at eight. I then wander back to the hotel for a restless nap and shower before dinner.

As we are walking to find a spot for our evening meal, it hits me—I don't feel well. Amira and I are to have dinner, drinks, and head to our favorite rooftop bar in Bangkok to hang out and sing our favorite songs with a live band, just like the first night we met. We have been planning this for weeks, and I have been looking forward to seeing her again since we split back in Cambodia.

"Don't worry, Jill, it will be okay."

Amira rubs the top of my hands as I nervously grip a Coca-Cola bottle. Throughout every nauseating bus trip, every stomach-churning moment before racing to the bathroom, and life in general acclimating my body to the plethora of intestinally antagonizing bacteria, my first response has always been to drink a Coca-Cola to calm my stomach.

But I'm not so sure all will be well this time. I'm nervous. I'm starting to feel like I did the last time I was sick, which is *real fresh* in my mind as it has only been weeks. Within thirty minutes, I have to go back to my hotel. This is not looking good. As I moan and roll around in my bed, I realize my prospects of not throwing up again are not in my favor.

What's the worst part of getting food poisoning in a three-dollar-a-night hotel in Bangkok alone? Well, that would be getting food poisoning in a three-dollar-a-night hotel in Bangkok…alone. I tell Amira to go on without me tonight, and that if I feel any better I will call her. But we both know I'm done for, and having Amira spend another night of her trip holding my hair back and watching me cry is more than I can bear. I'm going to suffer in silence tonight…as silent as I can when the walls here are paper thin, forcing my entire floor to hear me dry-heaving bile until five in the morning. To top it all off, the only bathroom is a public one at the opposite end of the hall.

I'm miserable—*miserably* miserable. By the end of the night, I can guess I've thrown up at least twenty-four times in the month of November. Dengue fever claims most of those counts, but tonight is a close runner-up. I call one of my closest friends from home and start bawling at the sound of her voice. Sometimes I can't help but wonder how cut out I am for this backpacker life.

I wanted to see a couple things while I was back in Bangkok this time around, but I'm afraid most of what I see is a toilet bowl and the bottom of a trash can.

Thankfully it only lasts twenty-four hours, so I'm able to make my twelve-hour bus ride down south. I'm beyond exhausted and feel like I've been hit by a semi-truck. *All is okay*, I whisper to myself as I drift off to sleep. *I'll be soaking in the sun on an island by morning...*

Koh Phangan, Thailand

A MOTORBIKE TO A BUS TO ANOTHER BUS to a tuk-tuk to a ferry and I have arrived. I am now on the beautiful…cool, rainy, and foggy island of Koh Phangan. Oh…*good*. I actually don't care, to be honest. I am still exhausted and dehydrated and haven't eaten since before I got sick two days ago.

"Rain all you want," I mumble to myself. "I'm going to sleep."

The Thai man on the boat then hands me my backpack, and I am instantly heated. Here's the lowdown before I go any further. Buses throughout Southeast Asia aren't big enough for you to keep your luggage with you. You can bring a carry-on to jam somewhere in your personal space, and the rest of your luggage goes in storage underneath.

If you are lucky or well-read with guidebooks, you will know not to keep anything of importance in your luggage that goes underneath because people will hide under the bus to search through your belongings and steal anything of worth. There's nothing you can do, and the companies post signs claiming they "are not responsible for any lost or stolen items."

I always pack a carry-on that I lock while I sleep containing my passport, money, camera, phone, journals—anything important to me. My backpack is essentially clothes, books, shoes, and my towel. I "rig" my pack in a certain way to know if it's been tampered with. Any sorry excuse for a person who would steal from people's bags under a bus won't be paying attention to how things are tucked and buckled. I have been lucky, until now.

Back to the pier on Koh Phangan, my pack looks and feels different. I haven't seen my bag in a while, as it was promptly transferred from bus to ferry. After my last forty-eight hours, this is not something I feel I can emotionally handle. I rip open my bag in the middle of the windy and somewhat rainy pier to check what's there and what isn't.

Besides the neat pack job that's totally shot to hell, all appears to be present. Knowing some stranger had his grubby hands searching through my things isn't the best feeling in the world. I shove everything back in and zip up as rain pelts the back of my neck, grumbling and swearing like a pirate the entire time.

I hop on the back of another tuk-tuk and tell the driver to take me wherever the other tourists are going. There are three British girls in back with me, all with baby faces, probably about the age of eighteen.

"Excuse me?" I prod. "Do you know where you girls are staying?"

"Oh, of course! It's called Delight Resort. We always stay there. We've been here three times already, and it's our favorite place to party!" one of the girls chirps, all bright-eyed and cheery.

I force a smile back. *Ugh. Party.* Shivers run down my spine. After the last couple days and lack of sleep, food, water, and stomach acid for that matter, I have only one thing on my mind—*sleep*.

"You should just come with us. We'll show you where to go!"

Despite my heavy exhaustion, I genuinely smile and accept her offer.

I am always taken care of.

Delight Resort is, well, delightful. It's centrally located and a three-minute walk to the ocean with beds the size of my whole room in Bangkok. I happily fork over the cash and lock myself in my room. And I sleep for days.

Jess isn't to meet me for another three days, so between trips to the 7-Eleven for yogurt and apples, milk and pea-nut-butter sandwiches, I sleep. I also have multiple Skype dates with Ray, catching up on our adventures and telling each other how much we're missed. Seeing him again in Asia is unfortunately not a possibility anymore. We prom-ise to keep in touch and can only hope to see each other again when the timing is right. Another casualty of world travel, something I've grown used to at this point: you meet incredible people but will more than likely never see most of them again. I can only be grateful for the opportunity of having them slip into my life—even for a mere moment—to forever leave echoes in my memories.

After a couple days my body starts to feel whole again, my stomach pieces itself back together, and the dark circles under my overly tired eyes slowly fade. All in perfect timing because right on time, Jess comes sliding back into my life again.

I see her at the end of the hallway, petite little Jess and her beloved straw hat.

"Jess!" I scream.

We run toward each other and hug. At times I think we couldn't be more opposite, Jess and I, but that woman lights up my life with such a fire and intensity. I missed her and her crazy passion for life and am delighted to have her next to me once again.

Even the locals love her. It never ceases to amaze me how many women talk to, touch, and even *hit* Jess. I can only sit back quietly and smile as Jess is continually smacked in the arm by the smiling women selling her mangoes.

Now I thought for sure that being in the south of Thailand after the rainy season meant "dry season," aka warmth and sun. I couldn't have been more wrong. My week on the island of Koh Phangan is filled with clouds and rain. But this has no effect whatsoever on our fun. We spend most our days bumming around the quiet and carefree island streets, and our nights sitting on the beach with beer and fire dancers.

We have, amazingly enough, clear skies and decently comfortable temperatures for the island's famous Black Moon Party, which is the only reason we are in Koh Phangan in the first place. Similar to the Full Moon Party, which has taken place on the island's Haad Rin beach every month since the mid-1980s, a Black Moon Party is held on a mountain in the middle of the island and carries on all night until the sun rises. Thousands of people from all over the world flock to the islands every month to attend and spend the evening dancing away to electronic beats and fire dancers.

～

By noon on my last day, the circus begins again. Jess and I hug for what feels like five minutes and wave farewell until I meet her in Sydney for Christmas, and all the while a hyper little man is jumping up and down behind me.

"*Okay?* Okay! Let's go! Let's go! GO GO GO!"

"Yeah, yeah, yeah," I mumble as I look at him with utter resentment. He takes my backpack and throws it on top of the tuk-tuk. "Good luck," I whisper to my things and climb in back.

Our tuk-tuk takes me and another group of travelers to a van, then to a ferry, which drops us off to another tuk-tuk that takes us to, we'll call it Travel Agency #1. We wait an hour. Then another tuk-tuk picks us up and drops us off at Travel Agency #2. We wait another hour, then another tuk-tuk and another travel agency. I walk up to the counter.

"Excuse me? Yes, are we done yet? You sell 'one' bus ticket to Bangkok, and we take twenty tuk-tuks. How many more tuk-tuks?"

She smiles, of course. "Yes, okay, last stop."

"No more tuk-tuks?"

"Yes, okay."

Whatever.

We wait around another hour as *Jackass: The Movie* plays on the only television (as if my night couldn't get any worse), then watch gratefully as our bus pulls up across the street. We cross through the mud puddles and rain to our tacky, neon-lit "VIP" bus headed for Bangkok. As another little man grabs my backpack to put under the bus, I look him directly in the eyes and say very loudly, "Yeah, hey, how about don't steal from me this time, yes?"

Ten hours later, three new Australian friends and I are enjoying coffee and each other's company at a restaurant in Bangkok at 5:00 a.m. I am rustling through my bag, which has *clearly* been tampered with *again*. One of the

Australians, Asha, despite having padlocked her bag, decides to check through her bags as well.

"My iPhone—it's gone." Her face is pale with disbelief.

"Really?" We all gasp. "Look further, maybe you put it somewhere else? Maybe you put it in there? Or how about there?"

Ten more minutes of frantic searching and she announces, defeated, "Nope, it's definitely gone."

At this point, I'm feeling quite grateful that I left nothing important in my backpack that went underneath. I decide to check my carry-on anyway, even though it was padlocked and under my seat the entire journey. Everything at first appears to be intact. Then I go through my organized little pouch, which holds my extra cash, passport, and emergency credit cards. I've checked this pouch maybe one hundred times throughout my trip, and things are always in the exact same spot because I *never* use them.

I really can't believe what I'm seeing, or maybe I should rephrase that to what I'm *not* seeing. *Missing.* I check again. And again. And again and again and again. My last and only credit card (my other one had its numbers stolen by some dick in Kansas during this trip)...it's gone, along with my U.S. dollars that I had as backup for emergencies. Gone. All gone.

"Robbed?" I mumble. Heads shoot up in response. "I've been robbed. They took my credit card. They took my cash."

"Are you sure? When was the last time you used it?"

"*Never!* Never in Asia because they'll keep the receipt and use your damn numbers, those bastards!"

This isn't good. I check again. Never having been robbed before and having kept something so important in the exact

same spot for months, my brain just can't wrap itself around
the fact that it's gone. It's gone. I have nothing, no Visa or
MasterCard—only a simple ATM card. Thankfully my flight
to Australia is already booked or I'd be stranded in Bangkok. It is nearly impossible to travel without a credit card.
How can I book flights? Or buses? Or hostels? Unless I just
show up, which has worked in Asia but won't in Australia.

I spend the morning searching Bangkok for an international phone, then feel my blood pressure rise as my
attempts to speak with Capital One's customer service representatives result in multiple dropped calls. Two hours and a
dozen calls later, all is sorted and my card is canceled. I head
back to Khao San Road to spend the rest of my afternoon
sharing drinks and some much-needed laughter with my
new Australian friends before heading off to the airport.

Okay, not ideal to be robbed on my last day in Asia, but
what can I do? I'll figure it out—I always have. This is all
I can tell myself in times like these. There is no point in
stressing out because there is *nothing* I can do to control it.

Admittedly, I'm slightly tired and cranky boarding my
plane to Australia, but I'm still happy. It's deep down, the
happiness—*like way deep down*—but it's still there. The
world has beaten me up and stripped me down, but I still
feel alive tonight. I'm going to Australia. I'm going to *Australia*! I fought and fought and the universe listened. The
world doesn't always play fair. Living the life of your dreams
isn't for the "lucky" or "spoiled" but for the *strong* and the
brave—even if you have to learn these things along the way.

Ask and you shall receive. Believe and you will see: there
are no rules but your own. Next stop: Australia.

Australia

Melbourne, Australia

W E ARE DEEP IN THE BUSH here in Australia's Tarra Valley. Tall blades of grass topped with little white flowers brush casually against our legs as we idle on our quads along this leaning hillside. I am with my friend's ("Karen from Australia") brother, Steve, who has kindly taken me in—despite me being a total stranger—here in my first days in Australia.

I met Karen in Chicago two years ago, on a regular day filled with teeth cleaning and daydreaming. I'd had the hope of Australia in my heart for years, with my desire to go only increasing exponentially with each passing day. It was my "promised land," a dream of mine that offered the *hope* of a new and better life.

Karen sat in my dental chair to have her six-month cleaning, completely unsuspecting of the curious young soul about to devour her life and viewpoints. I had been waiting to meet someone like her, someone—anyone—able to support my unreasonable and irresponsible dream instead of joining me in questioning it.

Karen, now in her early forties, came to Canada from Australia at the tender age of twenty-seven, not knowing a soul and broke as hell.

"My God," I sat back in my chair, astounded. "Weren't you *afraid?*"

She looked at me and said something that changed my life, something I'd never considered or believed up until that point.

"Nah, mate." She shrugged. *"It always works out."*

Huh.

I went straight home and wrote in my journal:

"Don't you dare let it go, don't you dare!

Why on earth would you keep living and not start planning this? You were not meant for small living.

You were not meant for mediocrity.

*You **know** this life is an adventure. How can you be so afraid? It's okay to be afraid—but have **courage!***

*Be afraid and **leap anyway.***

LEAP ANYWAY.

It always works out, always. Just as you start to think about it all again, there she is—Karen.

She did it, and with no money. Who says it won't work? When has it never worked?

Forget fear and just believe.

You must believe, Jill.

You must fight for your dreams.

Never give up.

You know it.

You know it is supposed to happen.

You know it.

God have mercy on me. Let me fly."

The next couple years Karen and I became close friends, along with a few other souls who had lived a version of the life I so passionately craved. These people became my heroes, encouraging me in times when my fear became so loud that it seemed only logical to back out. But they were always there, holding out a supportive hand when I was ready to come back again. They knew—they had all been there. And now here I am, in Australia, staying with Karen's family...all from a chance encounter just two short years ago.

~

Steve whips around quickly to look at me.

"All right then," he says in his thick Australian accent. "You have to go first. These quads are loud and they can hear us before we see them, and you riding behind me means you're missing out on all the action."

"Okay." I grip my handles.

"Now you've got to go fast, and don't hesitate. Just *go!*"

"Okay, no worrieeeeeeeees!" I squeal as my thumb presses heavily against the accelerator and my quad jolts forward. In an instant, the two of us are speeding along, plowing through thick fields of overgrown grass and brush.

It doesn't take long to see her. Her black head pops up over the tall grass, her ears perked into tips on the top of her head. Within seconds she's up on her feet, bouncing alongside me and then up in front of me on the path in a zigzag motion, her large tail flopping around like a helicopter behind her. And just like that, just as fast as I see her, she's gone again into the thick brush on the side of the trail.

I stop and throw my hands triumphantly into the air— my first wallaby. Wallabies are like the kangaroo's little sister—slightly smaller, and in this area of the country they are black—but other than a few slight differences, they are just like kangaroos.

Steve and I spend hours racing the hillsides of his parents' farm just a couple hours outside of Melbourne and only steps away from the Tarra-Bulga National Park with trees over a thousand years old. We see almost ten wallabies today, with heads bobbing and tails swinging, bouncing around the hillside as we race through with our quads—essentially scaring the shit out of them. Not nice, I know, but thrilling all the same.

And the air? Oh, the air up here is pure oxygen and pine needles. It hits me from the moment I open my car door, and I rave about it continually until I leave.

We spend the evening with Steve and his family at their farm, sharing a couple bottles of wine and my first home-cooked meal in four months. It's tradition for them to get together on Saturday night and enjoy good food and each other's friendship. Without hesitating, they take me in and treat me as one of their own. The whole ten days I spend in Melbourne end up like this, strangers and "friends of friends" taking me in and taking me out.

My next couple days in Melbourne, one of Australia's largest southern cities, are pretty quiet at Steve's suburban home. I sleep a lot and try to get used to being pushed another four hours ahead in time, making me now sixteen hours ahead of my initial time zone in America.

I wander the streets of Melbourne and try, somewhat miserably, to acclimate my body to the cooler weather. I had become quite comfortable in the balmy ninety-degree weather in Asia, and Melbourne is apparently having an odd cold streak of a crisp sixty degrees. Since it is the beginning of summer here, most heating systems have been shut down for the season, being replaced with an inescapably icy air-conditioning. Not owning a pair of jeans, or socks for that matter, I'm freezing.

I also continually rub my eyes in shock as I take in the prices in my new country of residence for the time being. Generally speaking, the price tags of most things here are at least *double* those in America. I have to get a job and fast.

Melbourne is a beautiful city (pronounced "Mel-bin") resembling an intriguing melting pot of, in my opinion, San Diego fused with a pinch of Europe. How could you not love that? With a population of a little over four million, it's quite large, full of high-rises and skyscrapers and hugging the waters of Port Phillip with the large Yarra River cutting through its center. There are trams and palm trees, beaches and yachts. Melbourne's tree-lined streets are often "quiet" compared to New York City and Chicago, especially because the millions of people here are much more sprawled out.

Wandering the heavily European-influenced streets, I discover countless alleys with city-supported graffiti artwork. Where there is no graffiti, quiet and aesthetically tasteful pathways are tucked between city streets packed with chic cafés and restaurants, succulent bakeries, and swanky shops. The pathways are so small that there are no cars or bikes, only the foot traffic of Australians slowly strolling by with no apparent agenda whatsoever.

I've searched for streets like this in every city I've been to on this trip. They are cozy and comfortable, void of car motors and honking, and I love them. I take pleasure in telling you that so far, very few cities top Melbourne when it comes to this lovely attraction. This city is where trendiness meets culture meets charm. It's no wonder I've never heard a bad thing about it. Melbourne seems to leave its people like its cafés and pubs…warm and happy.

∾

After a week of sleeping in and wandering, Friday night comes around once more, and Steve has arranged a fun-filled and somewhat unorganized bar crawl through the pub scene of Melbourne. True to Australian fashion, we start as soon as Steve walks out the double doors of his work. Some of his coworkers join us along with Leah, Steve's friend who has kindly opened her home and given me her guest bed for my last four nights, as Steve thought it'd be nice for me to stay with someone who lives a little closer to the city.

We spend the next nine hours combing the streets of Melbourne, encountering a little bit of everything from the sports bar to the Irish pub, the tourist trap, the trendy lounge, and the trendier lounge. Because this is Australia and full of "manly men," and because Steve is the only man sporting four chicks by his side, we skip the lines entirely and just walk in to most places. Can't help but love that.

My last days in Melbourne prove to be just as entertaining. Leah is also hosting another group of travelers from Adelaide whom she is friends with, so we spend a good deal of time in her home hanging out in her outdoor living room, drinking beers, and listening to music. No matter what time of the day it is, there is always someone to sit back and talk to. It is such a personal and cozy "hostel," only because it is not a hostel at all but a generous and warm introduction to Australia's people.

~

I would never consider myself to be a "needy" person (I do believe others have referred to me as "stubbornly independent"), but landing on the shores of southeastern Australia ten days ago, I was definitely in a different state. Never in my days of dreaming and planning for this journey could I have imagined how sorry of a state I'd be in, but sorry I was.

Besides being repeatedly sick, sleep-deprived, robbed, and possibly malnourished, I was tired, broke, and had been stripped of the means to fully take care of myself—sans credit card. My spirits had slightly fallen, but because of a couple dear friends from Chicago and because of *Australia*, it doesn't take long to begin feeling like myself again.

I stay at four different homes in Melbourne, all friends or family of Steve and Karen, each time walking through open doors exclaiming, "Thank you so much for taking me in!" and I am always met with, "Ah, please! No worries! We love having visitors." Australia essentially is like a big brother to me, taking me in without a second's hesitation, wrapping its arms around me and making sure I'm okay.

Melbourne, being my first official introduction to Australia, has been like its cool mountain air—incredibly refreshing. I feel as if I can breathe again, relax into my surroundings, and figure out my next steps.

I am now headed to the slightly larger, much busier, and hopefully warmer Sydney. Christmas is quickly approaching, as well as New Year's. I'm not loving being so far from home this holiday, but at least out of all the places in the world that I could be, I'm in a place as warm and welcoming as Australia.

It's good to finally be here. It's nice to finally meet you, Australia.

Chicago, Illinois

Late at night, when my exhaustion has kicked in, I sometimes find much of my optimism, along with my energy, has been sucked dry for the day. Worried, I search the Internet once more for some sort of encouragement that will appease my fears of the risks I'm about to take.

Most of the time as of late, I am searching for reassurance that I won't move to Australia and find a reality so much different than the one I have been dreaming of. **What if?** *thoughts plague my consciousness, particularly worries concerning the job market. And most of the time as of late, I am met with a somewhat disturbing message.*

Apparently I'm not the only worried one, as most online boards are filled with those already in Australia...and without jobs. The basic mess of words greeting me on my computer screen is comprised of the same repeated message, "It's hard everywhere..."

I've never been too big on the "taking risks" aspect of life. I never tried out for sports or plays. I almost went to college to study graphic design but found out it was very competitive, so I went for "safe" dental hygiene. I attended a community college instead of a university not because I wanted to, but because it was financially smart.

After graduating, I almost did "travel hygiene" to make a lot of money but went for Chicago instead—where I was close to home and my source of income was stable (still scary, but I moved with a job and a home lined up).

Of course now I am reaping the benefits of my choices. Most of my non risk-taking has made my life better, but I've never taken too many risks so I don't know. Risks in general are not considered smart, but some risks, when you are following your gut, are brilliant.

"It's hard everywhere…"

I leave soon. I'm giving up my life, my job, my home—and this is what supposedly lies ahead for me. My brain is screaming at me about my lack of judgment with this decision. The whole point of this trip was to live what some call "The Australian Dream" and also what others are saying…is dead.

Could all this be for nothing? Will I leave everything behind only to find a black void on the other side? I suppose it's a possibility. I bet there are people who give it all up to find their yellow brick road is nothing but an illusion. Only then will I be able to come home and rest easy knowing that I went, and I saw.

The thing is, I can't turn back now. What was all the fuss about then? Why have all the dreams and poems and conviction only to turn away now just because it's getting a little scary? Isn't this what "risk" entails anyway? What is bravery without some fear and sacrifice?

Once again, this is part of the deal. I keep searching the Internet for someone to say, "**Here**, here is your answer! I can guarantee you a job for six months that will allow you to live in Sydney AND save for another six months backpacking Australia. Congratulations!"

But that doesn't exist. This is the risk I am taking. This is my once-in-a-lifetime trip. I can go and see and stay or not *stay or go somewhere else or not go somewhere else. I can do whatever I want.*

The thing about life is it keeps moving forward: I'll eventually make a home, and hopefully fall in love and have a family. I want those things, but those things are also a "no looking back" investment. Once those things happen, I can no longer drop everything and move across the world. This is my chance. All I can say now is I am taking that chance and hoping with all that I am that it's worth it.

As I write these words, I can't help but smile. How can it not be worth it? I am going! I am moving to Australia. Maybe it'll accept me, maybe it won't. But even being out there a month, and knowing for the rest of my life that I went and I gave it my all, will be worth every sacrifice, every penny. So here I am, and there I'll be.

Cross my fingers, pray to God, there I'll be.

Sydney, Australia

I KNOW WHAT YOU'RE THINKING—we only just met, what do I know? I know, I know. I'd think the same things, the same quiet, judgmental thoughts. Thoughts like, "They can't really be in love, they need more time." Or "They just met. She must be infatuated. It's just lust based on surface things like good looks. How could she possibly be in love?" I know, I know.

I kind of had a gut feeling I'd like it here, but I didn't always feel this way. No, initially I wanted to skip right past Sydney and find a small town, get an easy job, and be a beach bum. But all the signs and people and whispers pointed me here, the same way they pointed to Chicago when all I wanted was New York City.

I had a feeling I'd like it here, but I was wrong.

Love. I love it here.

Why? Well, why do you love the sun? Why do you love good food, beautiful beaches, and amazing scenery? Why do you love swank and sophisticated restaurants with charismatic company? How about fascinating culture and new experiences? Add these loves together, and you've found my love for Sydney.

You see, we're in love, Sydney and I. Well, okay so it's a little one-sided; *I'm* in love with Sydney, and I knew it instantly. It wasn't any one thing in particular, but a feeling—a feeling I haven't felt since I moved to Chicago over three years ago. I knew, just like I know now. I'm in love with Sydney, and I'm staying...if only she'll have me.

~

I arrive in Sydney late Monday night. *Ugh, another hostel.* God, I am *so sick* of hostels. As I wait impatiently in line to check into my room, drunk teenagers with dreadlocks chase each other out of the building. I was so spoiled through almost the whole of Southeast Asia, staying at guesthouses and having my own private room with only *one person.*

Despite having an offer from Jess to stay with her aunt and uncle just outside Sydney, I book a hostel anyway for a couple nights in the city to get my bearings and take care of a few obligations. I have to find a job...like, *yesterday.* "It's okay," I say confidently to myself. "I can move to a new city of millions of people! I've done this before! Besides, I love a good challenge."

Ten o'clock Tuesday morning, only twelve hours after landing, and I've already made a few phone calls. My dental CV is ready to go, it's a beautiful day, and I've got a temp agency to go to. I wander into Capital Jobs in the heart of Sydney and meet with Char, a young English woman who is now one of four recruiters for me. She takes a brief glance over my resume, her face blank.

"Where's the rest of it?" She looks at me like I am wasting her time.

"Uh." I clear my throat. "Rest? Rest of...it's the one page. That's it."

She sighs. "Jill, I'm going to be honest with you. I could send this out, but you'll never get a job."

Harsh.

She immediately exits the conference room as I continue to sit, alone and stunned. *Is…is she coming back?* I don't move.

Char then reenters the room with a handful of papers—CV examples. This is my first big culture shock. Forget the laughing birds in the trees, the thick Aussie accent, the giant bats at night, and the schools of jellyfish in the harbor—she wants me to put my *marital status* on my CV! Not only that, but it needs to be three pages and include my hobbies, date of birth, and my nationality.

"Do you also want my shoe size?" I half smile. She looks at me, unimpressed, and hands back my CV, which now appears to be bleeding with red pen marks coating the inadequate, lonely single page.

Char, along with the other three agencies, doesn't recruit dental professionals. Most offices, it appears, do not want to hire and train a dental nurse—dental assistant in America—when she's almost guaranteed to leave within the year. I don't have the proper licensure to be a dental hygienist in Australia and don't have the time nor the finances to put in the effort to test for one. Fair enough. So now I'm a secretary.

"This is no problem," I reassure her. "I'll fix it up (shoe size and all) and have it back to you in twenty-four hours!"

This may be harder than I thought.

Feeling slightly defeated, I start to aimlessly wander around the city. I think what I need now is some fresh air and sunshine.

Sydney is beautiful, Australia's largest city with a population of over four and a half million. The city streets today are alive and well. There is rarely honking, the skyscrapers glitter and shine in the midday sun, and the faint ocean breeze ruffles the leaves of the palm trees above me. It's almost eighty degrees and it's December. It doesn't get any better than this.

I head straight for the harbor. As the trees clear away, I see the Sydney Opera House in all its magnificence. Its sleek curves and brilliantly white exterior radiate against a cloudless sky. I've waited so long for this moment. I'm standing at the harbor in Sydney, Australia, with the Opera House to my right and the Sydney Harbour Bridge to my left. I am finally here! I flip on my sunglasses once again as a mask to cover my tear-filled eyes. What an incredible feeling.

Today is my first date with Sydney! We walk hand in hand in the intense sun while I learn all about the new love of my life. Down by the harbor, a saxophone player is playing Lonestar's "Amazed," and I feel giddy with excitement.

I find a bench along the harbor to relax on and watch an entirely new world unfold before me: sailboats cruise through the harbor as men dressed in traditional Aboriginal gear and face paint entertain the tourists with the authentic bass of their didgeridoos.

As I glance down along the water's edge, something catches my eye. I gasp as my sight focuses on what's just below the surface, a school of jellyfish, maybe fifty or sixty of them. I walk to the dock's edge and stare in wonder as these mysterious multifarious blobs open and close. What a fascinating place this is, with an exciting city environment so much like my home in Chicago, yet worlds different and oceans apart.

On my way home, I stop by another harbor (Sydney has heaps of them alongside an assortment of beaches) and enjoy an ice cream cone and a whole new circus of fun. The birds here are aggressive. More than aggressive, they are *psychotic*. I watch, amused, as giant seagulls swan-dive onto a restaurant's outdoor tables and take the food right off its patrons' plates.

In one swift moment, I watch as a massive seagull swoops in and lands on a table while victim #1 and victim #2 stare in shock and horror. By the time they start to react to shoo him away, one large piece of fried fish has already been confiscated and the bird is in midflight. Victory is all his today.

I watch as this happens to other defenseless tables, snapping photos as armies of birds attack a table when its patrons leave and munch happily on the leftover scraps. Waiters and waitresses run over in annoyance (as they do this all day) to shove the birds off and clear the plates.

Feeling fully powered and reenergized, I kiss Sydney good evening as I retire to a land of computers at my hostel to fix up my CV. Let me rephrase that, to write an entirely new CV.

The next morning, I send out my new and improved, *very personal* "secretarial" CV to a handful of jobs and cross my fingers. It is now only days before Christmas. As it's the holiday season, most Australians are off work, giving me the absolute worst timing ever to find a job. The only thing I can do now is wait.

I pack up at the hostel and move to Jess's family's home, where we spend the next week celebrating the holidays. Each day I send my resume to as many places as I can, even though I know it won't realistically be looked at for weeks.

Mark and Anne, Jess's uncle and aunt, assure me my presence is not a burden and I may take as long as I need to find a job. I always feel a slight discomfort making myself "at home" in someone else's house, but I truly enjoy Mark and Anne's company, laughing daily as Anne rolls her eyes at Mark's dry jokes, and joining Mark every morning for his heaping helping of "porridge." (I am chastised for calling it oatmeal, even though it *is* oatmeal.)

Every afternoon Mark and I sit on the back porch for a beer and salt-and-vinegar potato chips to take in the day and wait for the kookaburras to start their afternoon comedy show. Those birds are my favorite—they sound like they are laughing uncontrollably. The first time I heard them in Melbourne I thought they were monkeys. Steve had a great laugh over this.

Jess's family has given me their spare bedroom for the time being, a coveted room I'm sure, with my own dresser and closet. I haven't hung my clothes or put them in drawers for months. My pack sits open in the corner, airing out its must and rot from months of travel, humidity, and general abuse.

I am almost used to the cockroaches and large spiders now, the accent is becoming easier to understand, and the best part of all is that I am becoming one of the crew with a whole new family of friends I've met through some of Jess's friends. Jess is gone most days, setting up her own Australian life again, as she is returning from living in China for eleven years, so at the very least, I am grateful for the companionship despite her absence.

Unfortunately, my deep exhaustion from Asia remains like a pesky hangover. I sit with the family Christmas morning, smiling as I watch them open gifts and deeply missing my friends and family. Jess was kind enough to buy me a couple things, although I feel guilty as I unwrap them because I've been too broke to buy her anything in return.

I'm always broke. I'm pushing the limits spending time with people here who are not backpackers but *real people* with *real* jobs, good jobs—Fendi-purse and Gucci-watch jobs. As if Australia isn't expensive enough. I look for serving jobs despite having an overall disdain for the career, but even those are completely booked by backpackers who came here just a little earlier than I did.

Living in the suburbs but spending time with friends in the city leaves me sleeping on couches, living out of my carry-on, and falling asleep on public transportation when I can't find a ride. This isn't exactly the life I had in mind when living here, but it's my only option at this point, as my unemployment dictates my every decision. I can't help but wonder how much it would change on a server's salary…

All I can do is wait and see what happens. Until then, my adventure continues as I learn to find my way in Sydney… if only she'll have me.

Sydney

Part II

ALMOST A MONTH HAS PASSED since my euphoric first date with Sydney, and I wish I could say I've received a single phone call or interview for a job...but this is not the case. Every day I am met with unreturned phone calls and an empty inbox.

I ring in the New Year at a lively house party only steps away from the Sydney Harbour Bridge, where I witness one of the world's foremost New Year's celebrations, watched on television by over one billion people worldwide. Its theme this year is "Make your Mark," reflecting on the past ten years and the consequences—good or bad—of our actions, as well as reflecting on how to make a difference in our future. Ironic, considering for me this year has been the culmination of years of hard work and my own set of decisions made, both past and present.

The displays have never-before-seen effects and fireworks that almost cause my heart to skip a beat. The harbor is packed with over a million people from across the globe, all coming together to witness the two displays of fireworks, one at 9:00 p.m. and the other at midnight, with six different launching pads along the coast and fireworks exploding off every inch of the Sydney Harbour Bridge. I stare up into the blazing midnight sky and giggle like a schoolgirl. I've never seen anything like it.

～

Despite the beautiful weather and my exceedingly active social life, I still can't escape the small but persistent gut feeling that my world trip may be coming to a close. I've grown close to this feeling; it's been a soft whisper greeting me daily for months now, growing steadily since the shores of Vietnam. I wasn't ready then—I knew I wasn't ready… but now I'm not so sure.

Through the friends and the parties, I slowly find myself living a life that is not my own. I am becoming a person I do not know, making choices I normally wouldn't make and taking chances I normally wouldn't take. I have grown to love these dear people, but the scene here is not me. It's beautiful and trendy with drugs, alcohol, and money weaving chaotically through every DJ-spinning, martini-sipping, coke-snorting, rooftop after-party. It's a beautiful collage of some epitome of untouchables, a web of everything I've envied from a glass window collection of unattainability… and now that I'm in it, all I can see is the illusion. It is everything I cannot be only because it is everything I'm not.

In this frenzied façade of luxury and nirvana I start to lose myself…blend into the madness, fade into the blackness. All I can do is lay my head down at night and listen to the quiet drumming of my heart repeating the same undeniable truth:

"You have to get out of here. Run. Run as fast as you can. It is time to go home. This is *not you*. Run. Don't become an untouchable."

But this is my trip…my baby. I've been dreaming of this my entire life, and it's over?

Silence.

But wait! Where is my happy ending? I'm going home? This isn't how I thought this would end…this isn't how this should end.

I know it's right, this guardian of a gut feeling, but I'm not ready to listen. I'm so afraid. What if I'm making a huge mistake? What if I show up in America and realize I should have stayed? I won't be able to come back—I won't have the money—and I'll be relinquishing my once-in-a-lifetime working visa.

I could always move to another town in Australia, try again to find the life I came here for, but the thought of packing up again and starting over is more than I can handle. If I leave now, then this is over, and if I'm wrong, I will regret this *for the rest of my life.* And regret I will, according to almost every person I speak to. Generally with a shake of the head and a disapproving tone, I'm told I will be making a *huge* mistake.

I don't know what to do. How do you know when to hold on and fight…and when to let go?

Things have changed…I have changed. I'm not exactly sure how yet in this very moment, but I can feel it. Something has shifted, like the turn of a page in a book, landing me in an entirely new and foreign chapter. I *have* to trust myself and listen to my inner voice, the same voice that refused to give up when reminding me of this trip in the first place, but my fear of regret is so powerful that it trumps any logic that may challenge it. And to appease my fear—I let it.

"Let go, Jillian, and forgive yourself of the notion that you are 'giving up.' Quite the contrary—you have conquered. And it's time to go home."

I'm not ready to let go. I can't let go...

I stare up at the ceiling as my sadness lies in streams on either side of my face.

Oh God, what do I do?

I wait for an answer, but the ceiling only stares back at me.

"All changes, even the most longed for, have their melancholy, for what we leave behind us is a part of ourselves; we must die to one life before we can enter into another."

—Anatole France

Sydney

Part III

I'm having a bad day.

The bus pulls up to my stop, and the driver nods to me that this is where I get off.

"Thank you," I mumble with an indifferent smile.

"Ah, no worries," he replies, and I step off the bus platform as raindrops splatter against my skin.

Just like a scene in an old black-and-white movie, I humbly walk the empty street in the pouring rain, too tired to care. I have accepted now the constant thought that weighs heavier on my mind with each passing day.

I am ready.

I've been ready.

I don't want to walk another foreign street alone, pack my bags just to unpack them again, ride another train, or have dinner with strangers anymore.

I know these past months I've been behaving like a free spirit, taking risks and flying uninhibited around the world. Free spirits possess a passion and a lust for adventure in a way most don't, but it comes at a cost. It can be a little lonely and exhausting. It's amazing and heartbreaking. Each day a certain effort is required. Comfort isn't part of the vocabulary. This isn't necessarily a bad thing, for it allows you to live for once with eyes wide open. But it's an effort.

And I don't want to do it anymore.

Other free spirits bow their heads in shame. "And here we thought you were one of us."

But I'm not. I never was. I didn't do this because I was fearless; I did this in spite of my fear. I mustered up all the courage and strength I had to live this life despite the fact that it left me shaking in fear. Why?

Passion.

Love.

Wanderlust.

Because I *had* to go. I *had* to see. I had to see what would happen when I faced the world on my own, with everything I own on my back and endless possibilities in front of me. I did whatever I wanted, went where I desired to go, when I wanted to go. No obligations, no rules. I had to see what would happen, and now I believe I've accomplished what I left home to see.

I know in my ecstasy I've fallen hard for Sydney, and I wouldn't for a second have believed you a month ago if you would have told me it wouldn't last. I think I love Sydney for all the ways it reminds me of Chicago and all the ways it is so incredibly different.

But it's not Chicago, not at all, and it didn't take long for me to realize that the spark it created wasn't a love for Sydney so much as a longing for home.

Some people's journeys take them far from home while others never leave the confines of their living room. Some last years and others last only months. Neither is above the other nor more grand.

The truth is we all struggle—we all have fears and some dreams to conquer too. I went about mine all at once with a fever and passion that couldn't be denied. Living this dream, traveling and living as a nomad alone in this world is a sacred gift I've given myself, and one I'll carry with me for the rest of my life.

I've ridden camels in the desert, climbed the stairs of the Eiffel Tower, watched the sun rise in Vietnam, and walked the silent graves of Auschwitz. I've been through this massive journey, a few wars and a few more celebrations—what a dream come true! What an immense, intense, amazing, life-changing, eye-opening, sacred voyage through lands and time and people's lives I'd never hold with my own had I never left.

This journey has changed me to my core. What if I would have let fear guide me? What if I had never left? I can't imagine. I can't imagine never having lived this life! I can't believe how close I came to letting this go.

But I didn't.

In fear and insecurity and pain I held on. And I have conquered. I surrendered to my destiny, and I have conquered the world. There are no regrets.

To live life with no regrets, that seems like true freedom to me. To survive this life through facing fears and breaking your barriers is the liberty that angels sing about. It's not easy or a short-lived endeavor to come to this summit, but to have arrived brings tears to my eyes. And isn't that truly living, as Albert Camus says, "To live to the point of tears?"

The decision to leave Sydney hasn't been an easy one. Day in and day out, I've written lists and made phone calls, all the while searching desperately for the "right" answer. I have been so afraid of making the wrong decision, never for a moment realizing that *to ignore your heart is a decision.* And I'm not going to do it anymore.

I don't know if I'll turn around one day and regret leaving Australia. I only know that in this moment, this is the best decision I can make in the name of being true to myself. I thought this would be a place where I belonged...I thought this was my happy ending, but I was wrong. So there's nothing left to do but keep moving.

My adventure is far from over. I'm giving myself another month in Australia to travel up the coast. I still have a couple more dreams to check off my list. I haven't bought my ticket home yet. I want to be able to change my mind if I so choose...because that is what this trip is all about.

And change my mind I just did. I am no longer traveling up Australia's east coast. A portion of the beautiful Sunshine Coast is tragically covered in water and in a state of emergency. I could skip that part and go farther north, but I've decided to mix things up a little more, add a little more adventure to my adventure. I'm going to Western Australia.

I'm not sure exactly when it hit me, my absolute readiness to return home. I guess it is the quiet, steady knowing that continues to grow stronger with each passing day. And I guess I'm still not sure—anything can happen. God only knows and only time will tell, but home sweet home, I may see you soon after all.

Sydney

Part IV

THE KOOKABURRAS have woken me up—again. It's five in the morning, the sun is just starting to *think* about rising, and those damn birds outside my window continue their chorus of hysterical laughter. Unfortunately, on the east coast of Australia, they are the only ones laughing. The country, along with its people, seems to be hysterically weeping, and much to its own demise.

Oh, I think of the years I spent sitting on my bed in the middle of the night, dreaming of Australia. I imagined befriending its smiling people with their "no worries" attitude as I traveled up the east coast. I imagined Australia and all it could be...only to arrive years later for some of its darkest days.

I sit with Jess's family in front of the television, watching the increasingly devastating situation in front of us: tsunami-like flash floods, water seventy feet above normal, cars being swept away in rapid succession, hopeless tear-stained faces. This—this is not the Australia I imagined.

I can't sleep now. Damn birds. I wander down to the living room and flip on the news. The flood crisis in Queensland is getting worse by the hour. The rain won't stop, despite the millions of prayers begging for its mercy. The death toll is rising, along with the number of missing loved ones. The last confirmed dead? A four-year-old. My eyes well in tears as the screen flashes footage of the damage, people waiting, stranded on their rooftops, a man holding on to a tree branch for dear life as the water surges around him.

A lump forms in my throat as the camera pauses on a street sign almost completely covered in water. The name "Ballina" is printed across it.

Ballina…Ballina…*how do I know that town?*

And then I remember. Before I arrived in Sydney I had been looking at Greyhound tickets to Ballina. It's close to Byron Bay, next to the Gold Coast…all cities I had planned on going to had I not fallen for Sydney—cities now covered in water. I was going to try to live in one of those areas, focusing primarily on Brisbane, and find a job.

I was supposed to be there.

I was a little confused—embarrassed even—about my sudden "switch" of not wanting to stay in Australia any longer and go home. Now I realize my love for Sydney may have lasted just long enough…to keep me *here*.

I have a somewhat damaged relationship with water; I love it and loathe it at the same time. A bad experience as a young teen left a deep fear ingrained in me when it comes to water and its currents.

Caught in a rip current, I was pulled out into Lake Michigan, screaming for help and desperate for oxygen as waves relentlessly pounded into me. The angry water battered my body, suffocating me as it pushed me beneath the choppy surface and pulled me farther from shore. For a moment, I considered stopping kicking—to get it over with, as I was sure I was going to die.

Turning toward the lake, I only saw more waves many, many feet above my head, barreling toward me. Filled with dread, I whispered out loud, "Oh Lord, please help me." With that prayer into the heavens and a couple side-strokes, I managed to reach the rocks alongside the pier, the destination I had been struggling to get to from the moment I realized I was in trouble. Numerous bystanders who had unsuccessfully tried forming a human chain out to me rushed to my side to help me onto the cement.

A sidestroke is a known lifesaving mechanism to help escape a rip current. I didn't know this. It was years before I found this out. I only knew to pray. Despite all I've been through with organized religion, despite all the times I wanted to believe in nothing at all, this life-changing event saves me over and over again. I will never forget what happened that day. Never.

Along with strengthening my faith, however, this experience also instilled a deep fear within my heart when it comes to water. I have no issue swimming in a body of water, but if there are any waves, I'll forgo the splendor of the ocean and retreat to dry land. A small sacrifice for the life I continue to live.

∼

The possibilities of "could have beens" are endless when it comes to the fact that had I not temporarily fallen for Sydney, I would surely have been in the flood zone. Maybe I would have been lucky enough not to be among the growing number of missing loved ones, but I would surely have been in the war zone with an element as simple yet as atrociously destructive as water—an element now stealing lives as quickly as the ground beneath their feet.

It would have been one of my worst fears realized.

Oh, I thank God for Sydney. I thank God for Sydney and all the ways it has captured my heart, and then its kindness in letting me go.

I know there is tragedy the whole world over, and traveling it only pulls out every ounce of compassion and awareness I'll have. I've always known Australia is a diverse country with danger in every corner when it comes to its natural resources. Bush fires rage to the west of me, floods devastate the north, and yesterday eight hundred people went to the hospital as hordes of bluebottle jellyfish swarmed the shoreline.

The people in Queensland are hanging on to all the courage and hope they have. They aren't exactly immune to natural disasters, but this doesn't make experiencing them come any easier. I whisper another prayer for the souls in Queensland and then add another for myself, thanking God for life. I know it's easy to forget—I sure do, all the time—but *love, life,* and *health*…with those three things we are the luckiest, richest souls alive. It's simple really, but so easy to forget.

I could have easily been there, in that disaster zone just up the coast…I almost bought the ticket. It's cloudy here in Sydney, and I miss home more than ever, but I'm not complaining. I'm alive, I'm safe, and I'm loved. I am the luckiest girl in the world.

Southwestern Australia

Augusta, Albany, and Esperance

I'M SPEECHLESS. My eyes are wide and disbelieving, scanning the world before me as five hundred thousand years of stalactite and stalagmite crystals glimmer and wink back at me.

Cathedral-like ceilings tower above me as hundreds of thousands of years of hardened crystals point in different directions. Many hang like frozen icicles along the top of the cave, while others look as if they have frozen mid-drip along the walls. Some formations extend from the ceiling to the floor, reminding me of the passage of time. It takes a stalactite one hundred years to grow one centimeter. *One* centimeter in one hundred years. This place is ancient. I am in Yallingup, at the Ngilgi Cave in Western Australia.

Astounded, I slowly make my way deeper and deeper into this incredibly ancient cave, craning my neck in every direction as I take in the sights before me. My breath becomes short and rapid as carbon dioxide makes its presence known, and I remember that this is a normal occurrence 110 feet underground.

We spend the next fascinating hour descending into the cave, climbing down 350 steps as the path curves around steep bends and low-hanging ceilings. The temperature is a cool and constant sixty degrees with one hundred percent humidity. Pictures are practically worthless in comparison to what lies before us. It's spectacular down here.

I didn't even know we were going to a cave today. Being nauseatingly sick of figuring out how to get to the next destination, where to stay, what to see, and how to see it, I booked two separate six-day tours that take me south and then north of Perth, highlighting all the must-sees of Western Australia. I didn't and still don't know much, if anything, about where we are going, which makes my first tour that much more unpredictable.

After spending a relaxing and mostly quiet nine days on the ocean in a peaceful little suburb of Perth, I book my tours with a company called Western Xposure. We begin in Perth, then travel 450 miles along the southwestern coast of Australia, ending in Esperance before turning around and making the trip back.

There are twenty-four of us on this bus, representing Switzerland, France, Belgium, the United States, England, Italy, Thailand, the Netherlands, and a large group of people from Germany. We are led by Chris, an enthusiastic, bubbly, and incredibly knowledgeable Australian woman.

Western Australia spans a third of this immense country, with a population of 2.2 million. Perth is the largest city, claiming over 1.6 million residents. Basically, it's all empty space and nature here on the west coast, practically untouched by tourism compared to the packed and glitzy east coast. I like both coasts, but am happy for the quiet change of scenery.

Our first stop of the tour is at an area called The Gap, made up of towering granite cliffs with crashing waves below. It is the actual site where sixty million years ago, Antarctica was attached to Australia. The rock here has been tested and perfectly matched to the rock at Windmill Islands in Antarctica. In fact, Australia continues to float five centimeters away every year.

In Hyden, a sleepy outback town 250 miles from the coast, there is an ancient rock formation in the shape of a large, forty-five-foot-tall wave dating back 2.7 billion years. Two hundred and fifty miles is nothing in the vast country of Australia, so of course we make the trek out there.

In our cold, air-conditioned bus, I have a feeling that the weather conditions outside are rapidly changing, as we leave the coast and the scenery transitions from green and lush to brown and mostly empty. I watch tumbleweeds and snakes indecisively cross the desolate country road we now travel and notice that the only remarkable attribute of this landscape may possibly be its vacancy and desolation. I attempt a nap, but the window I try to lean against feels like a hot metal plate.

None of these factors though could have possibly prepared me for the 115-degree body slam I receive as soon as I walk outside. It feels like I've stepped into a furnace. The heat wraps and suffocates my body as blistering hot air blows against my skin. Sweat instantly fills my pores and drips off my skin, and I am immediately exhausted.

But before I even have a moment to acclimate to the heat, my hands rush to protect my face as an onslaught of flies smack into me. Australians have a hand gesture they call the Australian Wave, which looks like an overly enthusiastic, slightly hysteric wave of both hands moving in all directions in front of their faces. As friendly as Australians are, I have quickly learned they are *not* waving at me. It is a miserable and desperate attempt to get the copious amounts of flies off their faces and out of their nostrils and mouths. To say the flies are attracted to your body's mucus is an understatement. From the moment you step outside, these intrusive bugs are a constant nuisance. I think it could drive a person mad. Chris, our guide, was born and raised in the bush and claims to have had flies crawl up her nose, get stuck in her sinus cavities, and eventually come out her mouth. Welcome to Australia's outback.

After spending ten minutes at Wave Rock (which feels like nine minutes too long in this heat), we head to the picnic area to eat. As people are finishing their lunch, Chris and I decide to take advantage of the time and go hunting. I've told Chris about my intense fascination and fear of spiders and that I haven't seen anything too exciting or dangerous in my six weeks here, so we decide to take matters into our own hands. We go searching for redbacks.

The redback spider is one of Australia's most venomous spiders. They are black and relatively small in size, with one distinctive, vertical red stripe down the center of their bodies—much like the black widow spider, which is part of the same family. Chris and I have hunted for them before but with no luck. We figure out here in the bush, conditions may be more ideal. We are right.

Redbacks are pretty nonaggressive and love to nest under wooden ledges in dark corners. Along with learning to count and tie their shoes, Australian children learn the basics of the multitude of dangerous and lethal creatures their country houses and most importantly, how not to put their fingers under any ledge of any sort—especially trash can lids—which is where we find our little family of creepy creatures.

I spot the first—a large mother redback protecting her egg sack—underneath one of the park's trash cans between the wooden slats of the trash housing. Her fire-engine-red stripe comes into focus. "I found one!" I jump up and down. Before long we find a second redback in the opposite corner of the trash housing, protecting her own large egg sack. Just what Australia needs, more dangerous spiders.

Heading away from the outback and back to the coast, we happily sing along to the Beatles as the terrain changes into a variety of forests, valleys, and mountains. Chris stops the bus so we can pile out with our cameras in hand to run to the fields and see flocks of emus and mobs of kangaroos bathing in the sun.

As I creep up, my foot snaps a fallen branch, causing a multitude of the kangaroos' goofy tan heads to pop up from the tall grass. *Hop, hop, hop!* Feet together and tails swirling behind, a dozen or so kangaroos seek shelter in the dense forest ahead. They stop near the trees' edge to check us out as much as we do them, and we watch as a little joey's head peeks out from his mother's pouch to see what all the fuss is about. We stop suddenly in our paths approaching the large, muscular creatures, as there is for certain at least one mother in the group and a kangaroo's kick can kill you instantly.

We spend another afternoon at a national park known as the Valley of the Giants with the famous red tingle tree that grows only in Australia. The enormous trees that grace this park by the hundreds have circumferences of up to seventy-eight feet and tower at about 250 feet tall, with an average age of about four hundred years. Some trees are hauntingly hollowed out, eaten from the inside by a fungus, then destroyed by ants and ravaged by fire, making the trees appear to be standing on a tripod of trunks.

One tree in particular, known as the Bicentennial Tree, stands at about 250 feet—and you can climb it. Now, I don't have any plans to climb it or not; I figure I'll show up and figure it out. As I approach the majestic giant, I think to myself, *why not?*

The "ladder" is nothing but a series of metal poles stuck unevenly in the tree's side, wrapping around the trunk all the way to the top. About seventy-five feet up is a small wooden platform, and then four more another two hundred feet up. At about twenty-five feet, I start to panic. It's slightly misty out, coating the metal bars with a slippery condensation, and there is no safety harness. If you slip, you will fall through the bars and depending on how far you've climbed, possibly plunge to your death. This of course enters my mind early on and doesn't leave. One rung at a time, I death-grip the cold, wet metal and baby-step up the towering giant.

As my anxiety builds and my heart starts to race, I resort to a coping mechanism to take my mind off the fact that our twenty-three-foot bus looks more like a micro-mini machine from up here: I count in French. I clutch the next rung, "*Un, deux, trois…*" pulling my foot up and pushing myself up to the next step. My hands shake and white-knuckle the next bar. "*Quatre, cinq, six,*" and up and up I go, counting all the way.

As I reach the top, shaking and sweating from the angst, I pull myself onto the fourth and final platform and am met with cheers and clapping from the handful of others who tempted this fate and climbed the monstrous tree. And the view from the top? Oh, the view.

This isn't the only time I push myself on this "adventure tour." The next day we drive to the Stirling Range to climb to the top of the almost 3,600-foot mountain known as Bluff Knoll. It's almost a two-mile hike each way, all up steep, slanted, granite steps...nonstop, for two miles—in flip-flops. The last time I worked this hard was for my half marathon over two years ago. My legs begin to quiver, sweat is dripping down my temples and back, and I run out of water only about a quarter of the way through, but at the top? Oh, the view.

I think Australia must've been God's playground when the world was created. As we relax at the top of the mountain, I lean over to take a photo of the everlasting flower, which looks and feels like it is made of paper and is known to retain its color and shape an unusually long time even after being picked, all the while laughing as our guide informs us not to touch the black, flesh-eating snails.

"You have *flesh-eating* snails?" I ask.

"Uh-huh!" replies our spirited leader with a smile.

I smile back. "Of course you do."

And do you think coming down the mountain was any easier? Not for a second. I tumbled and stubbed my toes and slipped and slowly moved my wobbly and weak legs little by little down the incredibly steep mountain.

I think often of a young woman I met in Thailand and her intriguing tattoo, "I did it for the view." I'm absolutely miserable during the last hour of my hike, but I did it for the view.

I had always planned on staying on the east coast of Australia, as most do, and only because of a tragic string of events am I here. I would have been on the main tourist trail, with skyscrapers and packed hostels. Now, my skyscraper is a red tingle tree, my hostels small and welcoming, and my days a refreshing exploration I could have never imagined.

Sitting on this bus, looking out at the mostly empty scenery around me, and living this unconventional and uncommon adventure, I couldn't be happier that my life's path has led me here. I needed this break. I needed to remember what it was like to *travel*, and do it mostly on my terms. And now when I look back, I'll remember the *real* Australia, and know that at the end of it all…I did it for the view.

Perth, Australia

*I bought my ticket home. Three weeks from now I will be home. I can't help but wonder if I've failed myself somehow… like if I would have done something different, then things would be different, that maybe somewhere along the line I may have made a mistake. This was my destiny. I was sure of it. I was supposed to find my life, my love…a place where I belong. Despite loving my home, I didn't really think I'd go back. That was the whole point: in leaving I was supposed to **find** something.*

The only thing now that gives me strength to continue is my faith in my intuition. My gut is telling me it's time. There is no other logic to follow. Once more, I have to listen despite not understanding why. What will happen now because of that, I don't even pretend to know.

Never could I have imagined actually ending my trip after six months, but maybe for that belief alone I can be grateful, as it gave me the strength to sacrifice all I had, to go.

Maybe this short time was all I needed to live this life, in my stars it was written all along…it just wasn't for me to know until now. The Buddha once said, "When you realize how perfect everything is, you will tilt your head back and laugh at the sky." I think of this often in my life now as I still struggle to realize I'll never have all the answers. We are never meant to know all the answers. We make our discoveries throughout the journey, and maybe, if we're lucky, we'll recognize that the answers can only be found when we are living our truth.

I have changed, and my priorities have changed—something I didn't realize until now. I have learned a great lesson: love is all that matters. Love.

*Despite being surrounded by people, I'm lonely. I've been lonely. I don't care where I am anymore—a bar is a bar, a beach is a beach—the only thing that matters is who's sitting next to me. I know most may know this by now, but my fierce independence has forced me to live my life with a wall up, never getting too close to anyone who would tie me down. That wall has been shattered by a life with **no one** to tie me down. Maybe a little bit of stability isn't so bad after all.*

Love is all that matters. So while I left the shores of America to find it, so shall I return.

Northwest Australia

Perth to Monkey Mia

I T SMELLS LIKE A NURSING HOME IN HERE—a nursing home combined with hints of old beer and musty feet. I am so uncomfortable.

This must be the unofficial meeting place for Perth's failed AA members. Sloppy, unappealing souls slouch along the building's concrete steps, drinking goon (Australia's term for cheap wine) as wafts of body odor and cigarettes slither through the double doors and fill the hallways.

A greasy little man with yesterday's beard and an unfortunate attempt at a rat tail welcomes me, assuring me of the building's high quality by enthusiastically informing me that in the next hallway, there is indeed a working Coke machine. I smile uncomfortably and try not to make eye contact.

Following the dingy, stained carpeting in the low-lit hallway on the ninth floor, I head straight for my sleeping quarters to lock myself in. I open the door into my shoebox of a room and am greeted with the heat and humidity of a sauna. The one rickety fan in the corner coughs and spits out hot air randomly in a mockery of my misery.

This wasn't supposed to happen. I'm not supposed to be here. I had a hostel booked in a trendy area of town for three somewhat peaceful nights before the northern part of my Western Australia tour begins. Instead, I'm at Perth's YMCA, the only place that could get me in on such short notice, and the only place I've ever seen that has the creepiness factor of *The Shining*.

~

Two hours earlier...

I walk in the breezy, air-conditioned glass doors of The Emperor's Crown hostel in Perth, exhausted from my tour and incredibly grateful for the next somewhat lazy three days of relaxing and sleeping in.

"Hmmmm, Jillian Webster...Jill-ian...Webbbb...ster... I'm not seeing you in our system."

Oh God, I'm having flashbacks to Italy.

Several heavy sighs and several hundred clicks of the computer mouse later, the jury is in: despite my reservation number and having already paid them, somebody forgot to book me into the computer, and they are full.

Just like that, my three days of sleep and comfort disappear.

I stand at the counter, unfazed. This is their problem, not mine. Multiple workers scramble at the phones, calling an array of already-booked establishments to find me a bed for the next three nights, and they finally end the overly drawn-out process with a phone call to the YMCA. *Of course* they can get me in; cockroaches won't even sleep there.

Now, *now* it's my problem.

Six o'clock the next morning, I lie awake and overheated in bed, desperately trying to sleep. The intense rays of the sun flood my room and lie across me, convincing me fully that *I am in hell*. The pre-trip and younger Jillian would have just accepted this predicament, not wanting to create any tension. That Jillian is long gone.

Enraged and indignant, I call my original hostel and ask to speak to the manager. I lay out my case, spelling out my disappointment and anger with the situation I'm stuck in because of their shortcomings. With a couple rebuttals and opposing arguments back, a couple elevated octaves of my voice, and a stomp of my foot, I still have to stay at the YMCA. But that wasn't the goal. The goal was to book my last night in Perth with the hostel after returning from my second tour, and to compensate for my misery, for it to be free of charge. Fish fish, I got my wish. Victory prevails.

Unfortunately, my victory dance is cut short as I turn on my television and am met with a series of concerned reports about the level-three Cyclone Bianca quickly approaching the city. Oh, a cyclone? Lovely.

Now I'm really worked up. I can't die in this shithole, I just can't. I meet up with some friends who are locals, and with their Australian "no worries" attitude, they assure me that everything will be okay. I latch myself to them anyway, which isn't difficult considering what overall lovely people they are, and spend the remaining weekend with them.

I only spend one night at the YMCA. It basically ends up being a really expensive "closet" for me to store my things. And the cyclone? It disappeared completely overnight. We were lucky. Which is tragically more than the northeast coast of Australia can say. One week later they are hit with a cyclone five times the size and strength of our little Bianca.

Monday morning arrives quickly; part two of my western adventure begins. The first couple days into the tour are somewhat tedious: the company a little dull, the food repetitive, and the general sights mundane, to put it kindly. One loud and boisterous Italian with a love of his own voice quickly becomes a thorn in my side, especially as his definition of flirting involves being an arrogant, chauvinistic prick. Ah, the joys of organized tours: being stuck on a bus with twenty-three other strangers can easily be a blessing or a curse. Thankfully, a couple people end up being decent companions for our short time together and *thankfully*, we are on our way to the good stuff.

~

The tropical, warm turquoise water is like glass this morning. Its waters lap over my shoulders as my childlike grin at the ladies around me mirrors a handful of smiles back. We are in the tranquil waters of Shark Bay, Australia. We are in paradise—again. The warmth of the early morning sun kisses our cheeks while the finches and parrots celebrate the day in the trees lining the coast.

I have been waiting for this moment.

After a long but entertaining weekend in Perth and two days of desert hiking in 105 degrees of miserable, albeit beautiful, arid, red-rock cliffs, I am like a child at Christmas here. I've had my fair share of hiking through nature and mountains and cliffs. I can rightly put my hand up and say, "Thanks for that. I'm done now."

A high-pitched squeal flies out of my mouth as my foot lands underwater on top of a panicked fish below. I whip around and am greeted by a large school of dark gray dorsal fins swiftly headed in our direction. My heart beats rapidly as I gasp, "Oh, my God, you guys...dolphins."

Within one highly anticipated minute, the dolphins surround us and slowly cruise past, tilting their large bodies on their sides to get a better look at us as we giggle and stare at the majestic beauties an arm's length away.

They don't stay long, but they return once more a little later and we get the privilege of smiling at a baby while it sticks to its mother's side, tilting its body upward, as its eyes are unable to look up.

We spend a good deal of our morning in the presence of these dolphins, large sea turtles, and pelicans, all exciting on my list of firsts on this trip. We aren't too surprised to see the dolphins around; a small crowd of us fed them fish an hour earlier, directed, of course, by rangers. But in these small moments of contact, there are no crowds or rangers... just a few quietly explosive minutes of nature at its finest. And that has made all the difference.

∼

Northwestern Australia is, true to the southwest, also incredibly diverse. We pass by a naturally pink lake, lie for hours on a beach made up completely of shells, and watch a meteor shower in the most beautifully packed starry night sky.

On a quiet and sunny afternoon, we stop in an area with a boardwalk stretching out into the ocean over stromatolites, which are among the world's first living life forms, dating back 3.5 billion years. Stromatolites are made up of

single-celled, densely packed organisms called cyanobac-
teria. Billions of years ago, they started trapping floating
sediments, which built their colonies of "rocks" and pro-
duced oxygen, leading the way for plants and then animals
to evolve 550 million years ago. They did this for over *two
billion* years. As I walk the long wooden structure over the
shallow waters and clumps of living rock, it's easy to forget
what I'm actually looking at. These "rocks" of bacteria are
our prehistoric ancestors. Absolutely mind-boggling.

Western Australia will claim my applause and love in
comparison to the east, but it is also so completely different
in such extremes that the two coasts should, in all fairness,
never be compared.

The truth of the matter is Australia has spoiled me to
my core. In my two months here, I've seen some of the
world's most beautiful beaches, one of the most outra-
geous fireworks displays, and incredibly diverse and varied
landscapes. I've befriended and stayed with locals—the
real Australians—and have made friends I'll keep for life.
I couldn't ask for more.

My world trip is now coming to a close. Wow, a world
trip. I've just traveled the world on my own. It feels like I'm
dreaming. But I'm not dreaming. I have never felt more
alive...and that has made all the difference.

The End...

I LIE IN BED AS VISIONS OF MY TRAVELS pass before me: tuk-tuks and camels, wandering the streets in Italy, dancing on the beach in Thailand, chasing wallabies in Australia, the view from the Eiffel Tower, Amira, Kate, and Jess, tears of happiness in Rome, tears of disbelief in Cinque Terre, my ghost in Prague, my pain with dengue fever, a pseudo-romance in Paris, lanterns floating toward the moon in Laos.

The memories are hauntingly beautiful, full of life, adventure, and living passion. Oh, I thank God for the courage and strength I've had to live this dream. I've conquered my fears and released myself forever from the bondage of regret, the burden of always wondering what could have been...

I will forever look back on these days and smile.

Home

"Waiting is painful. Forgetting is painful. But not knowing which to do is the worse kind of suffering."

—*Paulo Coelho*

Michigan

S ITTING IN THE DARK CAR, I watch as elusive, swirling
clouds appear and dissipate with my every breath. My
body is shivering—from the cold, from the anger, from the
sheer force of gravity pulling the weight from my bones. I
look to my friend sitting in the driver's seat as a whimper
escapes my mouth. "I'm sinking, Shan."

"What's wrong?" The curves of her cheeks are painted
in the glow of Panera Bread's parking lot lamps, her face
streaked with equal tones of worry and exhaustion. She's
heard me say this before, not too long ago, almost repeatedly
in waves since I've come home.

"I don't know what happened. At one point I knew it
was the right thing to come back to the States. I followed
the signs, I followed my gut. It was right—I know it was.
And then I *knew* it was right to move back to Michigan
where my family and friends were and a job that seemed
perfect…but now that I'm here, I can't escape the feeling
that it all feels *so wrong*. All I can hear in my heart is,
'This life is not meant for you.' I've lost faith in myself. I
must've been wrong. I must've."

Delicate white flurries begin to spill from the burdened

sky. I look down at my shaking hands and pull my coat sleeves over them for warmth.

"So where are you supposed to be?" She repositions in her seat to face me. "What are you trying to say? Do you want to leave again?"

I stare out my window, unable to look at her. "I don't know. I can't feel anything. I can't feel myself. Everything is fine, and everything is wrong. I feel numb. And worse than the numbness is the pain. The pain of being so lost is so consuming that all I can hear is the mind-numbing mantra over and over again, 'I'm lost.' And I don't know how to get back again..."

Michigan

Is this the reverse culture shock they talk about? Now what? I don't know which way to step, which direction to head. Do I want to work? Nope. Do I want to go back to Chicago? Not really. Do I want to do dental hygiene? Not at all. Do I want to go back to school? Nope. So now what? I'm directionless. I have nothing, no home, no life of my own, no car, no money, no job. I have never felt so black and bottomless in my life.

I don't know, I don't know what to do. What do I do? I collided with the universe. I just walked through and experienced the world and now I'm back. Yup...this may be the reverse culture shock they talk about. Numb, indecisive, unclear, uncertain...I have never been so blank. Please tell me, please lead me...what do I do?

I want to write. Write. Write. Write. I don't want to search for the next path. I don't want to search for love. I want my authentic life...the life I violently crave and the life that hides from me as fervently as I seek it.

Michigan

I'm frustrated. I'm bored. Oh dear. I didn't expect this. Where is my instruction manual? Where is that hopeful coaching on what to expect, who to listen to, and what voices to follow?

*I, of course, always think I am making the right decision by following my heart, but sometimes I suppose it's not always what it seems to be. Or maybe my heart is right all along, and I have to follow the beatings of each heart drum…slowly, slowly, slowly to its final ending. It's not over till it's over. I'm here now so I can be there then, wherever there may be. There is no other way around it. Sometimes you have to go through the agony to get to the other side. My world trip would have meant **nothing** if I hadn't gone through such a heart-wrenching process to get there. Because of my teardrops, my laughter had meaning. And such is life.*

I sit in this town and feel nothing again. Oh dear, I fear there might be something wrong with me. A tortured, confused soul, I never seem to find what I'm looking for. Does anyone else out there feel the same? Not quite a homebody, not quite a free spirit…or maybe I'm a free soul who has no idea that it is okay to struggle, it's okay to be afraid. I do tend to take life a little seriously, but maybe that's because to follow a conventional life into its limited boxes would surely be the death of me. I can't do that. I can't follow that conformity so blindly like it appears others do. I just can't.

So have it I will not. I will fight until I find the soles of my feet treading deeper grounds, grounds so soft I seem to melt into them, grounds so foreign yet so familiar I can't help but feel I've finally found where I belong. I will follow my soul until I find the life that fits. It's just taking a little longer, because that life hasn't been built yet. I will make this life what it has always meant to be.

So who could've known I hadn't changed? I was sure I had. Never could I have guessed I hadn't changed, not for one minute. I thought I was finished.

*Instead here I sit, wanting my nomadic life more than anything. I would give anything, **anything**, to live it over again. I want it so bad. I want it all, all over again.*

*How do you know when you've found it? How do you know when to hold on and when to let go? Every night my dreams scream at me that I'm losing control, that I'm running and hiding and fighting to hold on, and that above all, I feel trapped. What does this mean? I **know** I feel trapped. I can't escape the feeling with each passing day and every weighted breath. What? What are you trying to tell me? Is this the point when I should let it all go? Are you telling me it's over?*

How are we supposed to know what to do with ourselves? Are we supposed to be okay with all…this? I'm not. I try to be, oh, I try so hard. I try to have a positive attitude but it's not working. Every time I think I'm having a good day, something happens and it all comes crashing down.

And life keeps getting busier and busier. I can't make it stop. All the while, I'm on this rollercoaster, screaming for it to stop. I don't want this life. Not like this, not like this. This isn't me. I don't belong here.

*So how will I know when I'm finally where I belong? Then the answer comes to me: I'll know…**when I stop asking.***

Yesterday was horrible. Standing crowded under the dripping gazebo with lightning rolling in the clouds, I watched my emotions overtake me like an overwhelming sickness. I trembled as tears fell from my silent ache, and onlookers could only stand by and watch in horror.

The whole family was lined up for wedding photos. Everyone smiled and held each other for the camera…everyone except me. Like a ghost, I stood to the side and watched a life where I didn't exist. She gave an ultimatum. My mother refused to be in any family photos with me.

My initial thought upon seeing the woman I used to call my mother was that I wanted nothing more than to hug her. After I watched the one thing I dreaded most, all I could hear in my mind was: **I hate you.**

Oh, I would give anything to do it all over again. I'd push through the tangled crowds standing between us. I'd scream, "Wait!" and wave my arms frantically through the air.

All the faces smiling in a line would have to stop and turn to look at me; a look of horror would stretch across my mother's face. Better yet—resentment, because I would have ruined everything. I would have gotten my way, and she would have been punished…versus the other way around, where she walked away unnoticed, and I was a crumbled mess on the ground.

I would walk across to those faces, those faces I call my family, and the photographer would have to stop. I'd smile and laugh and search the eyes until I found hers. "Shame on you!" I'd smile again. "You were taking family photos without me? Tsk-tsk, silly family."

Then I'd join the end of the line with my hand resting confidently upon my hip. I'd grin from ear to ear, allowing the camera to shoot a photo I wasn't meant for. But the photo doesn't know that, and neither does the photographer. For one snapshot at least, I would have a family that will never exist.

Instead, nothing happened this way.

Oh, I wish I were a defensive thinker. Then when horrible things happen to me, I could react right away, judiciously of course, and at least cancel out some of the shame the person is throwing upon me.

But no, I'm not like that. My brain doesn't think that way. Instead, I sit there and take it, not knowing at the time that this horrible thing is actually taking place. I become like a virgin dish sponge thrown into a body of dirty dishwater, slowly soaking in everything until I sink completely to the bottom.

Deep breath after deep breath, I desperately tried in vain to regain my composure. My father gathered me into his strong arms as I trembled and wept. Others reached out to me but were stopped instantly by Shandra's stern voice, warning them not to touch me. If anyone else were to touch me in that moment, she knew I might crumble completely to lie in pieces on the ground. There would be nothing left of me.

I'm a little worried for myself today. The depression has trickled in, and I can't seem to find the strength to see my way out again. "Oh please, God," I pray over and over again. "Oh please help me. I am so sad."

I feel like I'm in a dream, like I hope nothing more than to wake up from this and everything will feel right again. What has happened? Who is this lost shell of a person? And as these emotions only intensify, all I feel is the weight of a realization that this may be the beginning of the end.

*I feel like I have started all over again. I was doing so well. I had so much strength, so much compassion for my mother. **I really felt like I had moved on.** And now, after what has happened, I am so devastated. Oh please, God, please help me.*

Michigan

*What has happened? How did I allow such a life to creep in? There was so much victory, so much **pride**. I was living dreams and facing fears and fighting the triumphant fight of learning to fill my own skin. And now? Oh God, what has happened?*

I stopped dreaming. I stopped fighting. I didn't want to put so much effort into my life anymore. I just wanted to sit back and relax, which I suppose is exactly what I've done. Only to realize when I sit back and let life happen, nothing really happens. I let life happen…I become created instead of creating. I end up taking the path most traveled, the path of least resistance. I end up living someone else's life by default.

*How did this happen? **How did this happen?** I came home, and it may be possible I gave up. And then I continued to give up. I tried to make it work at a time…you know what? This is futile. I'll know the answer when I look back in the not-so-distant future. But I don't know it yet.*

I keep trying to figure out how I followed everything I knew to be right and how it went so wrong. I came home with lots and lots of thought and effort. I knew it was time, and I was so tired. And it felt right, people even said, "Oh, wow, that is meant to be." And then I walked into this life with a constant, "This life is not meant for you." What the hell? I didn't stand a chance. I didn't stand a chance.

The thing is it's hard to see your way out when you're in

the thick of it. Sometimes you have to fight your way through and have faith that it's all according to plan. I did everything according to the best that was in me. I didn't fall into this life; I found this job that appeared perfect. And I needed it. I needed the money. It just never felt right.

So maybe, in the thick of it, I'm in a place that will lead me to the next, a place that is shaping who I am becoming and what I need, a place that will never be right but fills a certain purpose.

Maybe it's possible to be in a place that is so right because it is so wrong. It's meant to be wrong. It's meant to send me to the depths of mercy, wailing on the bathroom floor in pitiful despair. Because only on that bathroom floor, at that point in my life, could I ever discover the next path, or could I ever find the strength to live it. Only on the bathroom floor could I have the viewpoint that I've always needed to see.

So you can't judge the view from Mount Everest when you're still at base camp. You're not meant to stay at base camp; it's just where you are now, and where you need to be to get to the next summit.

I can't believe for a second that the great leaders of our lives, the heroes in our storybooks, the saviors of our dreams have all failed by coincidence. There's not a soul out there who has achieved greatness by waking up one day and walking into it. It's the law of the universe to work hard for what you want, to fight for what you want, and then to feel the rewards of accomplishment.

And then it doesn't last. It never does. The moment passes, you outgrow yourself and you start at the bottom again—level two, and forward on you march. It's the ebb and flow of life; it's the mission of greatness. You start at the bottom, you fight to the top, and then you grow.

I didn't know this in Australia; I didn't know this when I came home. Without even realizing it, I assumed I had reached my point of completion. There was the celebration of a dream come true, an outgrowing of sorts, then a "Pass go and collect two hundred dollars"—on to the next round. I didn't know I had left level one and started level two. I didn't expect a level two. I was still holding on to level one.

So I found myself a failure, and I sunk into a deep depression. The world looked bleak, and there seemed to be no way out. I was on the bathroom floor.

*I guess this is where the leaders tell you to accept that sometimes life is suffering and to surrender to that self-defeating tone of feeling weak, **because you have to feel it to fight it**. And then you make a stand.*

Why would I leave on a world trip, only to move home, only to leave again? Who the hell knows? I can't possibly see to the extent of the horizon, because I am still at base camp one.

*It has been one hell of a year. There was a lot of love, and a lot of sadness, a lot of tears, a lot of anxiety. It was life, not a dream come true. It was feeling the pains that come from stretching yourself for the first time in a long time. Before this, I had only known **yes** for a good long while. So I got a long and ruthless **no**, which seems to be the prerequisite for greatness. It's like life is testing me, seeing how bad I want it.*

So I put my hand over my heart and I feel it:
Thump-thump, thump-thump, thump-thump.
And I remember...

*I am **here**; I exist...for a reason. Why? Because why else would my heart keep beating? Why did it start in the first place? Why does it whisper to me pleadings that I would rather ignore? I certainly didn't put that beat into my heart, and I* *most definitely did not put those quiet yet persistent whispers there either. Why? Because I ignore them more than I listen, until my own insanity becomes more of a threat than the voice itself. Because I just **know** this is my truth. And above all, we must come to the realization that we must live our truth.*

So what do I do? I have been asking myself this question since I returned home from my trip and the "plans" for my life ran out. So I tripped and stumbled my way through as I figured out the hard way that we are never finished. The world as a whole is never finished.

That is why we are here, each and every one of us, to make a difference, to make a stand...to make a memory in the tapestry of life that we even existed at all. One thread...one thread can make a huge difference. We weave and bend through our lives and each other's days, loving and learning, hurting and breaking...only to eventually pick ourselves back up and start anew.

So, I'm going to start with right now, instead of tomorrow. I am going to go about my day today, and I am going to listen to my heart, follow its drumming as a quiet reassurance that I am here for a reason. And I'm going to trust myself.

*How can I explain it...thinking of these things for the first time in a good, long while—my heart just **yearns**. The tug I feel is almost strong enough for my heart to rip from its seams, pull itself out from my chest, and scream at me face to face.*

So now, despite all my fears, I place my first foot forward.

Michigan

Playing with the rubber band between my finger-tips, I look up and see my stepmother staring at me expectantly. The side of her face reflects the flashing glow of the television from the other room, where my father sits quietly on the couch. We are perched on either side of the bar in the kitchen, finishing our dinner and having quiet conversations.

"So, how did it go?"

"I…" I become silent, acutely aware of my pounding heart.

"You met with your mother today, right? How did it go? Are you okay?"

"No, I'm not okay."

We sit for a moment in silence.

"She was the one who wanted to meet with me!" I yell. "She said she wanted to 'lay it all out on the table.' She wanted to apologize for something. But the only things she apologized for were the times during my childhood where she went in and out of the religion. She feels none of this would have happened had she been stronger as a Jehovah's Witness. I, of course, told her this wasn't true, but I think it may be another burden she carries. She must feel accountable for the way things went…"

The grandfather clock in the corner rings nine o'clock. I take a deep breath and try to calm myself.

"We talked about the wedding," I continue. "She didn't understand why it was a big deal, as there were 'so many photos' I would be in. I told her I was a part of this family, and I deserved to be in *all* the family photos. I yelled at her and told her I wasn't going to allow this 'arrangement' to bully me around anymore.

"There were no straight answers. *Nothing* was laid on the table! I don't know how I thought it would go any differently. What could she possibly say to make it better? What could she possibly say to make *anything* better without her? There wasn't a solution; there was only dredging up a sad and painful past where there still aren't any answers. I told her I have never once regretted getting baptized, and I have never once regretted leaving. I told her, 'When you left that religion, your life fell apart. When I left, my life came together. The way you feel when you are a part of that religion is how I feel being out of it.'"

"How did she respond?" My stepmom grabs my trembling hands for a moment, her face concerned.

"She stumbled a lot. I would confront her, and she would stumble. I think she wanted resolution. I think she wanted forgiveness. I didn't realize it until just now, but she said 'sorry' a couple times, and I never said it was okay. I told her I thought losing her because of religion was tragic. And terrible. And I wished it would go away. There were times I wanted *her* to go away. I wanted it to be over and I could go on with my life. There were times when I thought I hated her. As soon as she started talking about the wedding photos, the anger bubbled and boiled beneath my chest. The walls started to go up like a war was about to be waged, and I prepared myself to fight."

My stepmother doesn't say anything. She stands motionless on the other side of the counter and waits for me to continue.

"I'm sad that was the case." I look down at the now knotted rubber band. "She was looking for something today. I forgot to ask her what, but I know in her leaving that she didn't find it. I suppose I had the same hope, and I know I didn't find it. There were times I looked at her and thought, 'Remember, Jill, she is fighting her own battles. *Listen* to her.'

"I feel sad that I couldn't take her pain away. That she was in front of me and needed something I couldn't give. I feel guilty and sad tonight that she is possibly more sad. I can't know that for sure, but I do know that I am more sad. Is that even a word? Sadder? More sad?"

She half smiles at me but still says nothing.

"Deep down"—my voice begins to quiver—"I feel if I could have somehow made it better, maybe she would love me more, miss me more, be nicer to me when we are forced to be together."

I look up at my stepmother with weary, tear-soaked eyes. Her face concerned, she looks back through her own set of tears.

"I feel guilty," I whimper. And with that, a subtle squeak sounds from my throat as I choke back tears.

She stares at me and says straight and stern, "Jillian. None of this is your fault. You have *nothing* to feel guilty about."

At that, my head collapses into my hands, and I mourn the loss of my mother for the thousandth time. My stepmother rushes around the counter and holds me in her arms.

"This is not your fault, Jillian," she repeats as she rocks me back and forth. "This is not your fault."

And the tears of the past ten years all fell again on this day. They fell on my stepmother, and they fell on my father. They streamed down my face and soaked me straight through to my bones. And there we stayed, in this huddle in the kitchen, as I sat weeping, enclosed by my family. *My family.* The family that I will always have—unconditionally.

After a while, I lifted my chin and I dried my tears. For the thousandth time, I peeled myself off the ground, and I stood on my own two feet. And then I kept moving.

Michigan

L EANING OVER THE BATHROOM SINK, I splash my face
as suds of soap drop off my chin. I splash again and
again, then sighing deeply I grab the counter and look into
the mirror. Drops of water stream down my cheeks as a
film of defeat slowly permeates my heart.

She was right. I haven't found it. My mother told me when
I left the Jehovah's Witnesses that I'd never find the life I
was looking for, and she was right. I'm almost thirty years
old. I've lived my dreams, traveled the world in search of it,
and here I am, just as sad and broken as I was before I left.

What is it that tugs at me so fervently? Why is it that
I'm *still* so lost? And why is it that after years of living this
life that rejects me so, am I still unable to find my way out?
What is it? Where is this "life" where I belong?

Continuing to grip the counter, I look deeply into my own
reflection, and suddenly my whole life stares back at me: the
past ten years of love and laughter, teardrops and heartache,
goals and accomplishments, the college degree, the big city,
the world trip…all these years living this life, owning my
truth and standing up for what I believe in. But deep down
I was still searching, heartbroken that once again whatever
aspiration I was achieving did not fill the hole in my heart.

I take a step back as it hits me: I've never found the life
I've been searching for—*because I've been living it all along.* I

had it the moment I left. The moment I walked away from the Jehovah's Witnesses and started creating my own life was the moment I found where I belonged.

For ten years I've been building that life, passionate and free, experiencing what had once been a painful accumulation of could-have-beens and fantasies. This is it. This is what I've been looking for. I was too busy searching the world to see it was right in front of me all along.

I draw in a deep breath and giggle softly to myself, continuing to stare at the woman standing before me. This whole time I've been begging God, fighting in the dark with doors determined to remain closed. I cried out in my misery, clawing at the earth with my face buried in the ground. I hated this life. I hated the way it made me feel, the way it stripped me bare and left me to stand naked in the cold. This whole time I felt like I had nothing. I couldn't understand why it had been written in the stars for me to stay all along.

I left Chicago so that my life would eventually lead me back here. I needed to be stripped bare in order to learn to love my life at its very core. I had to lie on the bathroom floor so I could finally see from a new perspective. I have been given a great gift. Thankfully God was strong enough to listen to my tears and hold me while I grieved, giving me what I needed so that at the end of it all, I could finally find what I truly wanted: the life I've always had. Sometimes the journey is necessary—sometimes we need to break into a thousand pieces to find we were never really broken after all.

At that moment I finally let go and softened into my life; I was no longer searching. And then God swiftly opened doors once determined to remain shut and set me free.

New Zealand

One Year Later

Wellington, New Zealand

B OLD WAVES CRASH WILDLY against the sharp boulders and ragged shoreline of the North Island's southern-most coast as a young boy skips along the water's edge with a handful of colorful balloons. He whips around and smiles as his parents watch from a beachside café, drinking their flat white and long black, New Zealand's signature coffees. Sailboats coast along the restless ocean as the snow-dusted mountains of the South Island loom mysteriously in the distance.

The crisp southern air swirls around us as I press my body tightly against his. Gripping the throttle of his motorbike, he navigates the winding, ocean-side road, and I crane my neck farther to look at our surroundings. Steep cliffs tower above us to our left, and the sea to the right of us glistens under the intensely bright sun. A charming assortment of homes, some shiny and new, others weathered from the elements, tastefully clash against the already contrasting pines and palms blanketing the hillsides.

Cruising faster now, we pass through altering layers of salty ocean air, then cool and crisp pine wafting from the trails leading deep into the mountains. Signs peppering the road warn, *"Slow Down! Penguin Crossing"* as seagulls hover and dip around us.

I tilt my head back and fight the urge to open my arms and lift my hands into the sky.

I feel like I'm dreaming.

It's overwhelming—this feeling, like that cliché in the movies where the character pinches themselves as she looks around with glassy, tear-filled eyes. I must be dreaming. How can a place like this exist?

I've been living here for eight months now. I've traveled this country extensively and viewed scenery much more beautiful than this, but there is something about this place, this city, this very moment in particular. *I've been here before.* I've smelled this ocean and these pines. I've touched these rustic cliffs. I've stood under this sun. These houses…these people…it's like a scene out of a movie I've watched in my head my entire life. It's the movie I've been fighting for, the life I always knew I'd see before me…even though I had no proof it existed or I'd ever find it. I know this place, and in an almost inexplicable way, I feel like we've been reunited.

∽

After my revelation in Michigan, the incessant battles between my head and my heart were abruptly silenced. It was as if I had spent my entire life in a crowded room with thousands of people talking at once, and in a single moment, I found the strength to rise to my feet and shut the door.

The funny thing is I had grown friendly with every single one of those voices—those voices of adventure, of fear and insecurity, and the voices of truth. They had become the peers of my youth, each voice swirling around me like a hurricane, pulling me ceaselessly in different directions. They all disappeared that afternoon in Michigan, and they have never returned.

Rereading all my journals from the past ten years, I've found page after page filled with confusion and pain, "notes to self" on how to escape the sadness, how to forgive my mother, and more importantly, how to forgive myself. All journals trying desperately to be content, pleading with myself to let go and be a free spirit who trusts in life and the way it seems to go. So unhappy, so discontent, so bitter and confused...back and forth and back again, all in attempts to ignore a part of me that refused to be silenced. Fighting constantly...to be anyone but myself.

Looking back, I can see now how I carried my mother's rejection around as if it were my own. I must've believed her. It's almost as if her statement that I'd "never find" what I was looking for was a life sentence, etched into the back of my eyes so that no matter what I saw before me, it was never the life I was looking for.

To think that whole time *I could have stayed in that dark night,* forever fighting to "release the grip" and let go, so I could finally live this life—love this life, and that could finally be enough. I would have never realized the grand potential of my dreams. I would have remained shackled by my fears, and the woman I am today would have never existed.

Within weeks of my epiphany, opportunities I couldn't have imagined came flying at me from every direction. It was only a matter of months before I found myself traveling around the world once more with a visa to live and work in New Zealand.

I felt like I had been given a second chance. I was finally free enough to experience the world the way I had initially set out to three years ago, a chance to see the world through the eyes of a free spirit—the eyes I knew had belonged to me all along but were hidden by my own confusion.

It didn't take long to fall for New Zealand. I left America with no expectations and when arriving here found that I was effortlessly happy for the first time in my life. With outstretched arms and a smile across my face, I was finally at peace enough to be living in the moment instead of running from it.

That was when I realized New Zealand was my gift for holding on. It was, in its essence, the life that had been calling out to me years before my initial world trip. I had come full circle. That was it—I knew it. It was what all the whispers in the dead of night were about. It was never supposed to be my first world trip or Michigan, for those chapters in my life were only meant to guide me here.

To be truthful, it was never about New Zealand either. *It was about the journey required to get to New Zealand,* to that life calling out to me from the other side of fear. It was about the determination to stay true to that steadfast inner voice when everything seemed hopeless or when the world had let me down. It was about a life that could be only found *when I found my freedom.*

Had I given up, had I ignored my instinct, this life would have remained one of those dreams of youth that I strove for but never found. I would have labeled my first world trip a "means to an end" and Michigan a "failure." And how devastating that could have been, as all these journeys, despite being painful, were not only essential—they were a blessing. Because of them, I have been set free.

Over a year has passed since that fateful day I gripped the cold, wet counter and saw my life clearly for the first time, and I have never looked back. I have found peace within my heart and therefore have finally found where I belong. No matter where I find myself in the world, I am home. And I have nothing left to prove.

Ten years ago I was condemned for the stand I made. I was told I had made a mistake, that I was wrong. Ten years ago I was told I would never find the life I was looking for. But I never gave up. I placed one foot in front of the other, and I made a stand for my life, even though at times that meant standing alone.

I don't know what will happen next or where this road may lead, but that doesn't matter anymore. It never did. The only thing that matters is I am free.

I am *free*.

Chicago

I have a dream.

I can feel what it will make me feel,
I can taste what it will make me taste,
I can feel its life, fluttering within me.

What does a "calling" feel like?
Like this feeling right now.
Like a calling back to home,
like heaven pulling you.

It's like a soft melody you can't remove from your memory,
although you can't figure out where you heard the tune in the
*   first place.*
It's a long-lost love you've tried to forget.
You can't figure out why it won't go away,
but it's there,
and it's there for life.

You just know.

There is no logic behind it,
but you understand
for some reason not yet come to realization,

that it will be everything you forgot you knew.

There will be happiness and fulfillment you never thought you'd
  feel.
There will be a peace and acceptance you never knew existed.

I can feel the sun's warm rays on my face,
a hand in mine,
sweet perfume wafting through the air.

It will be late nights and long days and a book that will spell
  perfection.
It will be my final home.

And I'll feel the warm tears streak my face,
as I think of how close this dream came
to being a regret of a life never lived.
A soul never realized.
A spirit never freed.

It's going home.
It's a calling.

It doesn't follow logic,
it follows your heart.

Follow it and you will follow the gods to their final resting place.

Follow it and you will taste freedom.

Acknowledgments

THANK YOU TO MY BEAUTIFUL FAMILY: Phil, Bonnie, Charlie, Karen, Andy, and Molly. I wouldn't be where I am today without your endless love and support. Thank you to my closest friends who have listened to me talk about this dream for years and have loved me through my heartache: Shandra, Lindsey, and Kathy. Of course I must thank the beautiful souls I met on my travels: Kate, Amira, and Jess especially. And for those who made such an impact on my life but did not end up in the book—namely Rachel in Australia, you were no less important or special to me, and I will never forget you. Thank you to my cheerleaders and role models in Chicago, Karen and Barbara, for encouraging the young dreamer in me. I want to thank my brilliant editors: Kira, Suzie, and Colleen and my incredibly talented graphic designer, Jessica. It was an immense pleasure working with you all.

Last but not least, I want to thank Suzzette, my dear friend whom I've never met (…yet). It was your words, and your words alone that helped keep this dream alive.

Thank you.

About the Author

JILLIAN WEBSTER was born in Michigan, where she attended Lansing Community College for dental hygiene. She has written for *Access Magazine* and is now working as an international dental hygienist in New Zealand. *Scared to Life* is her first book. She lives in Wellington, New Zealand...for now.

19108455R00225

Made in the USA
Middletown, DE
09 April 2015